FAITH, FREEDOM & OTHER F WORDS

A JOURNEY BEYOND MUSCULAR DYSTROPHY

RHIANNON ANDERSON

ISBN: 978-1-969463-35-8

DEDICATIONS

To my Family, words will simply never be enough. Thank you for never letting me forget who I am and never letting me go on this journey called life alone. Thank you for your never-failing love and guidance. Thank you for not wrapping me in bubble wrap, for letting me grow, stumble, and learn how to get back up again. This book is only possible through your strength — choosing to keep living, growing, and creating memories even when life was uncertain. I love you all to the moon and back.

~

To Chris, Steph, and Hayley – this book wouldn't have been written without all of you. Thank you for believing in me when I couldn't.

~

To every person living with Muscular Dystrophy and their families, may you continue to forge your own path, believing that you are never alone; our journeys intertwine as much as they are unique. This book is for you, for your bravery, the moments no one sees but you. This book is for all of us.

FOREWORD

I am extremely honoured that Rhi has given me the privilege of writing the foreword for *Faith, Freedom, and Other F-Words: A Journey Beyond Muscular Dystrophy*. I was fortunate to have Rhi come into my life roughly 5 years ago. Since then, I have had the pleasure of forming a strong friendship through our mutual love of AFL, our shared experiences of living with a disability, and our passion for inspiring not only others living with a disability but also their families, friends, and the wider community.

After reading Rhi's story, you will reconsider the misconceptions society places on the disabled community, as you will read the words of a young woman thriving in adversity, not just surviving it.

Rhi is all about enjoying life and finding freedom in ways you never imagined. There is always joy, purpose and beauty that can be found even in the hardest moments of life which you will see by reading this book.

Disabled life definitely isn't easy, but with the correct attitude, we can rewrite the narrative to enjoy every single day to the fullest.

The unfiltered honesty in this book will, at times, make you laugh, then at other times make you cry, but by the end, it will leave you with a better understanding of navigating the world of disability.

I guarantee after reading Faith, Freedom, and Other F-Words: A Journey Beyond Muscular Dystrophy; you will see Rhi how I do: an incredibly strong, independent and inspirational woman who can't be stopped from kicking down barriers to achieve her goals. This is not a doom-and-gloom memoir; it is a celebration of the resilience of a remarkable young woman who won't let Muscular Dystrophy define her life.

Christopher Gillin
Gillin Boys Foundation co-founder

TABLE OF CONTENTS

INTRODUCTION

Spoiler: Turns Out, Life Doesn't Come with a Rule Book.

For the longest time, I've wanted to be a published writer. I still vividly remember sitting in my Grade one class and being asked to write a one-page story about what we did during the weekend. And guess what? I didn't just write one page; I wrote four, front and back. What can I say? I was a major overachiever even as a 5-year-old!

They say that being disabled gives you the gift of creative imagination, allowing you to envision a life different from your own—your perfect house, the ultimate fairy tale where you soar in and save the day, winning an Oscar in front of your idols. It's safe to say that I am no exception. I would often find myself lost in thought, staring out of the classroom window, daydreaming about all sorts of things: what it would be like to open that fairy door in the school forest, to fly with the birds, swim with dolphins, or win a gold medal at the Paralympics.

My short stories or blurbs in English class would span many pages. And those who read it end up engulfed on a journey back in time or into an imaginative land I had created in my head. Teachers, and specialists, would often tell my parents that I would become a writer. Despite my creative imagination, I never imagined that I would be sitting at my laptop at twenty-six, writing my first book. And, to be honest, neither did my parents.

They say life doesn't come with a rule book. But what they don't mention is how many people will still try to hand you theirs. From the moment I was diagnosed with muscular dystrophy, the world seemed eager to give me their version of the rules: what I could do, what I shouldn't try, who I could be. Teachers, doctors, well-meaning strangers—they all had advice. But none of their rules made sense for the game of life I was playing.

At first, I thought, maybe, they were onto something. After all, I wasn't exactly acing this whole "life" thing. However, their rules were about as useful as a chocolate teapot in the Aussie summer. So, I did what any self-respecting Aussie Rules Football fan would do: I threw out the rulebook, waddled onto the field of life, and decided to wing it. Sure, I've dropped the ball a few times—well, okay, a lot—but I've also scored some absolute screamers along the way.

If I were to be brutally honest, if I went by the medical rule book, I shouldn't be here. My younger brother should be an only child. My parents should be mourning yet another version of a life they didn't get to live.

If I were to follow society's rule book, I should be desperately trying to wear six-inch heels that make you question your existence and curse your genetics for giving you weak ankles. I should be a size 4, able-bodied stunner. However, I regret to inform you that I was a size 4 once, and I will never subject myself to a carb-free life again. I simply love pasta and my sanity too much. As for the able-bodied aspect, well, to that, I say it's a matter of perception. But we will delve into that a little later.

While rules have their value, there are countless societal rulebooks to consider. They are meant to maintain the checks and balances of life, ensuring as much predictability as possible. For many of us, the societal rulebook is simply unrealistic, and attempting to follow it often leaves us feeling lost and diminished from who we could be.

Yet, the greatest achievements don't stem from the multitude of 'Societal Boxes of Expectations' rulebooks. Instead, they arise from creating your own.

My story is unique. I'm not some famous actress, podcast host, athlete, spokesperson, politician, or content creator. I am just your average chick from Toowoomba, a country town outside of Brisbane, Australia, who just happened to be dealt some interesting cards. Cards that have, at times, been excruciating both physically and mentally. But, also, cards that have allowed me to develop a different outlook on the meaning of life. These cards have made me realise that there is no rulebook to life, as much as people think there is one.

This book will be shocking to some, as my outlook on life with a disability and what goes on between the pages is different from most. People often say they want to be left inspired, which, when saying that to a disabled person, often means "don't dwell on the hard stuff." Others also say that if we "dwell on the hard stuff" and admit that, at times, disabled life is no walk in the park on a spring afternoon with a Starbucks, then we are complaining, aren't inspiring enough, are ashamed, or hate our life.

This book is a no-holds-barred approach to the memoir genre. I hope it is bluntly truthful and sheds true light on what living with a disability is like, and how it unknowingly intertwines itself in the highs-and-lows of everyday life. There are only a handful of people in my life who know the whole truth about what it's like to be a disabled person navigating the world, and I hope that this book will help answer the questions that many may have, whether friends, family, or strangers.

I also hope that this book and my journey will help parents, teachers, and family members of those with disabilities realise that they aren't alone in their journey. I also desperately hope that the truthful nature of this book, while perhaps difficult to read at times, helps you break free from some of that toxic positivity and start to heal so you can enjoy everything that life has to offer.

For my fellow cripples—I mean, my disabled family, I hope that this book gives you the hope and the courage to throw the rule book out the window and realise that there is so much to life and how you live it should be up to you—no one else. Just because you have a label of a diagnosis over your head doesn't mean that is all you are!

I also hope that it helps you to realise just how far you have come in your journey, and while admitting to yourself that things are challenging, you can turn those difficult times into something that makes those hard times worth every minute. I hope you feel seen and that your thoughts, feelings, and experiences are somehow validated by reading this book.

For everyone else, I hope that this little story changes even just a bit of how you may view disability and what we are capable of. Or perhaps, even change how you view your own life and what you are capable of. I hope it enables you to challenge perceptions and viewpoints, and simply acknowledge the journey you have been on in your game of life. I hope it helps you recognise that everyone's story is different and unique in its own way, serving its intended purpose.

And this is my story.

SECTION 1
Unexpected Beginnings

You are in the perfect place, at the perfect time,
with the perfect people.
—Unknown

CHAPTER 1

NEW REALITY: MY EARLY DAYS

Life has a funny way of setting the stage long before we even realise we're part of the performance, doesn't it? Those nine months spent developing in the cosy "oven" of the womb lay the foundation for so many aspects of our lives.

Many of us find that our paths are often shaped by the aspirations and professions of our families. From an early age, we can feel the influence of our surroundings, leading us to consider becoming a lawyer, a doctor, or perhaps following in our parents' footsteps. It often seems like a big part of our lives is already mapped out for us before we even take our first breath.

When we think about life outside our careers, our parents often picture joyful holidays spent running on the beach as the sun begins to set on a hot summer day, or going on exciting hikes through bushlands and discovering a waterfall at the end. They fill our everyday lives with adventure, cheering us on during school athletics carnivals, even when we come in last. Sometimes, they can be a bit competitive, turning into "those parents," but it's all out of love and support!

Yet, the other side to this coin is the side where life doesn't go as planned. For 1.3 billion people worldwide, this represents a reality where dreams and hopes must shift. I belong to that population.

This will probably come as a shock, but my life's journey started in the womb. Like I said earlier, for every first-time parent, there's a mix of excitement and nervousness about what lies ahead. My parents were no different. They were filled with dreams of endless adventures and thoughts about my future. Would I dive into sports like my dad and play grassroots AFL or compete in Cross Country? Would I grow to be a deep thinker and creative like my mum? Would I be sporty or an academic? Or would I go through a rebellious phase, donning biker jackets and trying out smoking?

The anticipation and excitement of my parents and the entire family were through the roof as they eagerly awaited the arrival of the newest family member—the first grandchild on my mum's side and the second on my dad's. I wasn't the most active baby in the womb, but my mum didn't have anything to compare it to since I was her first child, so she didn't worry much.

I made my entrance into the world a little dramatically at thirty-eight weeks via C-section because Mum was diagnosed with preeclampsia. When I arrived, I was described as a floppy baby! It turns out that babies are supposed to be able to hold their heads up a bit, which was surprising since I was always told they couldn't at all. However, the more alarming thing was that the room was quiet. Filled only with the sounds of machines and doctors working, there were no cries to be heard—a silence that sent a chill through everyone.

The doctors quickly became concerned, and instead of placing me on Mum's chest, I was taken straight to the NICU. Mum looked at my dad and said, "Whatever you do, don't leave her alone." So, Dad stepped away to follow me to the NICU while Mum was being stitched up.

There, they conducted tests, primarily for Down Syndrome, due to the shape of my head. Being born in the last few months of the 90s, and I do proudly claim my identity as a 90s baby; testing in the womb wasn't standard yet. The tests for Down Syndrome came back negative.

Frustratingly, Mum had to wait quite a while to see me, her first child, after giving birth. I was born at 2:00 p.m. on the 29th of July, but it wasn't until 11:00 a.m. the next morning that she finally "chucked the poops" with the midwife. Her words, not mine.

Each time she asked, "Can I go and see my baby?", the midwives kindly reassured her that she would be able to see me "soon". They suggested she take a shower first and take a moment for herself. And it even got to the point when she was in tears! That was when a new midwife came in, asking if everything was alright. Mum explained, "I haven't been able to see my baby," and the nurse immediately replied, "What? You haven't seen her yet? Oh, my goodness, let's get you to your daughter right away!"

Without hesitation, she brought over a wheelchair and wheeled Mum to the NICU. Like any new mother, nothing, even major surgery, would keep her from seeing her baby.

She went to all sorts of lengths to be able to stay with me in the hospital in the first two weeks of my life, as I remained in the NICU unit. I was connected to nasal tubes, which enabled me to eat as I had difficulty latching. During those two weeks, my mum would always say she was still in too much pain to go home whenever the midwives asked, "So, do you think you might be ready to go home today?" The thought of leaving without her firstborn was just too hard for her, and she simply refused to give up on the dream every parent wants of leaving the hospital all together.

My dad, however, wasn't so lucky and still had to work each day, knowing his wife and his baby girl were still in the hospital. Remember, this was back in the late 90s, so paternity leave wasn't quite a thing just yet. He didn't have the opportunity to take those two weeks off, especially since it was around the time he had started a new job. Each day, he would turn up at the hospital after work and stay until he was practically kicked out because visitation hours were over.

Mum's luck eventually ran out after about a week. She was gently—but firmly—told she had to go home. I, however, had to remain in the NICU a little longer. I can only imagine how unbearable it must have been for my parents to come to the hospital every day to be by my side until the midwives gently asked them to leave when visitation hours were over once again. For a few hours each day, we were a family of three. Until evening came, and my parents went home while I stayed in my humidicrib, surrounded by strange sounds and unfamiliar faces.

Thank goodness you and I were too young to remember any of those times. And I may be biased, but I like to say I am blessed to have the best parents in the world. In those two weeks, they showed the kind of strength they would need for the rest of their lives. They just didn't know it yet.

When I finally received the green tick of approval to go home and finally leave the hospital, my parents felt like they could put that tough time behind them. We were ready to embrace being a family of three—or four, if you count our beloved Pomeranian, Maverick!

And it was pretty close to the perfect life for those first couple of years. My mum lovingly devoted the first few months to being home with me. When I was about six months old, she returned to work, and during those days, I spent precious time with my grandmother. However, after just a few months, my mum realised how much she had missed being with me and decided she wanted to be at home, nurturing and caring for me. Thankfully, in those days, a family could live relatively easily on just one income, which made mum's choice possible.

Growing up in Toowoomba, just west of Brisbane in Queensland, there's truly always something exciting to do and explore. Countless parks and lookouts are waiting for you to discover them, and there's even a charming little museum that celebrates the early transportation industry—a big part of what helped Queensland grow! There may or may not be a Lamington made on display, rumoured to have been invented in Toowoomba. Whether or not it is real though and how old it is, is open for debate, but no one is willing to break the glass and find out.

Summers are often filled with fun at the local pool, where you wish for the wave machine to be turned on and hope your parents can't resist your puppy-dog eyes, letting you go to the canteen to buy a box of potato gems and a delicious blue slushy before sneaking in one last swim before heading home. Summer in Australia, being at the end of the year, means hot Christmases, with evenings that feel slightly muggy. Families gather in the evenings to stroll from street to street, relishing everyone's Christmas light displays, eagerly counting down to Christmas Day with a chocolate advent calendar, which, for me growing up, was as thrilling as Christmas itself. It was one of those special times of the year when, aside from Easter, you could enjoy a little piece of chocolate for breakfast! The main park in town, Queens Park, also lights up with a fantastic display, showcasing various nativity scenes, all aglow, while choirs sing carols on the main stage.

In spring, Queens Park transforms into a soothing, colourful paradise of flowers, earning Toowoomba its nickname as the Garden City. The park bursts with flowers of all shapes and sizes, painting the ground with vibrant hues, from bright whites to soft pastels, while bees and a medley of birds creates a lively soundtrack as you explore the park at dusk.

Winters can be long and chilly, but they offer the perfect chance to cosy up by the heater, enjoying slow-cooked casseroles and freshly baked chocolate cakes. The mornings are enveloped in darkness, the soft crackle of the fireplace and the first signs of birds awakening, offering a level of peace and tranquility that only cold weather brings.

While Toowoomba is often referred to as retirement central, I believe it's also a wonderful place to grow up, and the ideal setting for my parents to fulfil their dream of raising a family together.

However, their "perfect" dream would come crashing down like a poorly crafted paper plane. In the glow of that perfect life, the early signs that something was wrong went under the radar for quite a while.

As first-time parents, they had nothing to compare my development to, so they were unaware that something more sinister was on the cards. I was in the lower percentile for growth. Although I reached all my milestones, I was a bit late to the party compared to the "normal" timeframe. That, too, flew under the radar, as some kids are slower to reach their markers, but nothing ever comes of it. Even the doctors were initially not concerned for that exact reason, thinking it was something I would perhaps grow out of as I became older.

However, the big telltale that something wasn't right was that I never crawled. Instead, I commando-crawled or belly-crawled. My arms and legs weren't strong enough, so I slid around on my forearms and belly. I didn't walk until I was 18 months old.

Once again, being the firstborn, my poor parents still didn't realise anything was drastically wrong; they simply thought it was standard and that I would develop my coordination and strength later. They held onto the hope that I'd eventually catch up. But as the months passed and the gap between what I should be able to do and what I could do grew wider, that hope began to fray at the edges.

My loving grandparents first noticed that something seemed a bit off with me. They lived in a cosy three-level home, with the main living area comfortably nestled on the middle floor. This little detail, however, meant that to go to the bathroom, I would have to become one with the stairs. I would have to make my way either downstairs to the bathroom off the second living room or upstairs, near the bedrooms.

As a two-year-old, navigating those stairs became part of my little adventure! For most kids, getting used to going up and down the stairs doesn't take much before they feel like a pro, and their ego makes them try the miss-every-second-step trick. But for me, those stairs were a challenge. I found myself struggling to climb even a single step. I would kick my non-supporting leg back as I made my way up, using my hand to help me stand upright with both feet firmly planted on each stair before taking the next step. While most kids would alternate their feet to go up, I moved slowly and carefully, tackling one step at a time and always leading with my right foot.

My grandparents eventually shared their concerns about how I was navigating standing, walking, and climbing the stairs with my parents, noting that when I stood up from the floor, I would walk my hands up my legs for support. Eventually, we discovered that this movement is known as the Gowers Manoeuvre—a sign of muscular dystrophy, which occurs when someone uses their hands to help them stand due to weak pelvic girdle and hip muscles. This little "trick," alongside the challenges with stairs and the concerned opinions from my grandparents, encouraged my parents to schedule an appointment with our GP for a professional opinion.

My parents relayed my grandparents' observations to our GP, who immediately recognised their concern. Figuring out what might be going on with me felt like searching for a needle in a haystack. She swiftly referred us to a neurologist, marking the start of what would turn out to be a long and challenging journey filled with so many unknowns.

When the unique ways I approached life were mentioned to the neurologist, they quickly decided to perform a muscle biopsy on the side of my leg. I was just two years old at the time—my first encounter with something resembling surgery, and I still remember that day vividly.

I woke up in the recovery room, all alone, surrounded by doctors and nurses, with my parents nowhere in sight. At that moment, being only two and having rarely been apart from my family, I felt scared and lonely. I called out for them as loudly as I could, a mix of pain and fear in my tiny voice. The pain, confusion, and being surrounded by a bunch of people I didn't know in an unfamiliar room overwhelmed my tiny brain. I still swear that this day was where I got my separation anxiety from.

Meanwhile, my parents were in the waiting room, thinking I was still in the operating room. They only found out I was in recovery when a receptionist casually said, "Oh, she's in recovery," as if it was no big deal! When my parents finally came into the room, they saw me flailing around, frightened and distressed, longing for their familiar faces. Safe to say, it was a challenging and traumatic experience for them, too, not to mention frustrating, since they weren't told I had been in recovery for some time.

The muscle biopsy results arrived not long after. My mum, who was seven months pregnant with my brother at the time, had a strong intuition that we should wait until he was born to find out the results. You might wonder how she made that choice, but throughout our journey, we've learned that trusting your gut is so important—It's often spot on!

The day we received the biopsy results was filled with more gut feelings. My mum remembers that morning as she prepared me for our two-hour drive to Brisbane. My dad walked in and gently asked how she was feeling. She was quiet and calm, but her heart was heavy. She replied simply, "I have a feeling that after today, our lives will never be the same." Oh, how right she was.

My grandparents joined my parents to help care for my little brother, who was just a few months old. They were there to look after him while my parents went into the meeting room. Of course, they were also there to offer emotional comfort to my parents. Waiting for our names to be called must have felt like an eternity! I was so wrapped up watching the Teletubbies that I didn't even notice the nerves creeping up on my parents. Besides, how could I even begin to understand or comprehend where we were or what was happening? I was only three years old!

My specialist was considered one of the top muscular specialists in the country, but also had some of the best bedside manners we have encountered from a specialist doctor. He genuinely cared for each of his patients. Each time he had to deliver news that would alter the course of someone's life, and particularly ours, he was incredibly kind, warm, empathetic, with an undertone that spoke of concern. When he came to talk to us about the results, the expression on his face was enough for my parents to sense something wasn't quite right.

He also didn't sugarcoat his words, like the time he said, "It appears your daughter has muscular dystrophy."

In the early 2000s in Australia, my family had never even heard of it. Naturally, we had the routine cliché questions that anyone receiving a diagnosis would ask. We wondered, "What medication is available?" "How can we fix this and make it go away?" But this wasn't just a simple cold.

The doctor kindly explained that the results indicated muscular dystrophy, but they couldn't pinpoint which type it was due to the limited technology at the time. He shared that it was a progressive muscle-wasting condition that would worsen as I aged. While the prognosis was uncertain, it wasn't very promising, especially for those with more aggressive forms like Duchenne, who often didn't make it past eighteen years old.

And just like that, my family's dream of what life would be like as a family of four imploded with shock, denial, sadness, and fear. Their firstborn was faced with a terminal illness, bringing a lifetime of uncertainty. The bubble of what they thought I would do in my life was suddenly dangerously close to bursting.

On our way home, we stopped at Maccas (a.k.a. McDonald's), where my family sat in stunned silence. My mum's head was already swirling with more questions and things to research; my dad's guilt, feeling like somehow it was his fault, was almost too much to bear. Meanwhile, I enjoyed my lunch, utterly unaware of the pin-dropping silence and loud thoughts of those around me, and that my life would take a drastically different turn than that of other kids my age.

One of the most surprising things to learn was that muscular dystrophy was often seen as a condition mainly affecting males. So, when the lab work confirmed that I had muscular dystrophy, it was a shock not just for my specialist but also for my family.

Before I continue, I am sure you may be scratching your head wondering what muscular dystrophy is. Just to clarify, it isn't the same as multiple sclerosis (MS). Also, I'm not a doctor (thank goodness!), so my insights come from my own understanding and some handy help from our good friend, Dr. Google.

Muscular dystrophy (MD) involves muscles—straightforward! The term "dystrophy" means tissues or organs waste away. The muscles in our bodies are made up of various proteins and collagens that aid in regeneration, repair, growth, and building strength. This fascinating process lets us tackle challenges like climbing stairs, running along a beach, lifting heavy textbooks, simply scratching our heads, and tying our shoelaces. However, in the case of Duchenne MD, muscles lack a crucial protein called dystrophin, which is essential for muscle repair. Without it, the muscles don't bounce back after use, making navigating life feel like pushing an immovable boulder.

MD, in many patients, depending on the type, can also affect the heart, lungs, and diaphragm, eventually making it impossible to breathe or cough up mucus if you're sick, leading to a high risk of pneumonia, which... Well, you can imagine what happens when your breathing and heart aren't functioning properly.

After my diagnosis, my parents struggled to accept that there wasn't much that could be done, except for maintaining the strength I already had. Fortunately, the specialist referred us to Montrose Access, a wonderful organisation specialising in muscular conditions. They provided a one-stop shop for everything needed during the early stages of MD, from orthotics to neurologists, occupational therapists, and physiotherapists—so much support was available!

Yet, even with all of this, my family felt a strong need for answers: questions like "How?", "When?", and "Why?" filled their minds. My mum threw herself into researching, often staying up late through nights shadowed by fear, despair, and anxiety as she sought to understand more about MD. One shared belief in the disability community is to steer clear of Dr. Google, since it often presents the worst-case scenarios and leaves little room for hope or optimism. For anyone grappling with a life-altering diagnosis, holding onto hope and optimism is essential, rather than drowning in extremes. So, you can imagine that instead of finding clarity or a glimmer of hope, she encountered a daunting reality that seemed hard to escape but was gradually becoming our new normal. My parents often consoled each other, desperately trying to lift each other up, yet one lingering question remained: "Will all of this happen to our baby?"

Nearly a year after my diagnosis, on February 18, 2004, my wonderful paediatrician referred us to a professor at Westmead in Sydney. After more investigations and testing, we learned I had Congenital Ullrich or Bethlem Myopathy, a condition linked to a deficiency of Collagen VI in the muscle. This isn't the collagen found in hair, skin, and nails. Imagine if it were, though; those collagen supplements from the supermarket would be stocked up in my cupboard for sure.

This new information finally gave us the direction we'd been searching for, which we hoped would also give us a plan to be able to tackle this condition head-on, ensuring I had the best quality of life I possibly could have.

Despite the uncertainty and the terrifying doctor visits and seemingly endless reports, what none of us realised then was that this wasn't the end of my story, not even close. Contrary to what many would automatically believe—that I wouldn't have a life—the reality is actually the complete opposite. That day in 2004, in that doctor's office, a journey began that would redefine strength, hope, and what it truly means to live truthfully.

Looking back, those early signs were like whispers—easy to miss but impossible to ignore forever. My body was speaking its own language, and soon, it would be loud enough that no one could pretend not to hear. It would form the basis of every decision, every thought process, and every fibre of my being. That neurologist appointment was the moment everything shifted.

But it wasn't the end—it was the beginning. The beginning of a woven tapestry of twists and turns that proves that life should not be defined by limitation, but instead, by strength, faith, and the kind of Dutch courage you don't know you have until you need it. Life had rewritten the "traditional" script, but maybe... just maybe, I was born to improvise.

CHAPTER 2

SMALL BUT MIGHTY:
A CHILDHOOD REIMAGINED

At Kindy, I was a bride—several times over, actually. There was one boy in my class who was always willing to "marry" me. We'd have a grand pretend wedding, me in a dress, made from whatever scraps of fabric or costumes we could find in the dress-up box, and him, in a mismatched jacket three sizes too big. Our ceremonies were quick—no time for long vows when lunch was waiting—so as soon as we declared ourselves "married," we'd both make a run for it, or in my case, a fast waddle, to grab our lunches. Afterwards, we'd spend the rest of the time conquering the playground equipment or digging up entire worlds in the sandpit.

Growing up with a disability brought a unique perspective to my life. Having said that, the plus side to being a four-year-old with a disability was that the world hadn't left its mark yet. And as a result, I was oblivious to the fact that I was different from my friends. We were simply a bunch of kids building sandcastles and playing Go Fish and tag. Naivety presented the opportunity to simply enjoy every day as it came. Life was simple and fun, and everyone treated each other with kindness, the way life should be, no matter our age.

To be honest, I was like my peers in many ways. Due to the slow-progressing nature of my condition, my differences weren't starkly obvious to me and many others my age. I was just another kid navigating the world one-scraped-knee and playground-adventure at a time.

I could run around, albeit slower than everyone else, but I was oblivious. I could climb slowly and sometimes not as high on the playground equipment, but I managed. I made my own bed for nap time like everyone else, even if it did take me a minute, and I often gave up on making sure the fitted sheet was tucked under the mattress.

Basically, I was your average toddler—full of tantrums but just as full of imagination and adventure.

One thing that did make me stand out from my peers, probably more so than my physical differences, was my separation anxiety. When it came time to say goodbye to my mum at the start of the day at Kindy, I would cling to her and kick and scream like it was the end of the world! To this day, I still have, perhaps, a slight degree of separation anxiety. At times, I still feel a little anxious being away from my family. But hey, at least I no longer kick and scream about it!

Sure, there were things I couldn't do or struggled to do, but when you're four years old, you have no concept of difference. You don't wonder why people your age can do things that you struggle with. Either way, I was filled with naïve determination and went about my day loving life. I refused to be left behind and would waddle as fast as my legs could take me—never wanting to miss a minute of all the fun on the swings or that cool science experiment using cornstarch and water that looks like a mix between Play-Doh and slime but turns to water the minute you pick it up, magically entertaining everyone for hours on end. I still remember its smell to this day.

But my childhood wasn't all about finger-painting and nap times. Part of the parcel that comes with the disability life, especially if your condition is progressive and terminal, is regular doctor visits. This was a significant part of my reimagined childhood. Instead of blending in, spending hours on end exploring, playing with my impressive Barbie doll collection, dressing up as a princess, or running around outside to play cops and robbers with my younger brother, many of my childhood memories also consist of doctors' rooms and hospital hallways.

Because we didn't move to Brisbane after my diagnosis, every six months or so, my parents would put me and my brother in the car and drive an hour and a half to Brisbane to meet with the never-ending team of specialists. It became a routine—a rhythm of medical check-ups woven into the fabric of my growing-up years.

Given the long line of specialists to see, we would start our day, bright and early, to be at Montrose Access by 9:00 a.m., if not earlier. Montrose felt like it was on acres and acres of land near a soothing stream, lined with tall gumtrees. Green sports fields bordered the long driveway; for a kid, it felt more like an adventure than a hospital visit. I would stare out the car window, counting trees and imagining stories about the animals hidden in the trees, not to mention what would be for lunch as my reward for going to the doctor. On the other hand, my brother was usually less than enthralled by the scenery—he was more interested in how long we'd be stuck there and what snacks Mum had packed.

First on the list would be pre-appointment testing and a check-up with the occupational therapist (OT), who became almost like another grandma to me. She was always up for a chat and would greet me with a warm hug. The testing began by timing how fast I could run up the hall and back. This appealed to my competitive streak, and I would run as hard and fast as possible. Because of my age, I couldn't tell if my time was any good, but I believed my OT and my parents when they said, "Wow, that was fast! Amazing job!" Let's be honest—why tell a kid, "Yeah, see, kids your age run a lot faster, but good job anyway!"

Other tests included trying to walk around on my heels and reflex tests. As a young girl, I always thought the tests were fun—mainly because, to me, they felt easy, even though to those on the outside, it looked like I was struggling. My brother would often sit on the sidelines, swinging his legs back and forth on a chair, clearly bored but supportive in his own way. He didn't have to go through these tests, but he was still part of the experience—watching, waiting, and sometimes, cheering me on.

However, as I grew older and the challenges started adding up, the tests, too, began to evolve. I was tasked with getting onto the ground and being timed to see how long it would take me to stand up. Originally, initially without assistance, but by the time I was around eight years old, I could no longer get off the ground without someone helping me or having a chair to act as leverage.

That was a tough pill to swallow—the first real moment when the "fun" of the tests started to wear off, replaced by the sinking reality that I was slowly losing abilities I once took for granted. And the questions began, slightly running through my head, "Why is this hard? I used to be able to do this no problem," and "What is wrong with me?"

Next, after testing, was usually a quick trip to the orthopaedist. He was a hilarious man and always took the time to listen to my random stories about school or just joke around. He was the one responsible for fitting me with countless AFOs—back in the day, I affectionately called them Moon Boots, because to me, they did look like the boots Neil Armstrong wore on the moon. They were splints made from plastic with hard foam inside, and your legs were held in place with Velcro straps. They were designed to keep my feet fixed at a 90-degree angle as I slept to slow down the tightness in my Achilles and stop me from walking on my toes.

The process of casting my feet in seemingly never-ending layers of cold and wet plaster rolls placed over a stocking and a skinny, long piece of flexible plastic running from my knee out past my toes took what felt like hours, but was probably more like an hour or so. After the plaster hardened, he would use a skin-safe electric plaster cutter to cut a line down to the plastic strip inside the mould, and free my feet from their plaster prison. I still remember the smell of the room lined with completed AFOS and freshly made plaster casts.

The last appointment to wrap up a rather long day was to see the neurologist. Being a specialist, she would usually run a little late, so to pass the time, I would often walk over to look at the river along the side of the building. It was so peaceful, listening to the movement of the water, the birds in the trees talking to one another, hearing the splashing of the hydrotherapy session in the indoor pool only meters away, wishing one day I would get the chance to swim in that pool.

Standing on the landing, looking over the water in the stream and hearing the splashes from the pool and the birds chirping, it was like time stood still; everything was calm, and there was no care in the world; nothing was wrong.

Eventually, I would get a tap on my shoulder, or a distant voice would call my name, snap me out of my trance, and, like a bad case of whiplash, I would return to reality. When I was young, the visits to the neurologist were fun; I felt so clever being able to do all the tests she wanted me to do—it was yet another challenge I had to win. From walking on my heels, jumping, seeing how long I could balance on one foot, reflex tests, resistance tests—you name it—I did it. She often asked me how school was going, and what my favourite subjects were, while I stood there balancing like a flamingo or hopping around like a kangaroo.

Like I said, it was fun. I didn't know why I was being asked to do all these challenges, but I thought I was doing a good job because of all the praise I was getting from both my parents and my neurologist.

After I had completed all the tests, there were times when I would then be free to rummage around the toy box in the doctor's office and allow my mind to wander into a different land. At the same time, my parents discussed the more essential things like disease progress, the results from the tests earlier that day with the OT, and any concerns they had about my day-to-day life.

There were times, however, as I got older, around eleven years of age, when at the end of my routine tests and a quick chat with the doctor, I was ushered out of the room while my parents wrapped up the appointment. To this day, I don't know what was discussed on those handful of occasions, but I could usually tell something wasn't 100 percent right, given the fallen faces of my parents and my mum looking like she was on the verge of tears. For a long time, I didn't know the severity of my condition and what it meant long term. And to be honest, for years, I thought everyone went through yearly visits to specialists, which is true, but not entirely.

Growing up, my parents only told me the necessities of my condition when I started asking questions about why I was "different." The simple explanation was, "When God was making you, he got his measurements slightly off, which means that you aren't as strong as everyone else." This simple explanation was something I could understand. However, given I was so young, it didn't register with me exactly what that meant.

But that was the whole point. It was an answer that ensured I wasn't burdened with knowledge that would sink the Titanic, of what I envisioned life to be twice over, and especially made sure that I could continue to be a kid as much as possible. I was spared the more in-depth and scary details until much later on in life.

When I reached around twelve or thirteen, the most memorable shift came when the neurologist announced that I was doing so surprisingly well that our six-monthly appointments could become yearly. My parents were over the moon, and to be honest, so was I. I had begun noticing more and more how my disability was impacting my everyday life, and in many ways, I was starting to feel uneasy and uncertain. So to receive such positive news from my neurologist felt like a small victory— a rare win in a world often felt dominated by limits and losses.

For the first time, it felt like maybe, just maybe, I wasn't losing this race after all. A small glimmer of hope radiated through my family like a small ripple in a pond. I will never forget walking to the car that afternoon, and my parents beaming with happiness and excitement.

However, as relieved as I was with the positive news, and seeing my parents and my younger brother, who was probably happier that he was able to have another day off school, I was silently being crushed from the inside, which I kept to myself as I didn't want to pop the long-awaited hope bubble that surrounded my family.

Visit after visit became monotonous, the same tests, conversations, and charts showing percentiles where my little blip slipped further and further behind the mainstream blip. The tests became harder, and the time it took to complete the tests became longer. Getting up off the floor used to mean going from sitting to standing. Now, it meant lying on my back and then trying to stand as quickly as possible. Attempting to stand up from the age of eight became like trying to stand up with three bags of concrete on my back. I went from standing with little assistance to using a chair for balance, to then, by my early teens, having to smoosh my face into the seat, cricking my neck as I pushed my face and body into the chair, and inching my legs forward, tiny step by tiny step, before I could stand.

With my parents watching on, the echoing happy shrieks of my brother in the gymnasium playing on all the multicoloured boxes and crash mats, and the OT standing over me with her black stopwatch and clipboard in hand, I felt humiliated and embarrassed. I wanted so desperately for the gymnasium to swallow me up whole. I tried desperately to show my parents and the OT that I was proud and that it was "easy-peasy" while hoping that I didn't have a red mark on my head from how hard I pressed it into the plastic chair. Like any teenager, you want to be seen as in control, confident, and as least embarrassed as possible.

These tests were the epitome of humiliation and embarrassment—they felt soul-destroying.

Soon enough, I vetoed the test, with the task of going from floor to standing without human or chair assistance becoming impossible as I grew taller and weaker. Hopping and jumping soon followed, as did walking on my heels. The contractures in my elbows became more pronounced, leaving my arms resembling penguin arms. I often say now for shits and giggles that given my waddle walk and my arms, I may as well be a penguin.

What I thought was good, my body barely reacting to reflex tests, I soon understood was not a good thing. The only thing I was still remotely good at was balancing on one foot, so much so that after what seemed like five minutes, the doctor said to me, "Clearly you are still good at that. You may as well stop." It felt like they were more interested in seeing me struggle than succeed.

The endless tests soon became less about a challenge, and I felt like another number, where everyone was waiting and watching for me to give up or be forced to give up. I was being compared to the scientific presentation of muscular dystrophy, not of Ullrich, but of Duchenne.

Even more so, I wasn't seen as an individual and compared to my own abilities. I was measured against what science dictated where I should or shouldn't be.

It was in those moments that the innocence of childhood began to crack just a little. The childhood imagination, lunchtime adventures, and sandpit kingdoms were still there, but they now lived alongside a growing awareness that my path would be different. It wasn't just about waddling faster or climbing slower—it was about realising that some things might eventually slip away. And yet, even as those cracks appeared, there was a stubborn fire within me—one I like to think I inherited from my grandfather—that refused to let go of the joy, the imagination, and the fierce determination to keep moving forward, no matter how hard the tests became. Simply because I had no other choice. Life continued, good days or bad. I had to keep going.

One of the other places I became familiar with early in my disability journey was the respiratory clinic at the Mater Children's Hospital, later Lady Cilento, in Brisbane. Muscular dystrophy doesn't discriminate what muscle group it targets, and for many of us, it doesn't spare a single muscle, including the heart, lungs, and diaphragm. Ullrich MD not only affects the muscles that allow me to move and cook dinner for my family, but it also impacts my lungs and diaphragm. This not-so-little detail means that my lung function—the amount of oxygen I can inhale and exhale—becomes smaller, and my diaphragm becomes weaker. Belly breathing quickly became a thing of the past, with lower respiratory function becoming equally nonexistent, and I had to rely on my upper respiratory system.

If you would like a small glimpse into what that feels like for me, simply inhale to your limit, then slowly exhale 50 percent, then exhale another 10 percent. Now, that is your mark for a full breath. Make note of that marker and exhale the rest of your oxygen before taking an inhale to that 40 percent mark. Now, take a few breaths, breathing to that line. Chances are, you may be starting to panic or feel restricted. And there is also a chance that you are engaging your lower diagram or the lower half of your lungs. Try that 40 percent breathing, just purely breathing from up high in your chest, and try not to engage the lower part at all.

How does that feel now? Scary? Has your body started to panic, asking for more air? Does it feel even more restrictive? Are you kicking yourself for even trying this exercise? Is your body asking, "What the fuck are you doing to me?"

Breathing like this is normal for me. The body is a marvellous and curious thing in that it adapts to changes rather rapidly. My lung function has been ever so slowly decreasing for many, many years, and I don't regularly notice, so I don't feel panicked or like I can't get enough oxygen in. For me, I am simply just breathing in the way my body is able to. I only notice how difficult breathing is for me once I try to belly breathe. If I take a large inhale at the same time someone else does, I can hear the difference.

For a lot of us with MD, we eventually end up on oxygen and BiPAP machines to assist with our breathing as it becomes worse. I'm not a scientist or doctor, so I won't even try to explain what a BiPAP machine does exactly. I am also still recovering from referencing my Law dissertation, where I had around 150 footnote references, so just the thought of footnoting for a reference is giving me an eye twitch.

Anyway, to keep track of how much oxygen your body brings in to keep you alive, you undergo a series of lung function tests. This would require another trip to Brisbane to see the respiratory specialist, and you guessed it, another early start to get to Brisbane on time.

Perhaps the best part of the whole experience was this amazing room where the stale blue hospital walls were transformed into a space full of vibrant colours, where arts and crafts were plentiful to satisfy any dreamer, and video games were available for those who preferred imagining the wind in their hair and claiming victory in the Daytona 500. This little slice of heaven was the Starlight Room. You knew exactly where it was, as the red, 12-foot floor-to-ceiling double doors with an oversized star on the door handles were impossible to miss.

For those of us, outpatients and inpatients, the Starlight Room offered the chance to escape and, just for a moment, forget the doctors, the hospital, and the fact that we were "sick." We could be kids. Each one of us was a complete stranger, and yet, somehow, we bonded almost with an unspoken word simply because we understood what each person was going through. As we coloured in, tried our hand at making chatterboxes, or cheered on the people at the video game stations, we all engaged in small talk until, yet again, our parents or doctors came into the room and called us to know it was time for our appointments.

I will never forget the many times over the past ten or more years that I had to go to the Mater and would beg my parents to let my brother and me go to the Starlight Room. It was conveniently located right next to the main reception and waiting room on the wing, so my brother and I took every opportunity to go, run amok, and just be kids. I craved any chance I could get to have fun instead of the boring adult talk. Alas, the fun would be cut short mid-colouring as my parents would soon walk in, and with a nod, I knew it was time to blow out fake candles on a computer screen like my life depended on it, because it did.

The lung function tests are rather terrifying, especially if you are borderline claustrophobic. They put a peg with foam padding on your nose, and you must inhale as hard and fast as possible through this tube with a mouthpiece that contains a filter, and then exhale with just as much effort to expel all the oxygen in your lungs. The machines measure all sorts of things related to how much oxygen you get in, the strength of your lungs, and a range of other things that make no sense to me. Numbers and maths are clearly not my strong suit.

The range of tests they do and the different breathing styles they make you do seem to never end. Having to pant like a dog with the tube still in your mouth while they cut the air off using the filter for a few sections, then it, coming back on, and having to immediately take an inhale and exhale as hard and fast as possible is as mentally complicated as it is physically. Shutting the air off and not being able to breathe, given the peg is still on your nose, and being completely at the mercy of the person running the tests, truly demonstrates the definition of trust.

There were many times I nearly pulled away from the machine because of the anxiety, and the way the machine changes your breathing because of the mouthpiece makes it feel as though somehow you can't breathe, even when you can. For the first few years of doing the lung function tests, I would remain standing. Once, I tried so hard that I almost passed out because I truly got rid of all the air and then some in my lungs.

Much like the neurology visits, these appointments were also yearly, thank goodness. Also just like the OT tests, these tests started out fun purely because of the fun birthday cake graphics on the screen. The challenge was trying to blow out all the candles on the cake; I never could, hence almost passing out from desperation to blow out all the candles. Again, the inner competitive streak was in full force. However, as I got older, the conversation phase of the appointment became something I dreaded just as much as the tests themselves. Seeing the percentage on the screen get lower and lower and the little blip showing people my age gradually becoming higher, while mine once again went in the opposite direction, was crushing.

The older I became, the more I realised what those numbers meant; my lungs were getting weaker. And without oxygen, you can't breathe, which in my mind meant I was slowly suffocating, and I didn't know it because my body adapted whenever my lungs got worse by a few percentage points. As I write this, my lung function is sitting around 42 percent. At the moment, my respiratory specialist is satisfied that my sleep study results indicate that while I have mild sleep apnoea, it's not bad enough to warrant a BiPAP machine.

I have been told that nothing will really ever improve my lung function. However, I improved it by about 2 percent last time, and I put that down to consciously taking larger breaths and stretching out the lung tissue. Who knows the real reason, but I love nothing more than showing science that I am simply just not going to be part of the status quo, as much as it is a relief to me that I am not *like everyone else.*

Fast-forward to seventeen years old, yes, we will jump around in this book, but bear with me, I had my last appointment with the paediatric neurologist before transitioning to the adult system. I was excited, but at the same time, the anxiety was fast overriding the excitement. Neurologists with a specialisation or interest in muscular dystrophy in the adult medical system are rare, particularly here in Australia, mainly because it is equally rare that someone with MD reaches adulthood, let alone having MD to begin with.

After the usual strength tests, which were mainly just resistance against her pushing and pulling my arms and hands and checking the contractures in my elbows and Achilles, she then told me the news that

I had been wanting to hear for years. "I think you are doing amazingly well, and your condition has stabilised in the last few years. So, I think if you can keep up with looking after yourself, I don't think you should see any major issues until you reach your 40s or early 50s." This was music to my ears and gave me the biggest boost of hope that I had had since I learnt what MD was. I left that appointment crying tears of joy, as opposed to the regularly scheduled tears of uncertainty or straight-up dissociating.

However, the adult medical system is another beast. I call it the invisible beast. What I mean by that is for people with muscular dystrophy, finding a neurologist or a specialist with an interest or background in MD is virtually impossible, especially here in Australia.

Since I became an adult, I have seen a neurologist perhaps once or twice. The last time I saw a neurologist was when I was around twenty-three. I was referred by my respiratory specialist, who said he was fantastic and that it would be good to have a team assembled and to have regular contact with them in case anything out of the ordinary occurred.

It was perhaps one of the worst doctor visits of my life, not because of the information but because of the lack thereof. He told me he didn't know much about MD and was confused why I was seeing him. After a somewhat awkward conversation full of long silences, I asked him about treatments and trials. "There is a stem cell treatment being used in the US, and I have a friend who is benefiting from it. I would love your thoughts on it and whether it's something we should consider."

He replied, "It's something that isn't really offered here in Australia, but it sounds like you have done your research on it. If you can do more research into it and give me the research papers you find discussing the treatment, I will investigate it and see if it's something that could help."

He then slugged me close to $500 for the half-hour appointment. That costs more than the Gastro surgeons my mum works for. Of course, I recouped some of that money via Medicare, but it was still a ridiculous amount for a short appointment and to be told I had to do the research myself.

Not for the first time, I left the appointment frustrated and told my mum I would rather not bother with neurologists any more. At my review appointment with my respiratory specialist, who, unlike the neurologist, showed genuine interest in my symptoms and did her research on my condition and was passionate about my treatment and my quality of life, she was horrified and taken aback that the neurologist didn't show much interest or care surrounding treatment and my condition.

This is, unfortunately, a common occurrence: being treated as no more than just a number rather than a human. I don't think I can count the number of times I have begged and pleaded with doctors, showing and telling them that I have been able to stand up, off the floor with the help of my bed rather than a person, for the first time in over ten years to be told, "Hmm... yeah. That's great." in a dismissive tone.

Being a patient is often filled with frustration and alienation. You aren't taken seriously and are often just used as data, and any questions about treatments or trials are shot down without even an, "I'll look into it and let you know." when you know full well there are treatments out there. Sometimes, you question whether or not it is worth the hassle, not to mention the expense, of going to appointments to be told the same thing over and over, like a broken record: "We've got nothing to offer."

I believe the lack of answers and being seen as a human are also part of the territory of having a rare condition like muscular dystrophy. There are often more questions than there are answers, leaving you to stumble across dead-end after dead-end. It's unrelenting, frustrating, and tiring. Especially knowing there are treatments happening in other countries, and those exact treatments are still sitting with our government, which has yet to even look at the topic. You are left feeling alienated, not only by the people you are paying to "treat" you, but by the people your country votes for.

It challenges your resilience from the jump, not to mention your patience. You realise very early on that if you are to continue having a quality of life while maintaining your independence and mobility, it is up to you to start thinking outside the box, try everything you can, and leave your fear and, at times, ego out the door.

That isn't me saying doctors and medicine are shit. Quite the opposite! They are incredibly beneficial for most people, and I have received amazing care in the past. But to be honest, I regularly question—if I wasn't forced to get a mobility scooter as young as I did, would I be in better or worse shape than I am now? Was it inevitable based on the science? We will never know.

While I had a vastly reimagined childhood full of doctor visits, confusion, and uncomfortable moments, the ultimate test was juggling the world of school on top of the appointments and an ever-weakening body. This became the time that would send me down a road perhaps more unfamiliar and isolating than the stale blue of hospital walls.

CHAPTER 3

PLAYGROUND POLITICS: BULLIES, BATTLES, AND BREAKTHROUGHS

Ah, school. A time full of lessons, both in the classroom and in the playground. These can be the best or the most trying years of your life. It all depends on which side of the coin you land on. And, to add to that, you have no say in the matter. Well, perhaps the only influencing factor is your level of confidence. Or, as the kids of today say, your *rizz*.

If you were different—whether due to religion, skin colour, disability, or even having freckles, ginger hair, glasses, or braces—then you were basically walking around with a piece of paper stuck to your back saying, "Pick on me!" Everyone loves judging those who are sociologically different. However, I am about to burst your bubble: Everyone is different! Yes, even if you're identical twins. Shocker, I know.

So, why are certain kids being bullied relentlessly in school? I attribute it to a combination of factors. I may sound rather controversial, but bear with me: Usually, bullying is done by people who grow up thinking there is something wrong with being different. To them, uniqueness isn't celebrated or even just viewed as something that doesn't need to be pointed out every minute of the day. These viewpoints turn to mocks, taunts, and jokes, told amongst family members, which kids then listen to and believe are perfectly fine to think and say.

These kids, now, take that viewpoint to the playground. As soon as they see someone who looks "different," they are unsure of how to interact with them. Instead of having a good conversation about it at home, where it's explained that everyone is different and that it is okay, they are told that those people are simply *born* different. And that one statement can then lead to bullying.

That's my opinion, anyway. I could be completely wrong, but at the end of the day, as the line in *Cool Runnings* goes, "Everyone is always afraid of what is different." And that is, unfortunately, the case, and it has been so for many, many years.

I was fortunate enough to have gone through school before Instagram took off, before everyone owned smartphones and had social media accounts, when bullies would say insults to your face, not while sitting behind computer screens, typing curses on their keyboards.

I am grateful I didn't have to endure cyberbullying back when I was in school, although, I have had some of the most horrid things said to me via social media by grown adults! I have been told they hope I burn in hell, and that I am disabled as punishment from God. Some have even said they are praying God casts me down to hell ASAP, and that I am simply taking up society's space and oxygen.

If I wasn't in a good mental space, I would hate to imagine what those things would have done to me. So, my heart breaks for every person who has gone through cyberbullying at school.

A few months before the start of school in 2005, the occupational therapist and physiotherapist at Montrose recommended I use a mobility scooter to help with the long-walking distances and navigating the playground. So, I was four years old when I first started driving—a significant flex for a city girl!

I still remember being a daredevil on an occasional afternoon, once I arrived home from school on our driveway. Let's say a three-wheeler, doing doughnuts, and high-speed are the perfect combination, especially if you want missing front teeth.

I only attempted this stunt twice—and yes, I didn't learn the first time I faceplanted on our concrete driveway after my scooter tipped over. I also recall a few broken potted plants caused by a head-on collision on the patio. Perhaps, giving a four-year-old a "vehicle" wasn't the wisest decision to make.

Because I was so tiny, they had to source a custom foot block for my scooter to help me stay as flat-footed as possible while driving. It had something to do with balance, which is odd since it was a three-wheeler, and it did nothing to help with staying upright when doing doughnuts. But sometimes? You must go with the flow.

The emphasis on my feet reaching the floor extended to having a footrest under my desk at school, made out of two or three phone books—those big yellow books used to find phone numbers and businesses—that were taped together and covered in any old wrapping paper or contact paper. I wasn't the only one in my class who couldn't reach the floor, but alas, the physiotherapist and OT were adamant, so this makeshift footrest accompanied me until, at least, Grade 5.

There was also a concern about my grip and my hands getting tired from holding a pencil, so I had to use triangular pencil grips. Even though I kept insisting I was fine, the adults in my life were, again, firm about me using those bright orange grips. I took them off my pencil and kept them off until the OT and physiotherapist from Montrose paid a visit. Only then would I put the grips back on, unless I forgot. In that case, they would look at me with politely scolding eyes and say, "Rhiannon, you need to use these." I would still take them off later, especially since the kids in my class started asking why I needed them.

There were a couple of classes where a teacher's aide would come and sit with me to take over writing so my hands didn't get tired. I usually didn't have a say in whether they wrote for me. My hands never really became tired, and my handwriting was the textbook left-handed scrawl, which probably gave them enough evidence to say I was tired. Again, despite knowing your body, as a kid, you are rarely listened to because adults and specialists know best.

All these lovely things combined, along with my apparent waddling gait and the peculiar way I got up from the floor, made me the perfect target for teasing, especially since I was the only kid in the school who rode a mobility scooter and walked oddly.

The bullying started when I was in Grade 2 or 3, as far as I can remember. But because I was only six or seven years old, I was naïve. I couldn't figure out what they were talking about, which, in hindsight, was a good thing.

One of the first instances I can remember was at what we Aussies call the "bubblers," or water fountains for everyone else. I was filling up my water bottle at the bubblers when this kid walked past me and laughed; I wasn't sure what he was laughing at, so I just brushed it off.

A couple of days passed, and he walked past me again. But this time, he was with a friend in a higher grade than us. He turned to her and said, "This girl walks like this." and proceeded to do a silly walk that would have received critical acclaim if it was a part of the Monty Python *Ministry of Silly Walks* Sketch. I was still oblivious to the fact that I had any disability or that my walk resembled somewhat that of a penguin, so I just thought he was just being stupid. I looked at the person he was with and just shrugged my shoulders, not knowing what the deal was. She just shrugged back and smiled slightly, and carried on her way. I like to think she, too, didn't know what he was talking about, or if she did, she was able to realise that laughing at someone wasn't the best thing in the world to do.

From Grade 4 onwards, the bullying started to pick up. I helped a friend who was going through a horrid time outside of school—she didn't appreciate it, and, as a result, made my life hell.

I found myself being kicked relentlessly under desks, stood on in the playground, grabbed by the shirt, and my friend circle being made to believe I was some nasty person, when all I did was get my friend some help. What, perhaps, made it worse was that it was the first time an adult didn't believe me when I said my friend was hurting me.

The day she stood on my ankle so hard that she broke the skin and drew blood; we were out in the playground. She saw that I was trying to reach our teacher, who I hoped was still in our classroom. It was around a good 50 to a 100-metre walk from the playground. Because I didn't need to have my scooter with me all the time back then, as I could still navigate the playground and school grounds well on my legs, I was significantly slower than everyone else.

I tried to move as quickly as I could, but when she saw me waddling, trying to get to our classroom, she took off in a sprint. By the time I got to our classroom, she had already told the teacher her version of the story, and when I told him mine—that she walked past me and stood on my ankle with force, he said, "Both of you go and sit down." That was the only thing said, and the situation was never addressed again. He didn't come to check on my graze or send me to the medical room for an antiseptic or a plaster. He just dismissed it.

Those twelve months were horrid, and it took me years to try and process what happened, mainly because she spoke to everyone I tried to make friends with and said that I was some horrible person. As a result, I began to lose my self-esteem. I started to believe her and second-guessed how I helped her, if I did help her, and if what I did made me some horrible person who should have just shut up and not said a word. It took me about five years to understand that I had done nothing wrong; I helped a friend who needed help, and it wasn't my fault how she reacted.

The rest of my schooling career was also marred by bullying, but this time, it's based on my disability. The surprising thing was that the bullies were two of my closest friends. For the sake of this story, we will call them "Mindy" and "Carla."

Grade 6 was the first time they called me a retard. I had never been called that word until then. I was ten years old. They didn't call me a retard to my face but behind my back. I found out a few months later when Carla told me after the two had a brief falling out. She told me one day during lunch that Mindy said, "She's a retard—get it? Rhi-tard?'

My nickname is Rhi, and she took the opportunity to merge a slur about disability with my nickname. It felt like the biggest kick in the guts because these were the two people I relied on and thought understood me and my condition. They had helped me grab my lunch when I needed extra assistance and would come over for play dates after school.

It was shocking to me that instead of the bully being some random student, they were the ones who decided to treat me as if I were subhuman. Bullying and the feeling of being bullied, especially about something you are born with, is perhaps one of the things that you aren't told about when you first learn about your "difference," probably for good reason. No one prepares you for being picked on because of the way you were born. When it happens, you feel so low, insignificant, and invisible.

I tried my best not to react and shrugged it off, even though I went home crying. That wasn't the right thing to do. When they realised they weren't getting a reaction from me, they escalated and started to dehumanise me completely.

One day in class, they talked about me while I was right next to them. Unfortunately, I could hear everything since we were sitting together. And when I told them to stop, Mindy looked at Carla and said, "Did you hear that? It sounds like buzzing; I can't hear anything! Oh no, wait, it's just 'It.' What do you want, It? Nope, still hear buzzing!"

Yep, you read correctly. I was referred to, not as a person, but as a thing—as an "It."

To me, that was worse than being called a retard. It meant to make me feel invisible and worthless. And I felt that I most certainly did, all at eleven years old.

I wish I could say this was a one-time event, but unfortunately, it went on for what felt like months.

I remember a day when the bullying was relentless, and I returned from lunch to find all my stationery missing. For those who aren't Australian, in primary school, we would stay in the same classroom for all our classes each year and had 'tidy trays' attached underneath our desks to hold our books and stationery. I kept my ruler, a pen and pencil, an eraser, and a highlighter at the top of my desk daily; it made me feel organised and oddly satisfied having them arranged in a triangular formation with my ruler at the top working down to my eraser. But when I came in from lunch that day, my stomach dropped. My stationery and water bottle, along with my pencil case, which was always left in my tidy tray, were missing.

I immediately felt a wave of panic wash over me. How was I going to do work without any pens or pencils? As I got closer to my desk, I noticed a white piece of paper on my desk. It was addressed to "IT." I can still remember what it said: "To IT, where is your stationery? We told you this place was haunted."

As I finished reading that, Mindy and Carla walked in the door and smirked at me. I made a beeline straight for our teacher, but they cut me off, snatched the paper from my hand, tore it up, and threw it in the bin. Suddenly, I had no evidence of what they were doing to me.

The mental scars from the events of Grade 4 convinced me that the teacher wouldn't believe me if I told him what happened. So, I didn't bother talking to him, especially without that evidence. Fortunately, they returned my stationery shortly after destroying the note.

However, the damage was done; I felt alone, scared, ugly, and like a waste of space. The scars from the past became deeper and deeper with the lashes from the present. I was also in the throes of struggling with the death of my grandfather three years earlier. Very quickly, my mind was becoming quicksand, and I was that helpless little victim stuck in its grasp.

Around the same time, the muscular dystrophy felt that it was the perfect opportunity to challenge me even more and join forces with the beginnings of puberty.

Seemingly overnight, climbing stairs on my own was becoming nearly impossible, and sitting on the picnic benches at lunch was also becoming more challenging by the day. You can imagine my shock when I was placed in a classroom up two flights of stairs when the Year 7 students in my class went on their week-long Sydney-Canberra school camp. My mum was ready to call the school and say that I was staying at home for the week, but I was stubborn and adamant that I wanted to go to school. So, I told her I could manage the stairs.

I thought I could handle the week, but by the end of day one, after painfully navigating the stairs four or five times that day, they quickly became more difficult and dangerous to climb. Lifting my legs felt like trying to lift concrete blocks, and my body became exhausted. I gripped the railing until my knuckles turned white and painstakingly stepped up, one step at a time; it took me fifteen minutes to climb up the two flights. This often meant I was incredibly late for class, which didn't help my anxiety whatsoever.

Being unable to access my classroom and having the school automatically place me in an upstairs classroom felt like a sick joke. Not only did my peers think I was the perfect joke, but my school seemingly overlooked all the meetings and conversations about ensuring my classrooms were downstairs. A person can only handle so much.

And after relentless bullying and my body struggling, I broke.

I got halfway up the stairs that afternoon, after, yet, another day of relentless bullying: my stationery and pencil case stolen yet again by the same two people, my body was screaming for there to be no more stairs in my future, and my brain was screaming, begging for the name-calling and the stealing to stop.

I stood on that landing, my legs shaking from exertion and dread, and I burst into tears. I just wanted to go home. Then, all of a sudden, it was like my prayers were magically answered.

That afternoon, I told Mum what was going on, and she, too, had had enough of the relentless bullying and the fact that my school couldn't be bothered to make sure I could access a classroom.

She went to the teacher whose classroom I was in for the week. She immediately saw the concern on my mum's face and asked the question no one likes to be asked: "Oh, Tam, is everything okay?" Mum burst into tears, on the verge of a panic attack. She eventually managed to get out that everything wasn't okay and that she would keep me home for the remainder of the week. The teacher understood our frustrations completely and rushed to compile a list of work for me to do at home. The teacher was truly kind and compassionate and even asked if there was anything she could do.

I wish the same could be said for my Year 7 teacher the following year. She had moments when she was great. However, she taught based on intimidation; she only liked to explain things once—God help you in maths if you were confused—and if you were musically inclined, you were wasting time attending practice and rehearsals. On the other hand, if you were sporty and excelling in your chosen sport, you were the apple of her eye and could do no wrong, even if your parents helped you with a report when they were told not to.

Everyone else who received even slight help would be threatened with a failing mark, while the sporty ones were given A's. Being late to class or "forgetting your hat" or homework was a big no-no. I understand that she was preparing us for high school and encouraging us to become independent of our parents. Ironic, I know.

If you were quiet and soft-natured, you were a prime target for remarks and faced a more challenging time compared to the sporty ones. I remember this girl in our class usually speaking in a whisper, so you could barely hear her. Each morning, as our teacher marked off our attendance, it would come to, (let's call her, Sarah), Sarah's name, who quietly replied, "Here." Our teacher would then respond, "Come on, Sarah, you need to start speaking louder. Enough of this whispering. I can hear you at lunchtime, so I know it's in there." She would call Sarah out in front of everyone, which made her feel incredibly embarrassed and made her even quieter. One day, she was slightly louder than normal at roll call, and our teacher said, "Oh my goodness, Sarah, you do speak! We can finally hear you! Was that so awful?" This went on practically the entire year.

Since I was soft-natured and emotionally sensitive, the teaching method my teacher used did more harm than good. It sent my anxiety back to square one, which intensified when the bell rang, and Mum still wasn't at my classroom door to say goodbye in the morning because she was dropping off my brother at his classroom. My anxiety wouldn't settle until she arrived. If I got up to say goodbye to her, I would get in trouble or mocked by my teacher, so Mum would often walk past my classroom and wave. I would try to wave back, swallowing the lump in my throat and blinking my anxiety-induced tears away, while hoping the teacher didn't catch me looking out the door.

When we went on holiday, my teacher made it obvious she wasn't impressed, even though it was the last week of school before the Easter break. She kept saying that I would fall behind and that it would be my responsibility if I couldn't keep up when I returned. She even made cheap digs at my parents for taking me out of school.

So, I ensured I completed all my schoolwork while I was away, not because I wanted to start the next term caught up, but out of fear of the consequences if I wasn't at the same level as everyone else. There were days when she was fantastic and would laugh and joke with everyone, teaching us Double Dutch or laughing with us during the occasional time we would play Around the World at the end of a maths lesson.

As I mentioned earlier, her unique teaching style significantly increased my anxiety. With one scowl, I was back to nearly having a meltdown if I didn't say goodbye to Mum in the morning, even leaving the house in tears at the thought, fearing what was to come, or even obsessively worrying about forgetting my homework or hat at home. It took years for me not to have the obligatory school-related nightmares, but instead of forgetting an essay was due, it was leaving my hat or homework at home.

There was one week early on when a lot happened, and I feel like my brain has blocked it out, but I remember it was a terrible Tuesday, and I seemed to be picked apart by my teacher all day, even down to calling me out for dog-earing the corner of a library book I was reading. Yes, it is the biggest sin for readers not to use a bookmark, but I didn't have one, and I still cringe at the fact I did that! However, it got to a point where the picking and intimidation were so bad that Mum ended up organising a meeting between her, the teacher, and the principal.

That meeting was held on a Friday. And on Fridays, we would have a morning assembly with the whole school. As you would expect, I was an anxious wreck, knowing the meeting was to follow the assembly. Usually, I was somewhat good at hiding my anxiety, like playing a strong poker game, or at least I liked to think so.

On this day, however, I folded my hand. When it was announced that the assembly was over, it felt like someone had punched me in the gut, and my brain short-circuited. While everyone else prepared to head off to class for the day, I stood alone, a shaking, sobbing mess, borderline hyperventilating, unable to move on the indoor basketball court.

Another teacher, the same one who had been with Mum during her panic attack the year prior, noticed my distress and rushed over to check on me. I began talking to her, or at least tried to, when my current teacher noticed and shooed her away, saying I was okay. She then asked me what was happening in a less-than-caring tone. As I again tried to explain what was wrong, which was related to the events of the past few weeks and how I was struggling with the intimidation, she cut me off. She responded with, "Oh, just get over it, Rhiannon!" with a level of annoyance and an emotion I still can't identify. This response made my anxiety spike again, and I started crying like my dog had just died. I was convinced that the day would only get worse, and that she would take her anger and frustration about the meeting out on me.

Yet, to my surprise, after she met with the principal and my mother that same morning, she approached me during sports a while later. She apologised, stating that she didn't mean to upset me and that if she changed her teaching style for me, she would have to do it for others, which wouldn't be beneficial, especially since we had several class interrupters who would challenge her. I appreciated the apology, and she was great the rest of the day, even cracking a joke about how I poked my tongue out slightly while concentrating. I wish I could say that the rest of the school year went without problems, but unfortunately, for 12-year-old me, that wasn't the case.

One of the worst moments was when we had to make felt frogs with legs out of pipe cleaners for Art. We needed to cut out the felt pieces, stuff the frog with stuffing, and stitch the pieces together. There were strict instructions not to take the frog home; however, I spent a few days off sick and was at risk of not finishing the frog by the due date. For some reason, I missed the opportunity to grab pipe cleaners, so I had no choice but to take the frog home.

I didn't really know how to hand stitch, so Mum did a few very neat stitches to show me how to do it. The downside of having someone used to sewing up dance costumes—yes, I used to dance—doing the stitches and passing it over to someone with no experience was that it was jarringly obvious and unmistakable. My naïve self hoped that the teacher would forget her glasses were on top of her head when she came to mark the frogs, but I was wrong. The class silently worked away on another project when I heard, "Rhiannon, come here."

My stomach dropped to my feet, and I could feel my face reddening by the second. When I stood in front of the teacher's desk, her blue eyes pierced my soul.

"Where did you get the pipe cleaners from?"

"Home," I replied.

"Where did they get the eyes from?"

"Home."

"Who did the stitching?"

"Mum did some to help show me how to stitch, but I did the rest."

"Class, were we allowed to take our frogs home?"

"No, Miss," the class replied. Their eyes bored into the back of my head.

"Go sit down, Rhiannon", she said as dismissively as you would expect with a strong sigh, slapping my frog down on the desk next to her.

I made my way back to my desk, feeling embarrassed and afraid that she would fail me. Surprisingly, I passed, which is a significant relief. If she had failed me, it would have been highly ironic, considering she would give A's to other students and praise how amazing their work was, even when it is evident that their mothers helped them with their projects.

You might think that Year 7 was shocking solely because of the teacher. However, a new challenge would arise—my younger self hadn't learned her lesson about hanging out with people who relentlessly bullied whenever they wanted.

I was suffering from major self-worth issues, and had practically given up on making new friends since. Whenever I tried, the girl from Year 4, who bullied me, would always end up saying some nonsense, which would make them suddenly ghost me in the playground. So, when one of the girls, "Carla," who had bullied me in Grade 6, apologised to me at the start of Grade 7, I didn't think twice about accepting her apology and trying to go back to being good friends. However, it was like a yo-yo in the first half of Year 7; one minute, we were fine; the next, we weren't.

There was a time when Carla, Mindy, and I were sitting on the picnic benches having lunch, and they told me that they were going to the bathroom and would be back. I needed help getting off the chairs at this point, which they knew about, and said they would come and help me up before the bell rang. I should have seen it coming the minute they walked past me on the other side of the undercover lunch area. They saw me, and they just kept walking. I realised too late that they weren't going to come and help me. I was left stranded like a boat at low tide. The bell sounded to go back to class, and there was no one around me to ask for help off the bench.

So, for the next ten minutes, I strained and struggled, rocking myself to gain momentum before planting my feet and using what little momentum I could muster to try and stand up. Time and time again, I would rock, plant, and attempt to stand, seemingly to little avail. I tried clinging to the fence behind the bench for leverage. Nothing. I was beginning to freak out, and my mind started racing, thinking about how much trouble I would be in once I somehow managed to get unstuck and return to class.

To this day, I still have no idea how I managed to stand up, but I eventually got to class. As expected, I was around 10 minutes late. My mind convinced me I would be picked on by the teacher as soon as I stepped foot into the classroom, but I was beyond relieved for once that she completely ignored me and was busy talking to someone else. Fortunately, I went to my desk by the door to the classroom and made eye contact with Carla, who had left me stranded on the bench.

I told her, "I have been struggling for the past 10 minutes trying to get up off the bench. You said you were coming back."

"Oh, sorry, we thought you were fine."

"You know I struggle getting off chairs, and you said you would be right back. You even looked right at me as you walked past."

"Mindy and I didn't want to be late for class, and we thought you could manage it for once."

I had nothing else to say; the rage inside me threatened to boil over, so I slammed my mouth shut and forced myself not to say another word. I didn't want to cause a fuss, and I especially didn't want to say anything I would regret, such as, "Fuck you."

There was finally one day when I decided to say something. I was in a friend group of around seven or so, and still friends with, yep, you guessed it, Mindy and Carla. I had mended bridges with Carla, who apologised profusely and said she was following Mindy around because she was worried she would be treated the same, but she still wanted to be friends with both of us.

Eventually, Mindy became increasingly frustrated that Carla had mended things with me. She tried to make my life hell, and entered a tug of war with me, with Carla being the rope in the middle.

Desperate to stop it, I asked my mum what to do. She said, "Stand up to her and say we don't have to be friends with each other, but can still be friends with Carla."

Armed with my response, I headed into school one day, waiting for the right moment to use it. I didn't have to wait long; during the first break of the day, as we waited to return to our respective classrooms, Mindy called out to me as I walked past.

I can't recall exactly what she said, but I remember thinking it wasn't good. I pivoted on my back foot, approached her, and said, "You know, just because you hate me and aren't friends with me doesn't mean Carla can't be my friend as well as yours. There's no point in calling me names because it just doesn't work."

She replied with something, but unfortunately, I only rehearsed the first part and had no other comeback prepared. I wasn't used to confrontation, and instead of fumbling through another response, I looked her in the eyes, smiled slightly, and walked to my classroom.

It was the first time in my life that I wasn't scared to stand up, and the very first time I had used my voice. The first of many life-defining breakthroughs.

CHAPTER 4

GROWING UP, GROWING STRONGER: HIGH SCHOOL REFLECTIONS

High school is something that, often, everyone looks forward to! You're getting older, which means more responsibilities and, not to mention, an increased ego. For others, it can also be like hitting a reset button, as you are starting at a new school, which means new people, opportunities, and a chance to breathe and start over.

I could have started my high school journey early. But about halfway through Year 7, my parents became increasingly concerned about my mental health and the issues I was facing at school. They asked if I wanted to start at my high school early by finishing off Year 7 there before starting Year 8. My high school was a private school, which meant that Year 7 was part of the high school campus, way before it became standard for all high schools across the state.

However, I was stubborn, and I didn't know what was good for me. I was desperate to finish the year at my primary school rather than bail when things got tricky. I also wanted to graduate with my peers because, believe it or not, my friendships had improved significantly. I ended up finding an amazing group of friends who were just as quirky and fun as I was, and I didn't want to leave that so soon. So, I graduated from primary school and started at my high school in 2012, just like everyone else. Full of trauma, anxiety, and self-esteem issues, not to mention a body that I swore hated me just as much as I hated it.

The search for a high school wasn't as simple as snapping my fingers; having said that, it was a rather eye-opening experience. Fortunately, my parents gave me complete freedom to choose the school I wanted to attend. Their main wish was for me to feel comfortable and empowered, giving me the freedom to make choices about my own life. A luxury I had yet to experience, as disability life often meant others making decisions for you, especially when you are newly diagnosed.

I immediately got to work and came up with an initial list of schools that interested me. Without even giving it a second thought, I ruled out the largest state high school in town, as I had been there once for a 'come and try' day arranged by my primary school.

I felt lost; the school felt like a city within a city. And even though there were many disabled students, I strangely could still feel everyone's eyes on me. The need to be invisible, competing with the need to just be seen as me, was starting to make its presence known, even as an 11-year-old.

I knew deep down that a small school would be more my style. I wanted something quiet, calm, and with less hustle and bustle. I wanted something completely different from my primary school experience, which reflected what I desperately wanted in life outside of school: peace!

I also knew that a smaller school could help with my anxiety and potentially provide more support as my disability changed. The fact that I thought a small school with barely any disabled students would give me the extra support over a school with almost 2,000 students and plenty of disabled students blows my mind.

My parents also wanted to ensure that when looking through schools, I was prioritised over them regarding questions or concerns. After all, I was the one who was going to spend the next five years of my life there, not them. They even encouraged me to create a checklist of what I was looking for, and come up with a bunch of questions I could ask each school when looking around. I was ultimately empowered to make my own choice, which again, makes me so grateful that my parents wanted me to have a say in my secondary education.

The first school we visited was not the high school cliché that you would often see in Disney films. The hustle and bustle of hallways lined with lockers and colourful cafeterias was instead replaced by dark, eerie walkways with an almost depressed atmosphere. I felt uncomfortable from the get-go, and seeing how glum the students looked told me all I needed to know. What solidified that even further was that the staff member who showed us around spoke directly to my parents instead of me, and when it was time to sit and chat, my parents mentioned that I had some questions. The staff member wore a look of surprise mixed with annoyance. I already knew then that this school was not for me; they made me feel like a complete burden and a number rather than a person. Safe to say, I couldn't leave that place fast enough!

My checklist was simple. The school I picked needed to be accessible, have a strong drama club, small class sizes, a well-equipped learning support area, and a disabled bathroom I could use. My questions again—surprise, surprise—centred on accessibility, how exams would work and the possibility for extra time, locker heights, the time allowed between classes, how to obtain an exemption from sports and PE, where I could park my scooter during classes, and the option of having an ergonomic chair instead of the standard low chair in every classroom to make it easier for me to stand up.

Based on the epic flop that was the first school, I was expecting I would be in for the long haul, and have no choice but to end up going to the state high school. However, I had a rare streak of luck, and found the school that ticked all the boxes on my second try.

You know that familiar warmth you get throughout your body when you have just arrived home? It feels like you have been there a thousand times. You feel immediately at ease and comfortable, almost relaxed. That is how I felt, driving up the long, tree-lined driveway to a stunning, old, heritage-listed building—or what would be my new high school.

Everything within me just knew this school was it. The tour confirmed my feelings, with multiple students even coming up to me to say it was a good school and that I would love it there.

Concordia was bright and had a tree-filled quad in the centre of the campus, bordered by the four main buildings. I could access the upper levels via a long ramp connected to the library, and the disabled bathroom was spacious enough to fit four of my scooters. The chapel was small, but full of character and had a slight vintage charm. Students went out of their way to say hi, and hoped to see me on campus soon. A stark contrast to the dark and almost zombie-like feel of the previous school.

During the tour and our sit-down interview, the staff member showed more interest in how I was feeling and constantly asked if I had any concerns. She even went as far as to make direct eye contact with me and ask me straight out if I had questions as soon as we sat down for the interview, rather than speaking to my parents first.

I felt seen, understood, heard, respected, and perhaps, more importantly, I felt valued. All the things missing from my previous school and what I had been desperate to find after years of bullying. I felt like I had found my second home.

Like most others, I was eager to have a fresh start at a brand-new school. I felt slightly uneasy because I was genuinely returning to square one.

As much as I was excited to start somewhere new, the prospect of making new friends was daunting, with the echoes of primary school bullying still lingering over me. Dealing with an ever-changing disability while starting at a new school, even if you love it, can also be frightening.

A million thoughts raced through my mind: Will I make friends? What happens if I drop my books and no one is there to help? How do I ask a random person for help? What if my scooter battery dies? What if I can't reach my locker? What if I can't get up off the toilet? What if I accidentally run over someone's foot? Can I run over someone's foot on purpose if they are being a jerk?

Well, my first day started off with me nervously waiting while Mum put my scooter together in front of everyone. I felt what felt like hundreds of eyes on me, and looking around, I desperately wanted the ground to swallow me whole. I quickly realised my skirt was the longest of all the girls, the hem almost reaching my shoes. Just as I was feeling more anxious and on the verge of a breakdown that would rival any *Real Housewives* dinner party meltdown, Mum said a quick goodbye, and as she reversed the car back down the driveway, I noticed the locking mechanism on my scooter, which stops the front wheels from turning, hadn't been unlocked. That essentially meant I couldn't ride anywhere. I was stuck, surrounded by strangers, and my heart was pounding in my ears.

Almost as if it were divine intervention, my school buddy—a Year 12 student I had been assigned and met the day before—came around the corner. She saw me looking like I was on the verge of a mental breakdown and immediately asked if I was okay. I told her my front wheels wouldn't turn, and I needed help unlocking the clip at the front. She pretended to pick something up off the floor to avoid drawing attention, while unlocking my scooter and giving me my front wheels back. Safe to say, young me was very grateful for her discretion, because what teenager wants their troubles to be broadcast to the world, especially on their first day of Year 8 with a skirt that looked like a nun should wear it?

The start of high school ended up being better than I could have imagined. I was making friends, enjoying my classes, and revelling in the fact I could get outside in the fresh air as I drove from class to class.

However, the bubble burst in the second term, which started around April. The year prior, I was diagnosed with scoliosis after months of back pain when I would get up out of bed. My curvature was a C-curve at the top of my spine with a curve of 52 degrees. My General Practitioner (GP) referred me to one of, if not, the best spinal surgeons in the state.

The highway to Brisbane was like a second home at this point, so the trip down was a breeze. The surgeon's office was small and minimalistic, creating a calm environment with a view down the road below.

Sitting on the examination table in a hospital gown with my parents seated nearby, we anxiously waited to meet the man people claimed to be second only to God. With a waitlist a mile long, it wasn't difficult to see why. He was kind and patient, listened to our concerns, and explained what was happening to my spine in a way we could all understand. He, then, said to us that surgery was the only option as the curve was too extreme for a brace to do anything, and the brace was hard plastic and super uncomfortable. He also explained that surgery wouldn't be straightforward. It would be a long, eight-hour procedure, followed by a night in ICU, and anywhere from seven to ten days in the hospital with daily physiotherapy and the need to relearn how to walk after bed rest.

This was the first time having major surgery, and I was terrified that he might have a bad day and leave me paralysed. Or worse. I was convinced I was going to die on that operating table.

He assured me he had been a spinal surgeon for decades and that I would be fine. I was so desperate for the back pain to go away, and after weighing our limited options, we decided to proceed with the surgery and scheduled it for April 2, 2012.

With the date set, I had approximately ten weeks to adapt to a new school, learn how to write essays, make as many friends as possible, and prepare my lungs and body for major surgery. Definitely not overwhelming in the slightest!

With muscular dystrophy, given the fact that respiratory and lung functions are often impacted, undergoing any sort of anaesthesia can be very risky. These risks meant that we had to arrange a lung function test before the surgery to ensure my lungs had enough capacity to handle the inevitable dip in function post-anaesthesia.

I think what happens to lungs under anaesthesia is it causes them to relax to the point of them weakening? I honestly have no idea the exact medical reasonings behind what happens. Thankfully, I am not a doctor, so for all our sakes, I will leave that one for you to Google.

On the same day as my lung function test, I also had to undergo a series of additional X-rays. They twisted, stretched, and contorted me around a solid bolster to capture as many angles of my spine as possible. Given my limitations, this created a lot of discomfort and, believe it or not, pain; after all, I am not a pretzel. Unless you are a Cirque du Soleil-level contortionist, there is no way anyone can shape their body into a C around a bolster, or half-lie on it and still have their shoulder touching the bed.

The last item on the agenda of pre-surgery checks was to undergo an MRI of my spine. I didn't think I was claustrophobic; however, I wasn't anticipating being inside a narrow cylinder, unable to scratch my nose or sing along to the music in my ears for distraction. It felt like the longest forty-five minutes of my life, with the buzz of the machine nearly drowning out the music they had playing, and Mum lightly scratching my feet to help distract me from the thought of choking on my own vomit.

I truly earned a strawberry and almond crêpe for lunch that day! And I absolutely enjoyed every single sugar-filled mouthful. There is nothing that screams surgery prep reward than a food coma!

Before we knew it, April had arrived. I had to stay in the hospital overnight before the surgery, as I needed to be prepped for the theatre by around 6:30a.m the following day. Given that I lived in Toowoomba and my surgery was in—yep, you guessed it—Brisbane, it made logical sense to travel down the day before. There was no way I would get up at two in the morning to be at the hospital for prep. No amount of caffeine would have made me conscious or sane enough.

Shortly after I arrived and got all the admission paperwork out of the way, or, should I say, my parents sorted it all out, I was then escorted to my room where they prepared my cannula. Due to my extremely small veins that like to play hide and seek, they needed multiple attempts to get the cannula in my hand. Given the fact that my arm can't extend out straight, trying to jab a vein inside my elbow is close to impossible, so on top of the hand it is.

One bruised hand and five or six attempts at finding a vein later, they asked if I wanted the hospital chaplain to come and pray with me. My faith was something I was still exploring, but having the chaplain say a prayer made me realise what I was about to endure. It heightened my anxiety and fear while also making me feel present and safe. It certainly was a strange mix of emotions that I wasn't expecting.

As you could expect, I began to cry, with Mum silently crying beside me and Dad trying his hardest to remain stoic, as the chaplain drew a cross on my forehead with his thumb, gave a slight smile, and then left the room.

The realisation of what tomorrow held became more real by the second.

Fortunately, for all of us, we were allowed a short reprieve from what would be home for the next week, as I was allowed to leave the hospital for dinner that night. We ended up next door at a restaurant that conveniently joined where my family would be staying for the week. If you have ever tried eating pasta with a cannula in your hand, you would know that it quickly becomes more about protecting your hand from unnecessary and unwanted jabs than it is to make sure the pasta eventually finds its way to your mouth.

That night, I barely got any sleep; between the other patients' monitors going off, nurses milling about, and my anxiety creating a rock concert in my head, the time till morning felt like slow torture. When the alarm finally went off, mum braided my hair while we engaged in small talk. The nerves were consuming both of us. Time seemed to speed up then, and before I knew it, I was saying, "See you soon." to my family and being sent off into Lala land, and hoping I would wake up.

The surgery itself was a complete success, with two slim titanium rods screwed into my spine, with long screws that would make anyone squeamish. My curve went from being 52 degrees to around 26 degrees. The anaesthetist was happy, the surgeon was delighted, and I was drugged out to the max with my body starting to itch from the morphine.

I woke up in ICU surrounded by my parents, my younger brother, and my grandmother and her partner, who flew in from New Zealand. They couldn't stay long as visitors were prohibited from hanging around in the ICU. However, it was still such a relief to wake up to a bunch of familiar faces instead of in a large, sterile room by myself.

The first time I sat up was only a couple of hours after surgery. The nurse told me that they had to wash my back and remove some of the last patches of antiseptic and pen marks. I was still half out of it, but present enough to notice the pain and how sensitive my back was. I couldn't help but cry out in discomfort as it felt like the nurse forgot I just had my back opened, drilled into, and stitched up again. I was fighting the urge to vomit and cry as they finally laid me back on the bed from the pain of surgery and the rough hands of the nurse.

Soon enough, my support crew had to leave as it was ICU after all, but given my age, Dad was allowed to stay with me that first night. With the hustle and bustle of patients coming in from car accidents overnight, neither Dad nor I got much sleep at all, with me waking each hour asking, "What time is it?"

The following week in the hospital was filled with many visitors, laughs, and discomforts. Around day three or so, they removed my dressings, the catheter (is that too TMI? Hmm, my bad), and the epidural. The most painful part of the entire experience was removing the dressings. Because of all the fine hairs on my back, how sensitive the incision still was, and how strong the adhesive was, the nurses had to ever so slowly peel off the dressing while using an alcoholic wipe.

The pain was unbearable, like someone was using a blowtorch with thousands of tiny needles. I screamed bloody murder, repeating, "Kill me, please kill me, please make it stop," as my mum held my hands, trying to reassure me by saying, "You are okay. Keep taking deep breaths. It will be over soon."

I screamed so loudly that a nurse heard me from down the hall and came rushing to my hospital room, asking my dad if everything was okay, thinking something was majorly wrong. Once Dad explained to him that everything was fine and that I was having my dressings removed, the nurse smiled slightly and said, "Ah, yes, it can be excruciating and uncomfortable. Which surgeon did she have?"

When Dad said who the surgeon was, the nurse replied, "Oh, thank goodness. He only does one strip down the spine and two across the back to anchor it. Other surgeons do a full wrap around the torso." When Dad told me this later, that knowledge made me grateful that I only had the three strips to deal with.

Once the epidural and catheter were removed, it was time to stand me up and get me walking. The rest of the time in the hospital was spent doing laps to and from the 50-meter-long hallway using a hospital walker, where you can stand up straight and rest your elbows while grabbing the hand grips.

Walking after three days in bed was like dragging dead weight, and trying to lift my feet was like playing tug-of-war with the ground. The times between rehab were filled with my brother going to the parents' lounge and sneaking chocolate yoghurt cups, biscuits, and cheese for us. So much so that when the time to be discharged came, the fridge in my room had an ample supply of snacks that had to be consumed.

To go home, I had to walk the length of the hallway unassisted without a walker. I felt uneasy on my feet, still adjusting to the hardware in my spine, with my feet and legs feeling like dead weight. Each step took a full minute; each meter felt like a kilometre. I was so scared of falling.

Looking back now, it feels like my fear made my brain almost talk me into falling. I had to hold onto either my mum or the nurse at times to regain my balance.

I wanted to go home so badly. I missed my bed and the silence of sleeping instead of listening to beeping machines. I deeply missed my 12-month-old Border Collie, Milly. All these things spurred me on, and I found another gear as I slowly but surely completed my there-and-back-again lap of the hallway, finishing it in around ten minutes.

The surgeon was satisfied and gave me the green light to go home on Day 6, which surprised him as not many people are ready to leave that soon. What can I say? I like to be an overachiever.

The journey home was slow, with Dad being extra careful not to drive over any potholes that could jostle me. I arrived home two hours later to see my dog jumping for joy, and the entire house was filled with helium balloons that my uncle had set up.

The next six weeks were spent walking for ten minutes, initially, and increasing the time by a minute each day. That experience was nowhere near as bad as having adhesive slowly removed from my back, but it still wasn't pleasant. Lap after lap around the kitchen, holding onto Mum, felt like it relieved some pressure off my back. Slowly but surely, walking became easier; my feet and legs felt lighter, and my back became less uncomfortable, leading me to graduate from walking around the kitchen to visiting the local park.

I returned to school for just half a day at the six-week post-operation mark. Before returning, I received three large plastic sleeves filled with get-well-soon cards made by nearly everyone in my grade, along with three extra-large cards signed by everyone as well. All my nerves about going back to school and feeling like the odd-one-out quickly began to fade, and I was excited to see my classmates. My anxiety lessened even further when I returned to class mid-morning, and everyone came over to give me the gentlest hugs.

Slowly but surely, my strength began to improve, so much so that my mum remarked my walking looked the best it ever had, with hardly a waddle anymore. My half-days at school turned into full days. And before I knew it, I was back in my familiar school routine, and life started to look good.

It felt refreshing to have, what resembled, a "regular" teenager's life. Wake up, go to school, come home, eat, do homework, shower, have dinner, go to bed, and repeat. It had been a while since my life felt mundane, and I welcomed it, even on the coldest winter days, wearing merino wool leggings tucked underneath my skirt.

Gradually, I felt my confidence return as I found my love for Drama, and I auditioned for the school's production of Godspell in Year 9. Acting was pure escapism for me. It enabled me to forget I was disabled and become entirely someone else. For years, I wanted to become a professional actress because I loved the challenge of becoming someone else and yet, finding a piece of me in them that I loved.

Being a part of a school production is the most cliché thing about being in high school. Everyone has fond memories, regardless of whether they were on stage or working behind the scenes. To this day, my parents talk fondly of being a part of their school's production of Grease, Joseph and the Amazing Technicolour Dream Coat, and Sherlock Holmes. My drama teachers believed in me so much that after auditioning with a group to sing in the chorus—even when I couldn't sing to save my life— she asked me if I would audition for a role.

As an aspiring actress, and as a 13-year-old, I felt this was my moment. However, because my singing sounded like someone gargling mouthwash,

I wasn't offered a leading role. Instead, I was fortunate enough to be cast in a tiny part involving one scene and about half a page of dialogue. I was ecstatic, and my disability didn't hinder my ability to perform.

Rehearsals were held several afternoons after school for months. They were long and tedious, especially if you weren't part of the leading ensemble. One day, when my body was fatigued, I stood on someone's foot during a rehearsal of a singing and dancing sequence that involved the entire cast. It was enough to buckle my knee, and down I went—in front of the whole cast. I felt embarrassed, but the slow descent to the ground was so comical that I laughed instead of crying out of humiliation. Maybe there was a touch of embarrassment, but I didn't want the teachers to panic or make everyone awkward. Luckily, my laughter broke the tension immediately, and everyone was laughing along with me.

Perhaps, the most embarrassing part was falling in front of the lead, who was a genuine all-rounder—good at sports, intelligent, could sing, dance, act, and play the saxophone like you wouldn't believe. All the girls had a crush on him, and I must admit I wasn't immune to the charms of the Year 12 guy playing Jesus. Thankfully, it didn't seem like he saw what happened, but he did witness the teachers helping me off the floor, so my face turned redder than a punnet of tomatoes.

Opening night rolled around, and I was a bundle of nerves. I wore a musical t-shirt, blue footless tights, and a denim skirt, with my hair teased to within an inch of its life. My makeup was colourful and bright, a mix of blues, yellows, teals, and purples. It truly felt like stepping back into the 80s.

My entire family, extended family, and friends sat in the front row. If I didn't know any better, I would think they were ready to try to make me laugh and break character. Thank goodness, you could barely see the audience from the stage!

Soon enough, it was my time for my one scene. I played a rather arrogant woman while the main cast told her story. At one point, I get pulled backwards, and a group of people become demons and drag-me-down-to-hell, *Ghost* style. In rehearsals, I nearly fell over from the force of the two guys grabbing me by my shoulders. But on show night, they somehow decided not to touch me at all and let me walk backwards by myself. Whether that was a decision made by the drama teacher or the two guys, I don't know. It left me stunned for a moment, as I braced myself to be pulled, but I composed myself and finished the scene, relieved I didn't land on my butt in front of an entire theatre.

That relief was short-lived, however, when it came time for bows and exiting the stage. As a chorus, we had to "run" off down a ramp that was on the side of the stage. Knowing that I physically couldn't run any more, I was terrified that I would be pushed over on stage and get trampled on, which was my worst nightmare. So, I decided to make a break for the ramp early, but not too early that it would be obvious. It was more like making people think I was slightly off-beat. I preferred to look like I made a mistake with the timing, rather than say hi to the ground in front of hundreds of eyes.

However, I still left too late. I just reached the top of the ramp when people were suddenly on either side of me. I tried to make my way down the ramp swiftly yet safely. I reached about halfway before I felt a pair of hands on my back; the next minute, I was pushed against the wall and ended up doing a solo Mexican wave as I fell. I slid on my face, my right hand curling underneath itself.

As I lay there, coming to terms with being shoved and the pain radiating through my face and hand, I was immediately grateful that the ramp had a half wall, so I was blocked from the eyesight of the crowd. The two leads were still on stage, goofing around and dancing to close out the show, which meant everyone was watching them, and not us leaving the stage.

However, I knew my family would have seen what happened and were desperate to get to me. I was silently pleading with them in my head not to run over and make a fuss. I was thankful they must have read my mind, and didn't come rushing over immediately when the show hadn't ended yet.

I lifted my head and saw my friends by the door next to the end of the ramp, trying to check on me and get me to move to the door. The fingers on my right hand felt like someone had stepped on them with a stiletto heel, and my forehead felt like a match had been lit on it. I was half lying on my stomach, and my left arm was stuck underneath me so that I couldn't go anywhere and hoped the lead would pick me up as he exited the ramp at the show's end. Instead of picking me up, he and the other lead stepped over me and kept walking. Looking back on it now, I am so grateful he didn't pick me up because it would have made it evident to the audience that something had gone wrong, even though I would have preferred being treated backstage.

When the lights were up, my parents and friends were right by me. I thought I had broken my fingers due to the pain and swelling; fortunately, it turned out to be a sprain, and I was sporting a gnarly carpet burn on my forehead and a slight black eye.

My drama teacher came running when she heard me say g'day to the floor. Once I told her what had happened, she was furious, and by the accounts of my friends and others in the ensemble, she gave everyone a tongue-lashing for pushing me and about being mindful of others. I felt terrible that they all got a stern talking-to on what was meant to be a celebratory green room after finishing the opening night.

I was still adamant about performing in the upcoming day's matinée. I caked on the makeup and extra concealer to hide my carpet burn, buddy strapped my index and middle fingers, and off I went to the theatre. The performance went perfectly, even though I decided to skip one of the dance sequences, as I was still a little weak after my fall. I didn't want a repeat of the night before.

I aimed to be professional on stage; however, everyone is known for "corpsing" at least once or twice. My corpsing moment happened during one of the final sequences when we had to do the peace sign. Because my fingers were taped together, I ended up doing the Spock hand gesture. I burst out laughing, and so did one of the other chorus members, who joined in doing the gesture to make it look like part of the choreography.

Perhaps the most embarrassing moment came after the musical run. The audience was gathered by the exit, chatting, when I saw someone I knew. I went over to her and started talking about how cute the male lead was, saying, "Hey, how cute is Jesus?" What I didn't realise was that his mum was standing right there, listening to my entire word vomit. Once I realised that, I waddled as fast as my legs could and hoped his mum wouldn't tell him! To this day, I still wake up early in the morning and cringe majorly, remembering that moment.

School life returned to normal quickly after Godspell ended, much to my, somewhat, relief. The stress of multiple rehearsals a week and trying to stay on top of my schoolwork was intense, and I often felt like I wasn't doing well enough either. Fortunately, I still managed B's and C's on my assignments, and apart from the faceplant on opening night, the musical went perfectly without a single line being forgotten. So, I guess you could say those few months went amazingly despite the stress. I was just eager to return to normalcy.

I think it is safe to say that around 99.9 percent of high school students struggle with self-worth and self-esteem at some point. It doesn't matter if you were in the popular group, the rejected group, disabled, musical, or sporty; no one is immune to self-worth issues.

For me, my self-worth and self-esteem problems were carried over from my primary school days. I still bore the scars of bullying like they were 10-kilogram weights in my bag. Whenever someone looked at me too long, I became nervous, thinking they would say something or laugh at me.

It's ironic that I tried to stay invisible while desperately wanting to be liked, leading me to pursue joining the popular group. I was so eager that I ignored their subtle attempts to ditch me at first—like not saving a seat for me in class, barely helping me open heavy doors, or even excluding me in selfies. I overlooked all of this because there were days when everyone was friendly; they would save a seat or walk with me.

One day, while they were ignoring me, I asked the only person still talking to me what the problem was and if I had done something wrong. She told me, "You are too needy. You need too much validation, and they are over it."

It felt like a gut punch. Not only was I labelled "too needy" for requiring help in primary school, but now, I was deemed "too needy" for seeking validation. The second gut punch was that several group members constantly sought reassurance about their appearance, weight, and hair.

My requests for reassurance stemmed from years of feeling inadequate and not wanting to be a burden. I just didn't know how to voice those feelings at the time so people could understand.

Later in high school, I came around the corner at lunchtime, and the entire group abruptly stopped talking. You could literally hear a pin drop. No, you could hear the boys next to us discussing going to the gym after school. I later discovered their conversation was about planning a party and a sleepover at someone's house. I found out when the photos were posted on Facebook. Their excuse was that there were two steps, and they weren't sure I would be comfortable. I was met with crickets when I suggested they could have just asked me instead of assuming. This alone should have served as a warning to avoid them altogether.

There was one time when they said I was "too serious." What they meant was that because I didn't drink, party, smoke, or wear clothes that might raise eyebrows even in clubs, and I spent time in class learning instead of gossiping, I apparently needed to "lighten up." Bear in mind that when this was said to me, I was around fifteen or sixteen. That conversation should have been the last major red flag to make me to ride my scooter away as fast as possible, enough to impress Tom Cruise.

Along with the friend drama, there was also the dating realm. Oh yeah, in case you weren't sure, people with disabilities can have relationships and go on dates. If there is one thing that doesn't discriminate, it's love!

I was in Year 11 the first time I went on a date. I reconnected with a friend from primary school, and we hit it off right away. He attended the school next door, and on top of messaging pretty much 24/7, we would occasionally meet at the fence after school to chat. One night, he asked me out, saying, "Roses are red, violets are blue. Will you go out with me because the love is true?"

Looking back on that now, I gag at how corny it is, but as a 15-year-old, it was sweet enough to make me sob. I think it was mainly because I didn't believe anyone would want to date me. Everywhere I looked, there were abled couples, while disabled people often sat alone. Interabled relationships weren't even portrayed in literature, film, or television, so I believed it wouldn't be possible. When he asked me out, I was overwhelmed and so happy. I also believed that someone loving me could help me love myself. Anyone who has had self-esteem issues knows just how wrong that statement is.

Our first date was at the cinema. Cliché, I know. But at the end of the date, we wandered around the shops for a bit; yes, at that time I could comfortably manage a stroll around the shops, before making our way back to the cinema where my brother was with his mates. I was meeting him near the arcade to head home.

My date and I were chatting when there was a moment of silence. He just looked at me, started inching closer, and tilting his head from side to side, somewhat mimicking a chicken. He was taller than me by a good 30 centimetres, so it was a rather funny and confusing sight until it dawned on me what he was about to do. I can tell you I had never moved that fast; I was like a duck that just found a pond. I waddled away as quickly as my legs could waddle. He just had to walk normally to keep up with me. I told him my brother would be leaving the cinema, and I didn't want him to make fun of me.

I didn't want to admit that, even at fifteen, I was slightly old-fashioned and thought kissing on the first date was a bit strange. I also didn't want to confess that I was terrified of my first kiss.

Our first kiss did happen two weeks later, on our second date. I pressed my back against an arcade game to avoid running away since I really wanted to kiss him; I was just nervous about being terrible at it. I closed my eyes right away while he stood in front of me. I again had to resist the urge to waddle away. When he kissed me, because of our height difference, and since I didn't think to lift my chin, he missed half of my mouth. I remember thinking, "Hmm, this is odd." My brain short-circuited out in confusion that I didn't think to kiss him back. Later, when I finally thought, "Okay. You can do this. Go kiss him," I looked up and saw some girls from school at the cinema, watching the entire awkward scene, muttering and grinning. I turned a shade brighter than a tomato and decided to just stare awkwardly at him while he played a racing game. If the look he gave me was any indication, I looked like a stunned mullet staring at him, deciding whether to kiss him or not, and then making a random joke about the game he was playing.

Like the majority of first relationships, it ended as fast as it began. We dated only for four weeks before breaking up in textbook high school fashion.

One night, he FaceTimed me, which wouldn't have been a problem. However, he was with his mates, and I hadn't washed my hair in days, was in my pyjamas and clearly not looking my finest self. For a 15-year-old girl, that is your worst nightmare when talking to a boy, with his mates present who you have never met!

Unfortunately my overanalytical brain, mixed with hypervigilance, combined to see his friends in the background laughing and muttering to each other as they looked in the direction of the phone.

Given my past history with bullies, I immediately felt embarrassed, and once again, felt I was being picked on. So, I quickly looked for some random excuse to end the call. I was already feeling singled out, I didn't want to add crying in front of them to their list of things to laugh at!

My boyfriend took that moment to message me asking what was up because I had seemed quiet during the call. Instead of keeping things to myself, I told him the truth: "I felt really uncomfortable, your friends kept looking at the camera and laughing at me and whispering to each other, and I was hoping you would have backed me up, but you didn't. And that really hurt. It felt like my feelings didn't matter, especially since you know my history with being bullied".

After going back and forth via messages for ten to fifteen minutes, with him defending his friends, of course, as to be expected, he then texted, "I've had enough of this; I'm going to bed."

I sat at the end of my brother's bed, a sobbing mess, not wanting to disturb our parents. As you could also expect, my brother was absolutely furious, and at times, I was confused about who was comforting who, but he gently reassured me that everything would be okay.

For the next two weeks, my supposed boyfriend went full ghost mode. I may have turned into a desperate girlfriend messaging asking how his day was, if he was okay and even sending him photos of my brother's birthday cake. I still heard crickets. That was until he messaged me one night, saying he was never ready for a girlfriend anyway and that we should take a break.

You could imagine my shock, anger, and surprise a couple of weeks later, when I had to go to his school for a history conference. He walked into the auditorium holding hands with a slim blonde. My heart broke into more pieces than I thought possible. I felt so disposable—almost used.

What, perhaps, made the situation worse was finding out about his "bet" with his mates. In typical high-school bloke fashion, their bet was whoever could lose their virginity first would earn "top dog" status. Even though he told me it was just a joke, and he didn't date me to see if I was "easy," I still felt used and downright foolish; naturally, it confirmed that little gremlin inside my head telling that I was ugly, and undateable because of my disability.

You can imagine my extra surprise when a month or so passed, and his relationship fell apart. What did I do when I found out that information? Yep, you guessed it! I was seriously considering giving him another chance when he started hinting at giving us another go. See what I mean by major self-worth issues?! I asked my "friend" group for their thoughts on the subject.

That lunchtime, I received several pink notes, each with a response. One note in particular stood out to me: "Rhi should take him back or lower her standards in men because not everyone will want to date someone who has the baggage of a disability." A few notes echoed similar sentiments, just delivered slightly more sensitively.

Reading this didn't hurt; once again, it made the little gremlin in my head louder by reaffirming that I was unlikeable. Perhaps, what's worse, if it could get worse, is that I kept those notes for several years afterwards, almost as a constant punishment for being born "different."

Year 11 was the gift that kept on giving! I ended up having my gallbladder removed and had to spend another week or two off school. I was relieved because it allowed me to just press the pause button on life for a bit. School was quickly becoming more of a *Days Of Our Lives* drama between dealing with friends and my ex. Add on the stress that came with entering my last couple of years at school, I was desperate to just disappear for a bit.

However, I was definitely not relieved about having to undergo more surgery and dealing with yet another stint of rehab. Albeit nowhere near as intense as the recovery from scoliosis rods. And if you're wondering whether this surgery was related to my condition, I can safely say that my gallstones weren't directly linked to muscular dystrophy, rather my intense love for mayonnaise.

I feel that, in many ways, returning from surgery and the notes from earlier in the year marked the tipping point for me. It was time to start standing up for myself and truly believe that: I deserved better.

The icing on the cake was when my supposed friend group claimed they would go to the bathroom and would be back, but instead, ended up sitting there, hanging out, and taking selfies. The bathroom was the only one upstairs, and I quickly picked up on the hint. Additionally, one guy in my grade told someone in Year 7 that I was a retard, but by that point, that word rolled off my back like water off a duck's back. He ran for the hills when the Grade 7 kid came over to me to repeat what the guy had said to him. I couldn't help but laugh. If you are going to say something like that, at least have the guts to say it to my face, not get some junior to be your messenger.

I began to sit alone at lunch until one of my best friends in Year 10 would come and find me, and we would have lunch together. It is safe to say our friendship was one of the best things to have come out of my time at high school. However, more on that later.

While all this was happening, it was around the time to start seriously contemplating life outside of school and what I wanted to pursue professionally.

If you have been paying attention, I will be sounding like a broken record when I say: I always wanted to be an actress; it was something I loved. I was always that person who would watch movies or TV shows and want to learn everything about how they were made. It only took a few people to tell me that everyone wants to act, and considering that I was female, in Australia, and faced the little "issue" of being disabled, I felt like I had no other choice but to close the door on that dream.

I still wonder why I gave up so quickly. Why didn't I completely ignore them and try my hardest to become an actress? Perhaps, it was because I was a major people pleaser, and if people didn't agree with what I wanted to do or the things I said, I felt as though I was letting them down or that they didn't support me.

However, we can all agree that's far from the truth. My parents have always been incredibly supportive of everything I have done. Obviously, that didn't mean they would jump out of their seats when I told them, "Hey, I want to act!" or "Hey, I want to ride horses." They were more calculated rather than impulsive and would offer much-needed feedback or considerations.

As someone who was beginning to really struggle with self-image, I was desperate for external validation. I was hoping when I told Mum about wanting to be the next Merryl Streep, she would jump out of her seat. So when she said, "Hmm, that sounds interesting. However, have you thought about..." in a nervous tone, I felt troubled and would usually no longer want to do what I had asked her about.

At that point in my life, I was desperately seeking acceptance, reassurance, and support. Even though I already had it from my family in spades, and they would support whatever I wanted to do, I didn't realise it then due to how much I was hurting.

One of the stronger feelings that is often not talked about when living with a disability is the sense of being a burden, especially if your parents are your primary caregivers.

They help you dress, assist you with cooking at times, sacrifice their own wants to take you to appointments, and mourn what they envisioned life would be like. You see the pain in their faces, the quiet grit and tenacity to always show up for you, and you can't help but feel guilty, leading to a desperate need to keep them happy. You start thinking that if you can keep them happy, perhaps you will be less of a burden. This often means giving up what you love. Seeing even a glimmer of nerves or doubt in their eyes makes you read it as though they aren't happy. Yet, in truth, they don't want to see you get hurt or face even more rejection than you, perhaps, already have.

So, after closing the door on the dream of becoming the next Nicole Kidman or Peter Dinklage, I began searching for something that my disability couldn't interrupt or take away. Ironically, during my desperate search for a career, it was my love for the performing arts that led me to a path that was like chalk and cheese.

I fell in love with *Criminal Minds*, so much so that I aspired to be a criminologist. Alas, I was hit with another setback; in Australia, or even Queensland, so many people graduate with criminology degrees, but there was only one criminologist for all of Queensland. I scratched that idea off the list, but I still felt that the legal industry was where I wanted to go.

That's when I discovered Law and the idea of becoming a lawyer.

It was like a light bulb went off in my head, and everything suddenly made sense. Law was a way for me to give a voice to those who didn't have one—something I had desperately needed years prior and still needed.

I felt that becoming a lawyer was also something that didn't rely on my physical strength, and given that muscular dystrophy doesn't impact the brain, it was a career I could pursue regardless of how my condition progressed.

Despite my severe self-worth issues, I was still incredibly opinionated and would regularly debate topics with anyone willing to engage. All things considered, Law ticked all the boxes of what I was looking for. It also marked a box I didn't realise at the time: to be seen as worthy.

I jumped in with both feet, or rolled in, to legal studies at school. I loved almost every minute, and when I truly discovered my passion for Law, my teacher encouraged me, perhaps, slightly more than the others in my class. Partially because, by that point, I had decided I wanted to study Law at university, and I told my teacher, who immediately said, "I see potential; we just need to refine it."

My teacher's consistent feedback on my essays was that I understood the Law and its principles; I just couldn't express them on paper in a way that made sense. The other most common feedback was "too much waffling." Even for my very last assignment in legal studies for high school, I still couldn't master the art of not "waffling."

Because of my newfound love for Law, and the fact that I am a glutton for punishment, I undertook a HeadStart Program at the local university. HeadStart is where you complete a university subject while still in school, and upon successful completion, guarantees entry into a course that includes that subject.

Yes, it is as daunting and stressful as it sounds.

Managing Year 11 subjects alongside friend issues, self-worth issues, relationship problems, and dealing with gallstone attacks followed by gallbladder removal is a lot. Adding a university subject on top of everything feels insane. However, I loved a challenge, and the guaranteed entry into university was too tempting to pass up. And with that, I enrolled in Legal Writing and Research.

As a result of participating in HeadStart, the school granted participants the option to drop a school subject, allowing for a free period or study line. The program still provided us with enough points to graduate with an Overall Position (OP) score alongside our OP-registered subjects. In order to be awarded an OP, you had to undertake a certain amount of OP-registered subjects to make up 20 credit points in your final two years of study, and then sit the QCS exam prior to graduating year 12.

For those confused, an OP is a mark out of 1-25, with 1 being the highest and enabling entry into any degree or university you wanted. A score of 25 meant you were like Patrick Star from *SpongeBob SquarePants*.

Initially, I used my free period to work on my university assessment, as the due date coincided with my hospital stay for gallbladder surgery. After my return, my free periods became an intricate blend of university and school essays. At the same time, my afternoons at home were spent doing homework for the next day or figuring out how to write a university-grade essay.

By the skin of my teeth, I passed my HeadStart program and was guaranteed entry into law upon graduation from high school. This alone lifted so much pressure off my shoulders, allowing me to enjoy my final year of high school.

In Year 12, I began to see the light at the end of the tunnel, not just because I was graduating, but also because I slowly started to recognise the character of the people I was hanging around with. I was gradually, and I mean, *gradually*, finding my worth.

After months of coming home, crying to Mum at the start of my senior year about how the same friend group was mistreating me and purposely sitting on the oval for lunch, knowing I couldn't get to it, she suggested seeing a psychologist. The stigma around seeing a therapist was that only crazy people did it, so as soon as Mum suggested it, I shut it down.

My emotional turmoil each day began to strain our relationship and Mum's unwavering patience. One day, after several weeks of crying every afternoon about the same issues with my supposed friends and rejecting all of Mum's suggestions, she finally snapped.

"That's it, Rhiannon. I can't do this any more. We have the same conversations every afternoon about what the girls are doing. I have suggested taking you to see someone, reading a book during lunch, finding Tristan (my friend from the grade below me), and making new friends, and you won't take any steps other than sitting and watching the girls have lunch, hoping they'll see you and sit with you. I can't offer any more suggestions. And I can't keep discussing this because it isn't good for either of us. You need to find a way through this because you can't keep coming home upset every day."

At that moment, even though she never intended it that way, the voice in my head said, "You've even pushed your mother away. No one is coming to help you. You are alone and need to find a way through this and navigate life on your own."

Again, she never intended that at all, and when I told her how I perceived it many years later, she was heartbroken and apologised profusely for making me feel alone. We both shed many tears together that day.

Still, that statement woke me up and prompted me to start inadvertently recognising my worth, all while simultaneously reconnecting with friends who genuinely cared about me and had similar interests.

I began taking a book to school and, sometimes, sat with another friend while reading. I even started to enjoy my own company and relished sitting alone during lunch breaks in the middle of winter, pressing my back against the warm bricks that had soaked up the sun all day to defrost.

I would remain alone until Tristan would find me, and we would spend the entire lunch break bantering and joking about his passion for chess or discussing the latest gossip in our grades. There were times when he and two other friends of mine would sit together, either in silence or engaging in small talk, just happy to have company instead of all of us borderline outcasts sitting by ourselves.

I cherished our little group and Tristan coming to find me, him peeking around the corner with a grin that would make the Cheshire Cat proud.

I started to enjoy sitting by myself in class. If I had to sit next to the group of girls to work on our assignments, I would immediately plug my ears with R&B hits and go into my little bubble since we were allowed to listen to music.

There was a time when they would ignore me and then switch and become lovely, especially when they wanted help with their assignments or needed to borrow an eraser or a pen. It took me a while to figure that out, but once I did, and they asked for help, I said, "I'm not even sure what I am doing, so I don't think I am the best person to ask. Sorry."

It felt strangely liberating to say no and slowly begin to put boundaries in place, even for a major people pleaser such as myself. I cherished the times I was alone rather than feeling like I needed to be around people, just as much as I cherished the time when I was with those who genuinely wanted to be around me.

I finally arrived at a point where I didn't care what people thought about who I sat with, the fact I didn't drink or smoke, or that I loved to study.

I eventually found immense peace, delving further into my schoolwork, and with my career set, school became a place of serenity, rather than up shit creek without a paddle.

To get through the more challenging days, I started to write into my school diary every Monday morning the speech that Rocky gives to his son in the last movie, in front of Adrien's. I would see and read that quote each time I opened my diary to write homework, check due dates, or cross off things on the mile-long to-do list. It gave me extra motivation, confidence, and self-belief to keep trying and find a way through the challenging moments.

Still, to this day, I quote that scene and know it by heart:

"Let me tell you something you already know. Life ain't all sunshine and rainbows. It is a very mean and nasty place, and I don't care how tough you are; it will beat you to your knees and keep you there permanently if you let it. You, me, or nobody is going to hit as hard as life. But it ain't about how hard you hit. It is about how hard you can get hit, and keep moving forward, how much you can take and keep moving forward. That's how winning is done! Now, if you know what you are worth, then go out and get what you're worth, but you gotta be willing to take the hits and not pointing fingers, saying you ain't where you want to be because of him or her, or anybody. Cowards do that and that ain't you! You are better than that!" – Rocky Balboa

The last few weeks of high school were an entanglement of emotions, encompassing fear, sadness, and excitement.

The mad dash to prepare for the final round of exams intensified the stress but subdued the other emotions flowing through everyone. Ironically, my last exam was in legal studies. It was an essay under exam conditions, and we were permitted exactly half a page of notes. I needed a B+ or an A- to raise my overall grade to around a B, if I recall correctly. As I was entering law school the following year, I was eager to finish high school legal studies on a high note to boost my confidence.

My notes filled half a page precisely. I had written out my entire essay because the school and my teacher were not cruel; we were allowed to know the topic in advance and practice. I removed all filler words, leaving only strong points and essentially my entire essay, albeit without proper grammar or sentence structure. We were permitted feedback on our practice essays, so I entered the exam confident I would do fine. I still remember that, thanks to my strong note strategy, I finished my essay about half an hour early, the earliest I had ever completed an exam.

Due to hand fatigue, I was often granted extra time, usually finishing long after everyone else had left. This time was different; I could sit and reflect on the last five years and the fact that I had completed my last high school exam. I remember, while immersed in thought, my teacher walked by, grinned, and whispered, "I can't wait to finally be able to bump your grade up." She already knew from my practice exam that I had performed well enough for my overall grade in the class to improve. She was eager to see me succeed in legal studies and often became frustrated for me whenever I didn't do well enough on my essays. Therefore, that final exam was a relief for her as much as it was for me.

I left that exam room elated that school was essentially over, but it was bittersweet knowing that it truly was the end. I was leaving an environment that felt like a second home, despite the struggles. I was departing from teachers who felt more like friends and friends who had become like family.

That last week of school was essentially used to teach us about the outside world. We learned to change a tyre, cook, and had presentations from universities, trade schools, the police, and the Red Frogs. Supposing you aren't Australian or don't live in Queensland, the Red Frogs are an organisation that helps people during "Schoolies" week by assisting partygoers in finding medical help if needed, getting back to their accommodation, providing bottles of water, and even cooking breakfast for those too hungover to get out of bed. I counted my blessings for my disability, as I didn't have to struggle in front of everyone to change a tyre.

We learned self-defence from one of the best teachers at school, who was always everyone's first point of call should we need help. I still feel terrible because I thought that, because of my condition, I wouldn't be strong enough to hurt anyone. But my poor friend was recovering from an arm injury, and in a manoeuvre we did to escape someone's grip, I had to position her arm to apply force around her elbow. I recall the teacher saying you don't need much force, but I thought that applied to the intense gym junkies in the room. I felt like I barely touched her arm, and she immediately jumped and said to stop. Bear in mind, we weren't hitting or kicking anyone, simply learning how to escape someone's grip by practising a technique or having the teacher explain what to do if it became too dangerous.

A collection of staff and parents assembled a recipe book for us so we didn't have to rely on living off 2-minute noodles. Even though I am sure that as soon as we started university, those 2-minute noodles became a staple food group. That last week was full of laughs, memories, reflections, hugs, and tears.

Packing up my locker for the last time and putting away all the photos I had printed and stuck to the inside of my door, along with quotes from inspirational people, gave me extra time to look back. As I closed it for the last time, I looked out of the window behind it and stared at the stunning garden in the middle of campus.

That's when the realisation finally hit me.

I survived.

I made it through high school.

All the difficult times—the tears, the anxiety, the surgeries, the bullies, losing ability and strength, the news of perhaps not bearing children of my own, and standing up for the people I cared about most—these moments were all a part of finding who I was and getting to a point where I had to say: "Enough is enough."

Even though I was still waddling and emotionally wounded, the wounds were starting to fade, and I was instead finding genuine joy in life again, which in turn, planted a seed of self-belief that I hadn't really felt before.

Year 12 Formal, or Prom, and graduation culminated all the lessons I learnt from everything that happened at school. The most significant breakthrough, however, was physical.

When I was around twelve, I was told that I wouldn't be walking by the time I graduated from high school. But then, not only was I still walking, but I also walked in kitten heels across the gravel to get photos before formal, walked the red carpet at arrivals, and danced all night. That entire day, even being helped out of the car by a teacher who meant so much to me and to each of us, was the ultimate "Fuck you!" to those who kept telling me that I wouldn't be walking, not to mention all the research that suggested I might not still be on this Earth.

Graduation night was the icing on an already glorious cake. I was surprised with flowers and a bracelet from Tristan, and plenty of hugs from my family. Standing outside, talking to the teachers and thanking them for the past five years meant so much. They had always been there for me, treated me the same as everyone else, and even though I sometimes didn't feel seen by my peers, they always noticed me. I walked to get my diploma that night, and even though I held up the procession and my face turned bright red, I was immensely grateful for still being able to walk.

That night, as I drove out of the school for the last time, I checked Facebook to see that two of my supposed friends, who until, that last week, had somewhat reconciled, had unfriended me. That was the moment that strangely finally made me breathe. I was free. Even though I was already missing school and the fact that I wouldn't spend every day being escorted to my car or my locker, or see that Cheshire grin around the corner, I was so excited to finally turn to a new chapter.

My Schoolies week was a chance to reminisce and reflect on the past twelve years. For those who don't know, Schoolies is a big week-long party on the Gold Coast where recent high school graduates go to "live it up," celebrate, and sometimes, make some questionable decisions.

For me, I went to the Gold Coast in the second week when the Queensland partygoers had already returned home and the NSW crowd arrived, which is usually much quieter. Instead of going with friends and getting drunk out of my mind, I went with my family. We sat on the sand, swam, enjoyed good food, played board games, and shared a drink as the sun set with some cheese.

It was the first time I truly felt grateful for all I had experienced.

Of course, you can't experience the good without the bad. The bad often shapes us more than the good. Although I experienced so much good and had a blast during my school years, the hard times allowed me to delve deeper into discovering myself and what truly makes me happy. They made me realise that while I may have appeared "different," my differences could be my greatest asset.

Even when I felt like I was drowning from both physical and emotional discomfort, I began to see that I had a unique opportunity to challenge perceptions of bullying and disability. And to understand that, while life may be uncertain, what is certain is: how you survive the tough times.

And those difficult moments led me to Law and, simultaneously, unlocked a whole new side of life that I had to unearth and rediscover alongside my disability.

SECTION 2
Weathering the Storm - Storms and Survival

And once the storm is over, you won't remember how you made it through, how you managed to survive. You won't even be sure whether the storm is really over. But one thing is for certain. When you come out of the storm, you won't be the same person who walked in. That is what this storm is all about.

—Haruki Murakami, *Kafka on the Shore*

CHAPTER 5

GRIEF UNSPOKEN

Okay, so we have talked about my childhood, including the maddening highs and lows of high school, with humour mixed in for good measure. However, before we continue, I need to be real with you all for a second, and show you a new perspective to this journey. Because it's not just able-bodied people who get it wrong. Sometimes, even within the disabled community, there's this unspoken rule: if you say anything about your disability that isn't completely positive, you're labelled an ableist.

For those who don't speak disabled, the term "ableism" is described as discrimination or prejudice against people who have a disability, usually painting disabled people as inferior. Over the years, however, I have seen the term become altered. It has become a term used to shame those with disabilities who are trying to cope and live with their disability in their own way. If you want to work out, explore treatment options, or even just wish things were different for a moment, you're told you're rejecting your identity, that you hate your body, and that you're ashamed of being disabled.

But I don't completely hate my body. I don't always hate my disability. However, I absolutely despise the way I'm told I'm not allowed to grieve it sometimes. I hate that being honest about the hard parts is seen as a betrayal of myself and the disabled community.

So, call me an ableist if that's what honesty makes me. I'd rather speak the truth than drown in toxic positivity. Living life isn't about hiding what hurts or pretending everything's fine just to make others comfortable. It's about being real—even when it's messy, even when it's hard. Disabled or not.

We all go through the same things, just at different times. We all go through the highs and lows of life. Grief is a natural part of life; there is literally no way to avoid it. Grief, however, is also one of those complex emotions that so many of us think we can handle. But if we're truly honest, we, perhaps, haven't handled grief well at all.

For those of us with a disability, or muscular dystrophy specifically, sometimes, it can be like grief never truly vacates the premises. We grieve not only the loss of family pets, a relationship breakdown, or our favourite character's deaths. We also grieve over our bodies, as our disability robs us of more of our independence.

Muscular dystrophy causes your body to constantly get weaker, and sometimes, it feels like this happens overnight. One day, you're able to comfortably walk and get your weekly groceries; the next, your legs feel like lead, and you need to take a breather halfway to the shops out of fear your knee will give out. Sometimes, you are able to get up off the toilet by yourself; other times, you need a toilet frame to help you up. Otherwise, you're left with no choice but texting your mum to come and help you wipe your butt, get you off the toilet, or risk faceplanting and becoming trapped where you are.

For many of us, we don't know when it will be the "last" time of doing something, because of how fast muscular dystrophy can progress.

I felt the swiftness of my disease's progression from the ages of six to nine. I went from being able to sit on the floor cross-legged and stand up by myself to having to sit on a chair, as sitting on the floor and getting up became too hard.

I recall once being told off for sitting on the chair by a new teacher's aide, and I didn't have the guts to tell her I was allowed to sit on the chair, so

I sank to the floor reluctantly. I was there for only a minute before being tapped on the shoulder by the same teacher's aide, apologising and asking if I needed help, as another teacher's aide told her I could sit on the chair. I waved away her help and slowly and shakily managed to get back on the chair. I was desperate to, still, be like everyone else, and even though I did feel cool for sitting on a chair, I was in major denial that I was getting weaker.

I like to say there is a spiral of grief. Shock, denial, back to shock, anger, sadness, back to denial mixed with sadness, more anger, before you eventually arrive at acceptance. In dealing with a disability, you almost become accustomed to the first few stages, often hovering between the denial, anger, and sadness phases for a few weeks, months, or even years.

When I truly started to learn about my disability, what it would do to me, what it would take away, and what it was already taking away, I skipped shock and went straight into denial. I refused to settle for being labelled as "different" or "disabled." I always made sure I participated in school sports, cross country days, sports carnivals, choir, band, and dance—you name it. I was adamant I wanted to do it, because everyone else around me could.

My body felt fine, and even though I had the limitations of not being able to sit on the floor, and being more like a baby giraffe learning to stand on its feet as the days went on, I wanted to be a part of everything life had to offer.

I attended swimming lessons during the summer months and had to accept the fact that I was slower in the pool than everyone else. But I didn't mind because being in the water was when I felt physically free. I could jump, hop, lift people, do handstands, and swim laps without feeling like exercise was difficult. Mum had to come and help me get changed, especially when it came to taking off my togs at the end of the lesson, because I didn't have the strength to remove wet clothes from my body.

In the early days, I didn't think anything of it; I didn't think I was all that different until I really started to notice when people kept asking, "Why is your mum here?" and "Why do you always take forever to get changed?"

I would always participate in athletic days, getting a healthy head start for the 100-metre race in Grade 1, which was the only time I ran the 100-metre race. I was allowed to pick where I started, and I chose around fifteen meters from the finish line. No surprise, I crossed the line first, but the shouts of "She cheated!" started drowning out the claps and cheers from the teachers, including my mum, who was, again, there to help me. I was five and more naïve than in denial that things were wrong with me.

However, as time went on, sport began to become more of a challenge. And instead of wanting to face the challenge head-on, I became sad and angry as I learned more about why I couldn't high jump or throw a shot put more than ten centimetres. Not only was it a challenge, but it would have been a safety concern for me to participate. Let's be frank: if I tried to waddle up to a high jump bar, I would have jumped a centimetre off the ground and thrown myself into the bar, probably ending up with a decent concussion.

Instead of sitting out completely, which happened a few times for activities like soccer, my PE teacher put me to work. I would help him raise the high jump bar or set it back after it had been knocked off. After I stopped doing long jump and triple jump, I was given a rake and had to rake the sandpit between jumpers. Even though I was surprised that I enjoyed helping out during those days, a lump still formed in my throat, and tension remained in my stomach.

I was mourning the fact that I couldn't participate in something that was a "standard" for people my age. I was angry at the fact that I was standing out more and more, when at the time I wanted nothing more than to just blend in and disappear.

I would smile and laugh along with everyone who failed a high jump in rather spectacular fashion, scorpioning across the mat and landing on the grass. I would ask the PE teacher if he needed me to carry equipment back to the sports shed; however, I think he knew that it would probably take the entire lunch break for me to walk the fifty metres or so with equipment, so he thanked me for my offer but sent me on my way to grab my lunch.

On the outside, I appeared as if I was happy, loving life, and not minding that I wasn't participating in athletic carnivals or joining in for swimming carnivals. I was even laughing along with people who said they were envious that I could just sit all day and watch everyone else running around in the sun.

But, deep down, I was angry, frustrated, confused, and sad. I was silently mourning the loss of the ability to just be a kid like everyone else in primary school.

One of the hardest things about living with a progressive muscle-wasting disease, and particularly living with it at such an early age, is in the name. Progressive. I was never a "normal" or "healthy" kid in the usual sense of the word, but my "normal"—what I was used to—felt like I was the same as everyone else. I could run, jump, walk for ages, jump rope, play hopscotch, fly on the flying fox, sit on the ground, and pick up sticks in the playground.

I could do almost anything that kids my age could do. Albeit a little slower, or slightly different.

Until, almost overnight, I could no longer do those things and was relegated to the sidelines, watching everyone else have a great time. My only company was the breeze in the wind and the birds chirping overhead, who seemed to be almost mocking me with their ease of opening their wings and flying wherever they wanted to go effortlessly.

At some point, it stops being just a story about what happened to me. It becomes something that happens to anyone in my situation. It becomes what you go through, what you have to survive, when your body and, seemingly, the world feels against you at every turn.

You mourn every ability that becomes a challenge and then eventually impossible. Your thoughts are consumed with reminiscing about everything that you used to do, being frustrated that you can't, and willing your body to get both feet off the floor.

The anger that then fills your body feels as though you could probably move an entire wall of concrete, like Iron Man. You get home from school and scream into your pillow, so your parents won't hear you, yelling at your body for not working, and wondering why it could once do something but is now giving you the cold shoulder.

You scream at God for making you like this, ask why He is torturing you, and teasing you by dangling a carrot of ability, then ripping it from your grasp, seemingly in a matter of seconds. You even end up cursing your parents, desperate to find someone to blame for why you are the way you are.

The fear that comes when you learn that your disability is terminal, after seeing an email chain between your mother and the Starlight Foundation at around eleven years old, freezes your veins. The email details what you already know about why you are different and why you struggle in life, as well as the name of it. But there is one detail kept secret from you—the fact that you would be lucky to live to be nineteen years old. This thing, this disease inside you, robbing you of the ability to have a normal childhood, is also going to rob you of your life.

It feels like someone dropped a ton of bricks on your head. You don't tell anyone that you know this piece of information, and instead, choose to let it consume your every thought. In the next round of doctor appointments and lung function tests, you start paying closer attention to what people are saying in the room and the results on the screen. Seeing the numbers on your lung function test get lower and lower, your head then starts saying, "Am I going to suffocate slowly? Is this what this disease is going to do to me?"

You still don't say a word to anyone that you know. You don't want to add any more pain onto your parents, and you dare not scare your 8-year-old brother, who thinks that having a sister who drives a scooter is the coolest thing in the world because he gets to stand on the back of it for joyrides.

You mourn in silence. Every time you notice you can't walk as far as you once did, and you start needing someone to lift you up a stair at a time as they become harder to climb, you are filled with fear, anger, and sadness. You still have no idea that some day soon, stairs will become impossible. The disease is dictating your life, and it isn't something you can control or wish away.

You wake up night after night, crying yourself to sleep, not only for the fact that people are bullying you because of this thing inside you, but from the fact that you are at its mercy. Knowing you can't do anything to stop it, as it does whatever it wants to you physically. Realising it is slowly killing you, but no chemo or drugs will fix it.

You mourn the childhood you wanted but couldn't have. While you are required to have conversations and hear people talk about what your body can't do, being poked and prodded to test reflexes, and having someone hover over you, timing how long it would take you to get off the floor, other kids your age are, instead, talking about fairy bread at parties and the new Happy Meal toy at Maccas. You desperately want to go back to school to join in on those conversations, but at the same time, you don't want to because of the bullying and sitting on the sidelines. This all reminds you that you are still a kid, but not in the traditional sense.

You have to grow up fast; you have no choice. And with that comes a level of confusion. Having to almost be an adult and have adult conversations in a doctor's office, but at family dinners, be ushered away to play with your cousins who still want to play dress up because you are "too young" to stay at the table and have grown-up conversations.

The lines between childhood and adulthood blur together. When you get told off for being out of line for scowling at your uncle and dad over a joke, you are then told, "Know your place; you are a child, not an adult." You are confused because you are expected to then answer questions from the doctor and try to comprehend all the information about why things are hard, and why you can't do things everyone else can. But outside the doctor's office, it's like your opinion is irrelevant because you are a kid.

The confusion adds to the mental load—you become lost, and in a way, feel like you are floating in no man's land. Not feeling like a kid, but not feeling like an adult either, while in truth being only nine, ten, or even fifteen years old. Not only are you losing physical ability and the opportunity to have a "normal" childhood, but you also feel like you have been robbed of a sense of self. People only seem to pay attention to you if you are talking about your disability.

You become desperate to feel "normal," so you think that dance will, maybe, help. Like freedom of expression and being consumed in the music? Surely, it will be a good thing. And it is for a time. You make new friends and learn cool new dances. Adapting the dances to suit you and your ability doesn't really feel too difficult. You have already had to adapt to so much that it doesn't register in your young 7-year-old brain that things are different. You perform in your first dance recital, and are so excited to perform.

People have always called you a little performer. The glitter hairspray thickens in the room as you walk in with your auntie, who will help you get in and out of costumes. Again, your brain is too focused on the job rather than what is "different." That crashes down, yet again, when right before heading on stage, you step on someone's foot and fall over, pulling a muscle in your leg.

You either have two choices: you can bail and not dance, or pull yourself together and go and still have fun. The choice boiled down to one thing: that, even at eight, you weren't going to give up because you were in pain. So, you limped and waddled to the stage. There was a determination that could have come from one person—your grandfather.

While you are dealing with starting to recognise how you're different, and how your body is getting weak, grief takes a different turn. Instead of mourning your own body, you end up mourning someone else. Watching someone who you viewed as indestructible, strong, hard-headed, stubborn, and resilient end up going through cancer is more than heartbreaking.

Of course, being only seven, the concept is still surprisingly foreign. You watch your grandfather become thinner and thinner, to the point he is bedbound. You peek from around the corner as your grandmother and father lift him up out of his chair and half-carry, half-guide him to the hospital bed set up in the lounge room, looking out onto his pride and his farm.

The next few weeks, you visit him continuously, seeing the jaundice in his eyes overwhelm his kind blue orbs that would look at you with so much love. You celebrate your birthday with a phone call from him two or so days prior, talking about driving the tractor with him next time you see him, and talking about the snakes that were still bothering the chickens. He ends the call with, "Be good for grandma and your mum and dad, okay? I love you."

The morning after your eighth birthday, you find your dad is not at home, and your world suddenly comes crashing down. With one simple sentence, your world falls apart. Again. "Grandpa Bert is gone, sweetheart; he passed away at about four o'clock this morning," your mum whispers to you as she holds you in her bed.

Your heart shatters, your stomach drops, and you are consumed with a sadness that your younger self hadn't experienced before. You tell your brother, who had only turned five, two weeks earlier, too young to truly comprehend what you had just said. That was until that night, the realisation sinking in when your uncle came to pay his respects. Your brother wails and wails, the sound echoing off the walls, breaking your heart further.

You attend his funeral, sitting on a pew by his coffin, as he requested, alongside the other grandchildren. You stare at his Australian flag-draped coffin, trying to convince yourself he's not really in there. You listen to your grandma struggle through her speech and need help from her sons to get through it. You watch as the flag gets folded up and presented to your grandmother. "The Last Post" plays. The sound of the bugle is like a knife of lava through your soul. The tune almost sounds like saying goodbye as you stare at his coffin, wishing it was all a bad joke.

You look out at the crowd and find your mum. She looks at you with sadness in her eyes and nods, trying to reassure you with, "It's okay." You break apart, no longer able to maintain a resolve that you were proud of. You follow the coffin out of the church and are shocked that the crowd has filled the entire church and even flowed outside, with people listening to the service by the door.

Trying to mourn and comprehend death for the very first time, while also noticing your body becoming weaker, is almost too much for a child to handle. Instead of reaching out and asking for help, you don't want to add to the worries of everyone, so you choose not to speak about it. You are then actively engaged in two grief cycles: one over your own body becoming weaker, and the other, grieving over the loss of a family member.

The thing about grieving someone who is no longer with us is that everyone grieves and heals in their own time and in their own way. There truly is no rulebook or timeline for that. And that was the same for everyone around me.

All the adults around me were seemingly just getting on with life. This confused me because I still had all these emotions and was struggling to understand what I was feeling, but everyone else had "moved on." So, instead of being vocal about how little 9-year-old, or even, 10-year-old me was feeling, still struggling a few years after his passing, I kept it to myself. I didn't want to reopen old wounds.

Eventually all of these buried feelings spill over; you become angry and start lashing out at your dad for helping you go roller skating. Each time you almost fall, you yell at him that he isn't helping you properly, even though you have told him how to, and he is just doing what you asked. You yell because you are also embarrassed; you are the only 13-year-old on the rink who has someone behind them, helping them try to skate. It doesn't matter that there are many people who look like baby Bambi and are clinging for dear life onto the side of the rink; you are too caught up in your head and embarrassed thinking how "odd" you look. The many eyes on you as you go don't help much either.

Anger eventually consumes you, and you lash out at anyone and everyone. Even your brother simply asking, "What are you doing?" while you do your homework is enough to absolutely make you see red. You know it isn't fair, but there is a gremlin in your head that won't take a Valium and chill the fuck out. That anger coincided with the fact that it was around the time my body's strength took a dive, and I was losing the ability to do things I used to.

As the years go on, there are days, of course, that you are fine. It's almost as if "life" becomes a routine. Get up, waddle to the bathroom, get ready for school, go to school, come home, do homework, eat dinner, and go to bed. Rinse and repeat. It's almost refreshing, especially when it seems like your body has somewhat neutralised, and things feel easy.

You feel like you can afford to laugh again at things, joke around, and be gladly tossed around in the pool by your brother, not caring that he is younger than you and can lift you clean out of the water before you belly flop in spectacular fashion. What you don't know is that each time you go underwater, he watches to make sure you surface and are okay before allowing you to dunk him under.

Everyone is happy, as if the cloud of MD has disappeared somewhat into just a slight grey cloud in the sky. Not posing a threat. Just there. Almost as if a bridge between denial and acceptance was created, even if just for a brief moment.

As the legend goes, time heals all wounds. Or does it?

Grief never has an expiration date. Sure, as the years drag on and life goes on, the sadness and anger subside and become the emotion in the corner, showing up every now and then at times when you don't expect it. However, when you also have the usual ebbs and flows of life, on top of the grief that comes with disability, or even death, it is almost as if it becomes the ultimate juggling contest.

Allowing yourself to feel everything all at once is a recipe for ending up in a mental health facility. The emotions drown you so much that you don't know which way is up. So instead, and especially if you haven't learnt good coping techniques, you drown them out before they drown *you* out. By that, I mean you try not to process everything that has transpired over the past few years. That only gets you so far until more events happen, like being bullied relentlessly, and the emotions boil over.

Then, you're back to square one.

In the grieving of what you are losing physically, and the toll it is taking mentally, there is still a fire in your belly. A fire to continue pushing and being stubborn, and just get on with life, trying anything and everything. You try swimming and absolutely fall in love. Finally, you've found something that makes you feel weightless and can forget about your illness, if for only a moment.

In the pool, you can jump, hop, and do handstands—everything you can't do on land. Not to mention swim laps upon laps. You even go on to enter a swimming competition for fellow disabled people, winning in breaststroke and coming in third place in freestyle. You imagine going on to compete in swimming at the Paralympics.

That is, until you are put in a lesson with able-bodied people. Everything then comes crashing down. The high you felt, feeling as though you are good and capable of something, disappears. The clouds return when you are left ten metres down the pool, still swimming, while everyone else in the group is already forty meters down the other end, waiting for you.

The embarrassment creeps in, and the stinging reminder of being different is all-consuming once again. So, you pack it in, because at such a young age, all you can think of is difference being a bad thing, especially when you are trying to blend in. Ultimately, failing to see that is the best thing about you.

When I think back to that time, it's like watching a version of myself from the outside, like reading a story about a child that was stuck in a body that was changing too fast. A body that was hell-bent on trying to destroy my life.

It was clear that I still hadn't learnt my lesson about the grieving process because, for one, I still chose to keep my true feelings bottled inside me. There were times when I would come home from school after a relentless day of bullying, and I would be sobbing on my bed. My mum, concerned, would ask me what was going on. But I still couldn't tell her truly how I was feeling; about my body, my life, and how I was still struggling to process my grandfather's death.

My mum and I have an amazing relationship. We practically tell each other everything, so why couldn't I really tell her how I was truly feeling?

I would lie there crying like my dog had died, talking about school, briefly mentioning the physical limitations, and finish off by saying,

"The one person who would give me advice, who would listen to me and help me, is no longer here any more." I was referring to my grandfather.

Looking back now, this statement also must have felt like a kick in the gut for my mum, because she would always listen to me and give me advice, but I took her for granted, as kids often do at that age. If that hurt her, she masked it by the look of sheer confusion etched across her face. "Honey, Bert has been gone for several years now, and you were so young when he passed away. You guys never really spoke about things that were really troubling you. I am really confused."

At the time, I couldn't bring myself to respond to her because I was also confused. I couldn't figure out why I was still feeling the way I was feeling, that level of grief. Looking back now, I can completely understand. I felt vulnerable for the first time ever. It was the first time I experienced death, watched someone wither away, and went to a funeral. It terrified me, and I was drowning, trying to understand and move through the grief process.

I want to defend my family quickly, before getting on with my story. When I reminded Mum of this a while back, she couldn't stop apologising for not seeing what was really going on and understanding the message between the lines when I sobbed my heart out to her that day in my room. To me, there was nothing to apologise for. It was uncharted territory for her. Not grief, or the death of a loved one, but having to guide her kids through that process, and not being completely sure of what to look out for.

The thing is, like I have said before, grief isn't linear. Everyone has their own experiences and own ways of processing. Everyone copes and deals with grief in their own way. Granted, some manage it in healthier ways than others, but everything inside you is screaming for peace and a way to block out the pain.

At some stage, everyone comes out the other side. The skies are clearer, and life goes on. For all of us, life does just carry on, regardless of the situation that has caused the grief. You eventually find a way to dust yourself off, get dressed, put on some makeup, and go to work or even just make some breakfast that isn't last night's cold takeaway.

Don't get me wrong, grief never leaves us. Someone said, "Grief walks beside us. Some days, it quietly moves beside you, and life feels easy and peaceful. Other days, it feels as if it has a death grip on you, and you crumble into a thousand tiny pieces."

Being disabled, you find a way to let grief walk beside you very early on. However, it remains unspoken. Just whispers or yells between the two of you.

For me personally, why I didn't truly allow myself to not only process my grief, but really become honest with myself and my family, is that I was afraid. I already had a notion in my head that I was a burden and was causing my family pain. I thought if I were to tell them how I truly felt about life, I would just be causing more pain and would be an even bigger burden.

What I found, however, was that by doing what I was doing, the grief compounds. Life is more than just navigating being disabled. We all have the "usual" ups and downs to deal with on top of it. So, when you don't deal with that grief, and make some level of peace with it, and something else happens either related or unrelated to what kickstarted that grief in the first place, it becomes too overwhelming.

So what do you do? Again, you bury it—shy away from it. You then say, "I am fine," when you know for a fact that you really aren't fine.

I was drowning in my own grief and didn't know which way was up, like I was in a washing machine and couldn't escape. It wasn't until I reached a point when I almost made a decision in front of my brother that I couldn't reverse, should I have gone through with it, that I came to a realisation. Contemplating suicide was what jolted my system. My brother screamed out for my dad, and my dad ran over. The colour in his face drained; he said to me, "Just think about what you are doing, what it will do to your family. Everything your grandfather did to make sure he didn't go on your birthday will have been for nothing. Think about what it will do to your brother. It's not worth it. Please."

Was it the best response to someone holding a knife? Probably not. However, just mentioning my family and grandfather was like being struck by lightning. I realised I didn't want to leave; I just didn't know what to do with all these emotions at only eleven years old, and I had to find a way to swim to the surface.

I have always been a deep thinker, as well as a major overthinker and over-analyser, and that way of thinking has enabled me to try to find a way forward. I am also a major problem solver. I swear, 99 percent of the time, I am solving problems in my life that don't need solving. However, deep thinking, combined with problem-solving, equals progression.

I realised what was truly holding me back was constantly being mad at myself and my situation. My disability wasn't going anywhere, and it wasn't going to get better. So, I quickly needed to learn how to live with it, adapt to it, and accept it.

Even though I have always been a deep thinker and problem solver, there is only so much that you can do as an 11-year-old without a lot of life experience, and who is still cognitively developing. My skill set was limited, and what I thought I needed to "fix" mentally was even more complicated, as I had more negative subconscious feelings and thoughts than conscious ones.

That day kick-started my acceptance journey. It catapulted me into being at least open to the idea of meeting people like me, and to start turning my unspoken grief into what would propel me forward in life, instead of keeping me in that washing machine.

CHAPTER 6

SHARED JOURNEYS: FRIENDSHIP AND LOSS

If I had a dollar for every time someone said to me, "Find friends who are like you, who you can relate to," when I was growing up, I could comfortably retire twice and still have money left over.

As a part of my denial phase, I mentioned before that I flat out refused to even talk to someone in a wheelchair because that meant acknowledging my differences, too, which at the time, I just couldn't handle. I couldn't stand the thought of being "different." And whenever I did see someone in a wheelchair or similar to me, I couldn't relate because I always thought I "wasn't disabled enough" like them. Embarrassingly enough, I believed I wasn't like them at all. So, why socialise with them?

I was only around twelve or so at the time, and was consumed with major anger, resentment, fear, and, you guessed it, denial, so please excuse those thoughts.

Even the phrase "find people who are like you" often frustrated me. Purely for the reason that I've never heard non-disabled people around me be told the same thing. It felt like they were able to become friends with whomever they chose, so why was I being told to find people like me to be friends with? Wasn't I allowed to be friends with non-disabled people, too?

Little did I know, probably because I didn't want to hear it, that I was, well, truly allowed to be friends with whoever, but finding people like me would have enabled me to see the human side to disability. Finding people like me would have made me feel less like the odd one out. They would have understood everything I was going through, and I would have been able to rant with people who just "get it."

It's not like I grew up not knowing anyone like me. I was friends with a bunch of young guys with Duchenne who were about ten years older than me. Our parents met through a local MD group, and would catch up for coffee or the occasional dinner, and we would go along. There were times when we would all attend fundraising events and Christmas parties together.

I was too young at the time to build strong friendships with them or have honest conversations about what we were all going through. And there was a big part of me that struggled to feel like we were all 'similar', given the fact that I was still in major denial and perhaps in a little bubble of unawareness about my condition. Additionally, there was also the issue of being majorly socially awkward with people I was still getting used to, which, in a way, hindered my ability to become good friends with them all.

But as we got older, their conditions progressed, making it harder to travel. Our parents left the MD group, and we all drifted apart gradually. I was left spending my pre-teen and early teen years being the only person in my circle with a disability, which then, I believe, fed into my level of denial and not wanting to find people "like me."

There was also perhaps another feeling that was more prominent, lingering under the surface. It was no secret that in the wider community, being disabled was something that was considered "undesirable." It was like cancer; no one wanted it. If you were disabled, there was immediately a level of shame and embarrassment attached to it. I was even once asked if my disability was contagious. Granted, that was back in primary school, but the stigma of disability, and what it represented, was often treated with a level of disgust and most of all pity.

It also felt like having a disability put you at the bottom of the food chain, never seen as equal to your fellow human. As someone who has always been rather sensitive to the energy of others, you can see why even growing up knowing this information made me desperate not to be seen mingling with anyone who was disabled. The inner people pleaser and the desperate need to be liked by everyone was alive and kicking even back in those days!

Montrose Access ran a girls' group around once or twice a month, for girls with various types of neuromuscular conditions. You would go to the movies, go out for lunch, go to the library, draw, or make jewellery—basically anything fun. The aim of the group was to "make friends who are like you." I cringed so hard that I thought I would have frown lines at thirteen years old.

Eventually, after constant nagging by my parents and the Montrose team, I relented and turned up to the girls' group. At that point, I was about to do anything to make them stop raving about it. I thought if I went once, I could say I hated it and would be free to never attend another catch-up again. Mum asked if I wanted to take my scooter, but I was adamant about walking in. I refused to acknowledge I was disabled, and hated having to turn up to this thing, so out of defiance to the entire situation, I wanted to walk.

By the time I arrived, they were already making bracelets. My 13-year-old self nearly backed out of the room right then and there. Anything was better than making jewellery. However, it was as if a light switch had flicked on in my mind as we all sat around making beaded bracelets.

As time went on, I got comfortable, and soon enough, I was chitchatting away with a couple of the girls. I was expecting us to sit around and share war stories, but it was the complete opposite. No one asked, "What is wrong with you?" or "Why do your arms look like that?" No one judged when one of the girls needed help eating a sandwich. No one mocked each other for needing help with the simplest of tasks. We simply just got each other, and enjoyed the company.

On the way home that afternoon, Mum asked me how it went, and I refused to admit she was right about hanging out with people like me. Which pre-teen ever wants to admit that their parents are right? So I just shrugged and said, "Yeah, it was alright." When, in fact, I did enjoy it, even if I was the oldest in the group, and the activities were for people younger than me.

The next hangout was at Sizzler, a buffet-style restaurant that was a cult classic for decades in Australia. I was and still am a major foodie, so all they needed to say was "food," and I would say yes before they even finished getting the word out. This time, it was for the older girls, which meant I finally wasn't the oldest. However, it was a relief to see at least some of the girls from the first hangout, as it eased my social anxiety slightly.

One of the girls, who was about eighteen months older than me, turned up, and we happened to be sitting at the same table. It was like we had been friends since forever! And before we had even finished our first plate of food, we were actually comparing notes from our doctor's visits; what they said, how we felt, and even bitched about how stale the hospital blue colours were and how frustrating the hospital gowns are to put on. We spoke about how uncomfortable the AFOs were (remember, they were what I called "moon boots"), and the bullying we went through at school.

Once again, there was no judgment, and we weren't laughing at each other. We were laughing *with* each other, completely free to be authentically ourselves. We didn't have to try to look like we weren't struggling to carry our plates, or downplay what we were going through. We all felt seen, heard, understood, and felt. Most of us, perhaps, for the first time in our lives.

Suddenly, everyone telling me to "find people like you" started to make sense. It was about finding your chosen family. You instantly feel less alone, and even though your parents or blood family see you, perhaps, all the time, they can't relate completely to what you go through. Though, it is true that they are there for the doctor's appointments, support you through surgeries, and hear about the bullying, their feelings and what they are going through in those moments are completely different from your feelings and what you are going through with the same experience.

Don't get me wrong, they can also "get it," but the level at which they do is nowhere near the lived experience of what people "like you" get.

So, for so many of us, it's so important to have a sense of community that understands exactly what you are going through on a deeper level. You feel less insane, if I may use that word, for feeling the way you do towards life, God (or other similar higher powers), and your own body. Sometimes, they can even offer you hope and comfort, that even though things right now are messy, scary, and challenging, you will be able to get through it. And it won't beat you without a bloody good fight.

Australia, as compared to America, doesn't have a wide muscular dystrophy community. There are only about 40,000 of us, give or take, with MD or a similar neuromuscular condition, as opposed to about 250,000-ish in the United States. Comparing those figures, finding people who "get you" in Australia can literally be like finding a needle in a haystack.

In saying all of this, those who "get you" can, at times, also be people who are not disabled. It presents a unique opportunity where two different worlds collide, and it offers the ability to learn and feel integrated. I use the word "integrated" because it is becoming an increasing reemergence to say to classes or groups of people to stay with their own kind. And while I am all for finding people within your own community, you need to have friends from all walks of life to help you grow and evolve as a human being.

At my first ever job, everyone embraced me with open arms. There was never an awkward moment, and no one treated me with kid gloves. I was never spoken down to; I was just another colleague working to help people who desperately needed help navigating the legal system.

I remember one of the handful of times a group of us were planning a pub crawl after our work Christmas party. Based on my previous experience of not being invited to things, I just naturally assumed I wasn't invited and let my mind wander from the conversation, desperately hoping my poker face was in full force, and I didn't look like I had been stung by a bee. In my daydream haze, I heard someone say, "Are you in, Rhi?" My head snapped up so hard I almost got whiplash. I had to ask them to repeat the question to make sure that I heard them correctly. Had I just been invited on a bar crawl? Sure enough, I heard correctly.

That night was one of the most enjoyable nights of my life. I had never done a pub crawl before and was eager to finally experience the local nightlife. Clubbing is something nearly every 20-something-year-old does almost weekly. For me, I had yet to even have a taste of that world. My brother would always say that there was nothing special about it, but to me that was the epitome of being a 20-year-old, and I was desperate to step into that world for even just a moment.

As we started walking downtown (or in my case, driving downtown), we quickly ran into a little problem. The majority of the clubs and bars were up some flights of stairs, making it impossible for me to even get past the main door. My nerves were starting to go through the roof, and my head started spiralling with intrusive thoughts: "Will they just go in and leave me out on the street alone?", "Great. Now, they probably hate that they invited this disabled chick because they can't just go in and party", "See, Rhiannon? This was a bad idea! The first time you have a friend group that seems decent, your crippleness has to ruin it. Well done."

Instead, what I feared would happen never did. As we went to enter the venue, they simply said, "No, this one isn't good—there are stairs. Next!" They didn't blink an eye over the fact that they couldn't get into the bar. In fact, they were more frustrated because they were realising just how inaccessible the town was for someone like me.

We continued checking each club, and bar we stumbled across in town, before finally landing on The Tatts. It's a bar that has been around for decades and is still one of the most popular watering holes in Toowoomba. The only downside was that, at first glance, it wasn't wheelchair friendly. There were four steps near the front entrance; two right at the door, and another two in about a metre or so.

The guys in our group were adamant that I wouldn't be left behind, and I think they also were desperate for a beer, so they came up with a plan to get me into that building. I stood up out of my mobility scooter, and two of the guys picked up either end of my scooter and carried it up the stairs before coming to retrieve me outside. I was then carried up the stairs and placed safely back onto my scooter.

I was glad that the lighting was dim enough to hide the strong blush spreading across my face, and that the guys were too preoccupied with finding the bar in the venue to really take too much notice anyway!

That was until we stumbled across another set of stairs. And before I knew it, I was, again, being carried up the stairs, my scooter in tow. We failed to hear one member of our party yell out that there was a ramp nearby that I could have used instead. We also later learnt there was a concealed accessible entrance out the back, but it was in a dark alleyway and we would have needed to have someone go around the front and ask security to unlock the door. Usually, I'm humiliated by having to be manhandled in public—whether it's being helped out of my scooter, a chair, or yes, up a couple of steps—but that night everyone was drunk out of their minds and too busy trampling each other to get to the dance floor to even notice.

We stayed at The Tatts for the remainder of the night, with a group of us taking turns on the dance floor or grabbing drinks. I was no longer the wallflower, the person in the corner, often invisible to those around me. I was seen, valued, and included in conversations. That feeling was indescribable, and made the whole night even more memorable—if that's even possible.

Usually, when the music is blasting and the bass is strong enough to burst your eardrums twice over, everyone rushes to the dance floor. Now, I am not impartial to a boogie, but I remained on my scooter at our table—drunk people dancing on the same floor as someone with a physical disability is practically asking for faceplants, broken noses, and an alcohol shower.

Usually, the entire table will go dancing, and I will be left alone. But for the whole night, I was never alone—there were always a few remaining people at the table with me, partly because they also didn't want to get crushed by the number of people on the dance floor, and wanted to make sure I wasn't alone.

As we left the club and my dad pulled up to drive me home, my colleagues were adamant about helping me and my wheels back down the stairs instead of Dad helping me. They carried me, with my scooter quickly in tow, out the door, and I was gently placed on the ground, with the guy who helped me, not letting me go, until I was stable enough on my feet. With hugs all round and a quick "See you at work on Monday," the group dispersed to nurse potential hangovers.

For one of the first times in my life, I began to truly feel like I was part of a community—one that valued my opinions and my voice, and treated me no different from anyone else. They truly believed in respect and making sure that no one was left behind, even if it meant having to take almost all night finding a bar when they could have downed five beers at that point.

They felt like... true friends. They saw me, accepted my flaws and quirks, and made sure that me, as well as everyone else, was respected and simply treated like a human being.

Friends come and go; that is a part of life. Some people come into our lives to teach us a lesson before we can unlock the next phase of life; others are there for a lifetime. While I have people in my life who have taken more of an ensemble role than a leading role in my life, they have all shown me in their own unique ways that there are always people who are willing to be in your corner, and not everyone will give you a hard time for running over their feet.

That's the thing about friendship or chosen family. They are the people in your life who just "get it." You don't have to explain the reasons why you need help or even have to ask for it in the first place. They will just say, "I got you." No questions asked. They genuinely want to know about your life, not to judge or inspire them, but because they just want to get to know you, as they would want to get to know any of their other friends.

I've always wanted a large friend group growing up. In my little mind, it was a sign that you were cool and popular. Let's be honest—which kid doesn't want that? However, as I grew up, it was clear that the universe was telling me that I wasn't meant to be popular or have a large friend group. Believe it or not, I am relieved that I have four or so people in my life whom I could call my close friends. One from high school, one from Uni, one from Victoria, and one all the way in America.

My good friend from high school, Tristan, and I met by complete fluke after both doing the musical *Godspell* together. We were both in the chorus, and despite being in the same room for months during rehearsals and the eventual performances, we actually never spoke a word to each other until after the musical had ended.

I was heading to the pick-up zone, at the front of the school, one afternoon with my cousin, and I suddenly heard a quiet "Hi, Rhi." I whipped my head around and saw a guy kneeling by his locker outside, smiling at me and giving a little wave. I recognised him immediately, but wasn't sure of his name. Nevertheless, I smiled and greeted him back, then turned to my cousin to ask, "Who is that? We did *Godspell* together, but I don't know his name." She simply responded, "That's Tristan."

He was in a grade lower than me, despite us being the same age. Later on in our friendship, he would often mock me for being the younger out of the two of us, even if only by a few months. The grin on his face would make me so annoyed, which just made him grin wider.

Shortly after that two-second "Hi," that afternoon, we became instant friends. He was old-fashioned, smart, kind, and incredibly caring. But what made me gravitate towards him wasn't just the fact that he seemingly couldn't care less about my waddle walk, or having to be manhandled into my parents' car of an afternoon, or that I drove a scooter around like a mad woman. It was his old school charm and his wicked sense of humour.

He would walk me to my locker every morning as we got dropped off at almost the same time, walk me to lunch (before eventually I realised my group of friends were not really my friends and were horrible to him, and so, we would sit and have lunch together), walk me to class if it was on his way, and would walk me to my car when the school day ended.

He didn't do this because he was worried I couldn't handle getting to those locations without an accident, or that I was a fragile, disabled girl who needed to be taken care of. He did it just because he wanted to.

In Year 12, when I had a fall-out with a group of girls, I would often try to hide to have lunch. However, Tristan knew me too well and would always find me. Depending on the mood, he would either just sit with me and eat lunch without barely uttering a word, or if he thought I really needed a ribbing, he would say, "I told you they would do that to you. When are you going to learn, Smurfy?"

We were both, and still are, somewhat protective over each other. He wanted to have words with the guy who broke my heart, and I wanted to have words with the girl who broke his. We always had each other's backs, and not to mention, we would constantly be throwing quick-witted jabs at each other like an old married couple.

It was almost as if it was an unspoken rule that no one could give the other a hard time unless it was one of us. We would mock each other, and he would try and constantly scare the living daylights out of me. Not to mention, the nicknames that came about from mocking each other: him calling me "Smurfy" after a nasty sunburn on the back of my legs turned blue from the amount of aloe vera gel I put on them and in reference to my height, and me calling him BFG (Big Friendly Giant) because he towered over me—he was that tall.

He never once made me feel uncomfortable about my disability, nor did he ever make me feel like I needed to hide my struggles from him. He was always there when I needed to cry or vent, and wouldn't leave me until he knew I was okay.

When he asked me if I needed help, he was quiet about it, and there were times when he would simply pick up my bags and swing them over his shoulder. He would then call out, "Come on, Smurfy! Hurry up, stop being so slow," as I stood there, stunned, not only because he scared me, but also because he was picking up my bags along the way.

It is safe to say he is my gold standard for any other friendship. Someone who doesn't judge and doesn't make you feel like an inconvenience for taking longer to get somewhere or for being different. Someone who treats you just like everyone else and will mock you for dropping your ruler on the floor, keeping your ego in check, and making sure you aren't left out of the Valentine's Day chocolate giving organised by the school council committee.

Tristan showed me the kind of people I want in my life, and how I deserve to be treated. He never once judged me or asked me what was wrong with me. He never made me feel like I was different or wounded—that I needed pity. He didn't just see my scooter or my disability; he saw me for my personality. And that means more than he will ever know. Until now, when he reads this.

Now, that is also often said to be an ableist statement—someone "seeing past your disability" or pretends not even see it. To me, it isn't ableist; instead, it simply means the person sees us as human beings and treats us as such. And that is what Tristan did the entire time, and still does to this day, when we are able to find time to catch up, as we both lead busy lives and no longer live around the corner from each other. Ah, the joys of adulthood.

Regardless, he is the same as he was in high school. He still sees me as a human being, will still mock me for running into a table with my scooter, and will argue with me when it comes time to pay for our coffee. It is safe to say I am grateful to have him, and his wallet, in my life. I had to get at least one jab in there; it would be uncharacteristic of me to be all soppy!

I thought I would struggle to find more people like him, given my awkwardness and difficulty making friends. However, I couldn't have been more wrong. People turn up in the most random places, and you connect over the strangest things.

My friend from Uni, Steph, and I met over a forum chat for a Health Law class we were taking. We had to introduce ourselves, and for some reason, I ended up mentioning my scoliosis surgery. She replied, saying that she, too, had the same surgery.

We quickly discovered the coincidence that not only did we have the same surgery, we had it done by the same surgeon in the same hospital, the same year, and her surgery date was the second date that I was given before settling on April. We were also only a couple of years apart in age, with her being the oldest out of the two of us. It's safe to say we quickly found common ground and immediately organised a coffee catch-up before class.

You know that feeling when you have found your tribe? Conversations are effortless, and you just understand each other. We were both quirky, loud, adventurous, and, I reckon, see the little joys in life. I think we both knew we were going to be besties for life. She never pushed me to explain my disability, and when I told her, she would always want to know more, and would always apologise after asking a question, as if she was worried she had offended me. She is another person who just gets it. She doesn't make me feel uncomfortable or like a burden when we have to juggle chairs and move tables at a coffee shop so my scooter can fit. She will just help me and laugh with me along the way.

These two friends of mine, while not disabled, are still my people. They do something that not many others do. They don't take pity on me, they don't feel sorry, or feel the need to pitch their tone of voice up and speak to me like I am a 3-year-old. They ask me if I need help in the same way they would ask anyone else if they needed help: "Do you want me to grab that?" or "Are you okay?" Most importantly, they see me, which, in a world where you can easily tend to feel invisible, truly means everything.

Given my past history of reluctance to "embrace" my disabled community or be a part of it, as it were, it would be reasonable to assume that all the people in my life are without disability. That couldn't be further from the truth. As time has gone on, and I have become older, and indeed wiser, and worked on my own internalised ableism, there are indeed people in my life who round out my little circle, who all happen to be disabled.

There was a time years ago when I had a guy reach out to me via social media after watching my podcast episode on ListenABLE with Dylan and Angus. He happened to have Duchenne, as did his younger brother and two cousins.

Both his brother and cousins had passed away a few years prior to him reaching out to me. This person just happens to be the same guy who wrote the foreword at the start of this book: Chris Gillin. What I thought was just a simple "thank you" message turned into a blossoming friendship, and one that is also very dear to me.

We have never met in person; our relationship is the true definition of being pen pals. What is perhaps the most important thing about our friendship is the fact that we do genuinely just "get" each other. When one of us messages, saying we're having a bad day, the other person just "gets it."

Even though our types of muscular dystrophy are completely different in terms of how they progress, the speed at which they happen, and what muscles are involved, the fear, anxiety, pain, sadness, and frustration are all the same. We lean on each other in the hard times, and also celebrate each other's achievements like we just won the lotto.

You don't have to meet someone in person to be able to have a connection with them. It's already good enough that you can laugh, cry, and support each other without needing to feel like you have to always show up happy and bubbly.

The same goes for my friend, Amy, over in the US. She is a bit older than me, has the same condition, is married, and has two children who, at the time of writing this, are in college and are incredible athletes.

When I first saw her on social media, I was overwhelmed to see not only someone with MD, but someone with the same type as me, still walking, married, and with a family of her own—everything that I thought wasn't possible for people like me. She gave me hope that not only is having friends possible, but also finding that special someone who accepts you for who you are, is willing to be by your side, and help you every step of the way.

That may sound like the traditional, cliché definition of marriage; however, when one party has a disability, and a terminal one at that, it adds a level of extra baggage that the other person has no choice but to accept and be prepared to deal with everything that comes with it, on top of the regular marital issues that life brings. The saying "in sickness and in health" gets put to the test from the very first date.

Seeing interabled couples and even disabled couples isn't a common occurrence. Well, for me in my town anyway, so I always just thought it wouldn't be possible. That was until I saw Amy and her husband, Jamie, on social media. We have been friends for a good four or so years now, and it's another one of those friendships that mean the world to me.

Each person in my life has given me and taught me so many different things, but with Amy, the thing she has taught me is to always have hope and never assume life is set in one way. Given the fact that she is older than I and has experienced a lot of what disabled life looks like as a wife and older woman (I mean that in the best way, Amy!), I can often turn to her for guidance and advice. We often go back and forth in conversations, comparing experiences, traumas, and how MD has shown up in our lives.

I have met other people with disabilities and various types of MD, but Amy is the first person I have met with the same mutation and type of MD that I have. I can tell you for a fact, I am so glad I met her. She has kept my nerves at bay whenever I feel uneasy about how things in my day-to-day life are becoming slightly more challenging, and she has also provided an ear to listen to and bounce ideas off when I need to.

It's safe to say that we also cheer each other on and inspire each other to keep pushing the limits of what our bodies are capable of, and indeed, how far we will be willing to go to live the life we both desperately want, even if it means having to compromise and cooperate at times with our MD.

Having a terminal disability means that sooner or later, we will depart this life for whatever comes next. I had been so fortunate in my life to have been spared from going to the funerals of friends with a disability. I have seen people in the disability community pass away from their conditions, either via the news or through social media, more so these days. I had, in a way, landed in the realm of complacency, thinking that I would never have to experience something so difficult and confronting as that. Until I did two years ago.

If you remember a little way back in this chapter, I mentioned the group of guys that I spent some of my childhood with, who were a few years older than me, and had Duchenne Muscular Dystrophy. Even though we may not have seen each other in person, we all eventually reconnected via the power of social media, and would chitchat every now and again. It was always so interesting to see what we were all up to and how we all lived our lives.

One in particular, Mitch, was the loudest and most outgoing of the group. Almost every weekend, he would round up his mates and his carers and go to his favourite pub in town, The Irish.

He was a free spirit who loved Metallica and Jameson with as much passion as the wildest footy fan. If there was anything that Mitch taught me, it was that life should always be a party, and to never let your disability get in the way of a good time, and indeed, a good life.

He and I would chat, probably more so than I did the other guys, and one night he asked me if I was going to head out on the town. I was at the Uni Law Ball on the other side of town. When I received his message, I immediately thought about going. I was about to respond to him by saying, "Absolutely, I am at a law ball at the moment. But if you don't mind me being in an evening gown, and being way too overdressed, let me know where you are, and I will meet you there." However, my fears of being a burden still lingered like embers in a fire pit.

My parents attended the law ball with me, and I immediately became anxious and worried that I would be putting them out by asking them if they could drop me off at The Irish for a bit. Of course, when I told my parents about my concerns months later, they immediately said they would have dropped me at the pub in a heartbeat.

I also became self-conscious, thinking that I would stick out like a sore thumb if I showed up to a pub in a sparkly evening gown, like I didn't already stick out by waddling or being in my mobility scooter. I let my insecurities talk me out of going. I deleted my planned enthusiastic reply—the reply that I, deep down, wanted to send—and instead, replied with, "Hey hey, potentially, but not super sure just yet."

I ended up going home, eating Midnight Maccas and drinking a Long Island Iced Tea with my brother, as he was home from Gold Coast for a bit. We still chatted on and off, after that night, and would still mention plans to catch up. But six months later, in June 2023, a week after the passing of my Great Grandmother, I saw the post from his mum that he had passed away peacefully and unexpectedly. He was only thirty-two. Don't let the age fool you; the man lived a wild and full life, probably more than the average 32-year-old, for sure!

His funeral was the first time I had to confront the reality that is also my life. Arriving at the funeral home, for the second funeral I attended in a fortnight, I was numb. It didn't feel right to be sad or cry, simply because, in all honesty, we weren't best buds, more just passing acquaintances who would chat on the odd occasion. Having said that, he had a major impact on how I viewed life, and there is almost like an unspoken bond that comes with having MD, even though they are different types. It almost is like another "get it" moment. Besides, attending a funeral is never a joyful experience.

This funeral, however, was different for so many reasons. First, like I said before, it was the first funeral of someone with muscular dystrophy that I had attended, so it was very much like getting a glimpse into my future. That thought alone made it overwhelming. However, I tried to bury that thought and focus on the fact that I was there to say "see you soon" to an old friend.

The funeral home had several buildings on the premises, an indoor chapel and an outdoor chapel, and a building where mainly wakes are held. I have attended large funerals before, the largest being my grandfather's when the entire church was at capacity and people had to gather outside. I knew that Mitch was incredibly loved and had such an impact on the people around him; I knew it was going to be a big funeral. What I didn't expect, however, was that every building on the premises ended up being full to capacity, and people still gathered outside.

The reason I am telling you all this is that there was a designated space in the main chapel for people in wheelchairs, his friends, who also all had Duchenne MD. My family and I arrived a little late, and the chapel was at capacity, save for a few leftover spaces in the wheelchair row. I wasn't aware of this when I was ushered into the chapel on my scooter until I looked back and didn't see my family following me. I had to sit there by myself. Of course, I wasn't alone. I was next to the guys that I had spent a lot of time with when we were all children; however, that, in a way, made the process a little more emotionally complicated.

The funeral itself was, if I can say, the most "fun" funeral I have ever attended. There was a bottle of Jameson with a couple of shot glasses in lieu of flowers on the casket, with footy scarves included. The speeches, while still emotional, had all of us laughing. Metallica was the band of choice for the songs, which just made it feel like a party and a true celebration of life. You would expect a light-hearted funeral for someone who was close to knocking 100 years old, not a 32-year-old guy. But the truth is, it was the perfect reflection of who he was, and I personally will never forget leaving the service to "Enter Sandman."

As "fun" as the funeral was. It was an emotional juggle for me mentally. Here I was at a funeral of a friend with MD, and right next to me were a bunch of guys who all have the same condition, and who will all eventually succumb to the beast that is MD. It took me a minute to try and process that thought, as I looked down the line. We all ranged in age from 24 to probably early 30s. My heart ached for the guys because, even though I know I, too, will succumb to the beast eventually, for those guys, I felt that time is very much not on their side any more. So, I was worried about how they were mentally coping through the funeral, given that they were also all incredibly close with Mitch.

My thoughts then turned to my parents. They were watching other parents grieve the loss of their child, who had a similar condition to their own daughter. I worried if they struggled, knowing that it would become their reality one day, if nothing else happened before then. My parents and my brother are the three people in my life I worry the most about. I worry if they are okay with how life is going, if they will be okay when that day arrives, and how they will handle it when things get tougher and the concept of death becomes not an "if" but a "when." So, having my parents attend that funeral made me emotional, thinking about my own funeral.

I could see them so clearly, sitting at the front of the chapel, consoling each other, my brother trying to be stoic for them but barely keeping it together. The image was like a flash, and in one blink, I was transported back to the moment in time, listening to Mitch's brother and father speak. I immediately felt selfish for thinking of my own funeral, and tried my best to focus on sending Mitch out with a bang with everyone else.

Being friends with people with your own condition is a blessing, and at times can also be a curse. You are all living a similar timeline, death being something we all have to reconcile with and accept, but not letting it consume us so that we stop living altogether. It's that unspoken bond, that even though we may go without speaking for months and years at a time, when one is down and out and struggling, or indeed no longer in this life, we will always be there. Because we "get it." Because that is us—will be us. You have a connection that simply doesn't exist with other people, and while that may be a blessing, if you aren't in the right headspace, it can become awfully triggering when the time does come, and you have to sit there, deal with the regrets, and say "See you soon."

Everyone in your life is here for a reason; they are either here for the long road or here to teach you something that you need in order to go on. Friends become chosen family, and if you choose wisely, they become the framework that holds you up when you feel like life is falling around you.

The ones that hang in there for the long haul are the people who show you that you do matter, that there are people in the world who do care about you and love you, the ones who make life enjoyable. The ones who hang around for a moment are the ones that show you where you can improve in your communication, how to be a better friend, or they help you to realise that you deserve better. The ones who pass on teach you how valuable life really is, to never waste a single second, and how to really live for every moment, and when it is time to cross that bridge, to never have any regrets and truly celebrate life and all the magic and lessons it holds.

CHAPTER 7

THE WEIGHT OF WORDS: FINDING MY VOICE

Aside from my rapid problem-solving skills, especially that of how to get a mobility aid through a thick patch of sand, advocating for myself has become one of the most critical skills I've learnt. No, I am not talking about making it clear you take one sugar in your tea as opposed to the entire kilo bag, or asking someone to carry you over a puddle so you don't get your suede shoes ruined. I am talking about the more invasive kind of advocacy; explaining to people, particularly strangers, what is wrong with you or how you would prefer to be helped out of a chair or indeed back on your feet should the floor want to say hi to your face.

You also will inevitably have to explain why you want to walk that 5-kilometre fundraiser, train for an Ironman, learn a new skill, take singing lessons, or ride a horse. Not to mention, if you are on the National Disability Insurance Scheme (NDIS) here in Australia, that is an entirely different ballgame.

Advocating for yourself is like a never ending game of Monopoly, except that you never pass GO, and the banker seemingly loses your paperwork and withholds any chance of you ever owning Piccadilly Lane, because you're apparently not in a bad enough position just yet.

In the real world, advocacy is a different game we play. It's less about advocating why you want the boot token and more about explaining why you actually need help. But if you are like me, you will constantly be advocating as to why you need to see a psychologist, or why you need an in-home support worker to help you wash your sheets, because they don't believe your disability meets the criteria. For some, they even have to explain to the National Disability Insurance Agency (NDIA) why they need to be on the NDIS, because some people in a boardroom decided that their disability does not meet the checklist they have for what a "disability" is.

If you haven't already noticed, advocating also comes with a rather healthy dose of ranting, with a side of anger and exhaustion thrown in to keep things interesting. You know, as if things weren't interesting enough as it is.

Unfortunately, until the world can accept that disability comes in all forms, and everyone discovers the epiphany that everyone is, in fact, different, and that we all need help, advocacy remains as a necessary evil. So, finding your voice and standing up for yourself is crucial.

And there does come a breaking point for everyone. After being bullied relentlessly for years, and sometimes, feeling like I wasn't being listened to in doctors' offices when I tell them about how my ability was changing — for the better, mind you — only to have them look at me like I'd grown three heads and dismiss me, I started to lose the strength and confidence to speak up for myself. When you stop advocating for yourself, that is when you can end up in more uncomfortable situations than if you'd spoken up in the first place.

Given the slight fact that I was born with MD, and that my diagnosis happened when I was still a toddler, my parents were the ones who had to do the advocating on my behalf. They only knew of one person who was in a wheelchair, who was close friends with my Godmother. Instead of bombarding him with questions about his disability and "what was wrong with him" at school, they simply just accepted him for who he was and accepted him like you would anyone else. Now, that's not necessarily a bad thing, but I guess the disadvantage is that they didn't really know what the right questions were to ask when it came to talking with doctors and specialists about my condition.

I often wonder if my life would have been different if we had said no to me driving around a mobility scooter at the age of five. Would my life have been different if they listened when I said the stretches didn't feel like they were working, instead of saying, "Maybe you are just doing them wrong"? Would my life have been different if we had sought a second opinion on the impacts of exercise on my condition?

Finding my voice took me up until the later stages of high school. Don't get me wrong, I was able to explain to people how to help me off the floor, and I could ask for help to open a heavy door or pick up the pencil case I dropped. For some unknown reason, that came to me easily, even if I did apologise to no end. But when it came to my physical ability to participate in hobbies or sports, that is when my voice would quiet to a whisper.

Sure, I was given the opportunity, thankfully, to participate in sports in primary school, and when the students would inch forward before I hit the ball in a game of softball, it wasn't me who told everyone to back off. It was my teachers.

Looking back now, perhaps, I didn't advocate for myself because I had the best people advocating for me, and as a result, I never really had to learn how to speak up. Did they always get it right? Of course not, but they were doing what they thought was best at the time, and there is absolutely nothing wrong with that.

In a way, I also relied on everyone else to speak up for me because my confidence in my ability to speak was shattered. I found that whenever I spoke up about more important things, I was either dismissed or it led to me being severely bullied. So, I somewhat learnt that if I had a voice, I would be treated like rubbish; I left it up to the people, the adults in the room, to handle the tricky conversations.

It wasn't until around Grade 9 that I stood firm and used my voice.

It was cross-country day, and Montrose happened to visit on the exact same day. During our meeting, I mentioned how excited and eager I was about participating in cross-country, and I expressed my enthusiasm.

Concern was etched onto my physiologist and OT's faces at the statement. They immediately asked me, "Are you sure you want to do this? Remember, if you have a fall, and you break a bone, that will be it, you won't walk again."

Their concern should have been sweet and made me feel like they genuinely cared about me. But instead, it did the opposite. I was so annoyed that they couldn't see my capability and were putting me in the category alongside those with severe MD. I had to bite my tongue hard not to say something I would regret, and ultimately get myself suspended.

After a calming breath, I said, "I understand that you are concerned, but I know my own body, and it's feeling really good today, so I think I will be fine." They weren't convinced. And if anything, my response seemed to annoy them just as much as their comment did to me.

In order to be "allowed" to do it, I had to compromise: I would only do one lap, I wouldn't do it by myself, and if I didn't feel good, I would stop. I agreed to it all, and yet, I could still sense their unease. I felt rather annoyed because I thought for my entire life they were on my side, and I felt as though all along they didn't believe in me or the fact that I could accomplish something so simple to others, but like a marathon for me. Perhaps they were concerned about my naivety about the entire situation.

Nevertheless, I left that meeting feeling empowered. For the first time, I told an adult—and indeed myself—that I believed in my ability. That, despite their concerns, I was going to do something that seemed risky to them but was necessary for me. It was necessary for me because I loved a challenge, and I guess it was also a part of my denial or refusal to accept that I was getting weaker. I had something to prove to myself—I wanted to prove that I was still strong and capable in my own way.

My body so often was, and still is, a barrier, and I couldn't handle having people be a barrier too. If everything went wrong, I would rather say, "You were right," but have absolutely no regrets about doing something risky or physically difficult.

When you have a disability that will kill you, if nothing else does first, your perspective on life flips. It starts being a matter of doing everything you can while you can, and having no regrets. Even if you do fall flat on your face in front of a bunch of guys who were laughing at you mid-way through the cross-country course. Not once, but twice.

I can assure you I was also laughing, but more so at the fact of how the fall must have looked, and how pathetic it was to still see teenagers laughing at someone having a go.

Given my newly discovered rebellious streak, I slightly ignored the one-lap suggestion and powered through the entire three-lap course, with my cousin and friends helping me along the way and even piggybacking me the last few metres. I had succeeded in my quest to complete the cross-country. I may have finished, but let's just say I was fashionably late... by a couple of hours. The shades and decorations were being pulled down, and everyone had already left the oval and were eager to enjoy their weekend.

To most people, that would have destroyed them, seeing that their school didn't seem interested or invested in cheering them on. For me, however, I didn't care one bit about what was happening around me. My only goal was to complete that cross-country in my own way, in my own time, and with a great bunch of people, and prove to those who told me not to that I am more capable than what they think I am.

This was the second time in my life that I started to realise I was more capable than I thought I was. The first time after my spinal surgery, I was pushing my body out of desperation to stay out of a wheelchair. This time around, it was because I no longer wanted to listen to or believe people when they said I couldn't or shouldn't do something.

This was the moment where my determination and obsession with pushing my body and ignoring what people told me I could or couldn't do, revealed itself in full force.

Now, by no means am I saying to rebel and ignore every scrap of advice or concern ever shown or given to you, because usually, the advice and concern are coming from people who have lived longer or are more qualified than you. And there are things in life that even the great Houdini would have passed on. What I am saying, though, is that when it comes to your body, you know it better than anyone, and what you think it is truly capable of.

That day in Grade 9 when I was told doing the cross-country wasn't the best idea and that I shouldn't do it; had I stayed quiet, simply nodded my head, and did what the adults in the room were telling me, I would have missed out on one of the most incredible opportunities to break free from my own mind and prove to myself that I am more than just a girl with weak muscles. I was a girl who had it in her to defy the odds, push what was possible, and in doing so, go on to create even more incredible memories and opportunities.

It took some time, however, before I really thought about pushing my body again.

There is always a bit of downtime between the initial light bulb moment and actually executing it. I knew that my body was capable of more than I gave it credit for, and more importantly, responded positively to it in the strength department, but I just wasn't mentally up to the task.

Given the Friend 2.0 drama that continued, and with it shaving away at my self-worth bit by bit, I simply didn't feel like I was worth having another shot at a physical challenge or pushing myself. In a way, I was truly in survival mode and was using all the energy I had to just get through my classes and the drama without losing more of myself, or my sanity, in the process.

When I finally rounded the corner in Year 12 and started to find myself again, around the time I truly fell in love with Legal studies, I was in a better headspace to use my energy for more than just academics.

So, when cross-country rolled around again, and when I realised that it was the last time in my life I would get to participate in cross country, I knew I had to give it one last shot. This time, though, it was different. This time, it wasn't to prove to others that I could do something; it was to prove to myself that I was strong, capable, resilient, and worthy of moving forward and living life in the way I wanted.

I told my friends at the time that I wanted to do cross-country, and without blinking, they said to me, "Absolutely, let's do it." Unlike the first time when it was serious and my brain was in overdrive, repeating,

"Don't fall, don't fall. Just finish this thing,"—this time it was simply about enjoying being able to walk, feel the burn of lactic acid in my legs, and soak up all that Year 12 had to offer.

I had nothing to prove to anyone. I was completely free to enjoy the moment.

The entire 2-kilometre walk, my friends and I were singing along to music, laughing as we fumbled with the couple of stairs that were conveniently placed after an uphill section, which really made you second-guess your life choices.

We talked about what we were hoping adult life would be like, our hopes and aspirations, and what our parents all thought about our respective career choices. We were just a group of friends enjoying a long walk together, and yes, at times, they had to almost drag me or carry me when my legs started to turn to jelly. But no one complained about how slow I was or how much they had to help me upstairs, downhill, or while navigating tree roots.

I completely forgot that I was doing cross-country, and the feeling of just walking with my friends, my scooter left at the starting line, was something I had yet to truly experience in high school. I was simply soaking up the opportunity to do this, and the fact that my body was cooperating with me despite my muscles shouting, "What the actual fuck, Rhiannon? We hate you!" as we rounded the corner to start our second lap.

I was in a completely different space as we navigated our second lap. My body was starting to hurt more, my legs were becoming shaky, and my friends had to help me more and more. If we all noticed the mood becoming more serious, we just cranked up the music louder. Soon enough, we were all winding ourselves singing at the top of our lungs and receiving some strange looks in the process. We couldn't care, we were all just desperate to get to that finish line. Maybe, it was the fact that snow cones were waiting at the end that spurred us on.

What I saw as we turned the corner for our last 500 metres is something I will never forget. Having said that, it took me a minute to process what was happening; I was too busy giggling with my friends, trying to distract myself from the fact that my legs had pretty much run out of energy.

I looked up and saw everyone who had completed the event all walking around, instead of enjoying snow cones in the shade. My entire group were all wondering what on earth was going on. I thought everyone was packing up and leaving like last time, but what confused me was that there was still another twenty minutes or so before the bell sounded to mark the end of the day.

As we approached the 200-metre mark, that is when I realised what was going on, and it almost made me stop dead. The entire school had lined up on either side of the last 100 metres and formed a guard of honour.

I was absolutely stunned that the entire school, and most of whom I had never spoken a word to, had gone out of their way to do this. They could have easily just sat and enjoyed their snow cones not batting an eyelid. But instead, they decided to support me and help me through that last 100 metres.

As I made my way to the finish line, they started to cheer me on and clap so loudly I could barely hear myself think. They gave me the last jolt of energy to get through that last bit of the race, faceplant-free.

I was no stranger to love and support, but it usually always came from my family, and my head would always convince me they *had* to support me because they were my family, which is so not true; they supported me because they genuinely cared about me. But when I had an entire school stand and cheer me on and genuinely be excited for me, I felt like the entire school had wrapped their arms around me as if to say, "We see you, and we've got you."

So many people underestimate the power that their words actually have. Words can easily hype you up or rip you to shreds internally. I often think that the old saying, "Sticks and stones may break my bones, but words will never hurt me." is a load of bullshit. You can repeat it like a mantra, but in all honesty, it doesn't do much, especially if you have low self-esteem.

When you have been told you are a problem or a burden enough times, you begin to truly believe it. When it gets to that point, just the thought of asking for help in any capacity sends you shaking, and your voice becomes a quiet hum, like the wings of a butterfly in your ear.

My entire life, I have never truly been 100 percent independent. If I am to be completely honest, I will never be completely independent; however, I can get pretty close. That simply comes with redefining the definition of independence. A large part of that new definition is created through first being able to advocate for what I need.

Perhaps one of the most important things I have learnt as I have become older is the fact that using my voice and asking for help, and also using it to stand my ground, is an act of love and compassion towards myself. Over time, and after plenty of therapy, conversations, and self-development work, I have realised that my life becomes easier when I ask for help.

In turn, it has helped me create a better relationship with myself. That simply means I don't deprive my body or myself of what it needs in order to thrive and function with dignity and as little stress as possible. In my humble opinion, this should be the gold standard for every person, disabled or not.

In the past, I would have struggled for a good fifteen to twenty minutes trying to pull up my pants, stand up off the toilet, or even tie up my shoelaces. Now, I give it a couple of tries, and if my body isn't cooperating because it is a weak day for me, I will simply crow out for Mum to come and give me a hand. Or I will send her a funny GIF, because we like to keep things lighthearted and fun. Let's be honest, no one wants to engage in World War III with their jeans button or trying to pull up their pants on a cold winter morning, risking frostbite for the sake of vanity. I have too much to get done in my day, why would I use energy over a button or getting off the loo, when I could be using it for other tasks like cooking my family dinner, working, or judging my dog chasing her tail?

I have recognised that by keeping silent, I was keeping myself trapped and not allowing myself to live independently in my own way. For example, I used to feel uncomfortable going to the hairdresser by myself. I would need help getting out of the chair, to the basin, and sitting up to go back to the chair after having my hair washed. Instead of stressing about asking for help, my mum would go with me, and it became like a mother-daughter day.

However, I was desperate to try going by myself. Going to appointments or even simply going out completely by myself is a novelty, and so I desperately wanted to experience doing at least some mundane things on my own. So after trial and error, I finally found an accessible hair salon, and Mum decided to book a haircut at the exact same time as me, so she could be there if I needed any help.

Like usual, my brain conjured up many worst case scenarios, from being laughed at, kicked out, judged, or falling over as soon as I walked in the door, ultimately ruining not only my sanity but my nose in the process. After the standard consultation was over, she directed me over to one of the styling chairs. I was sitting at the consultation table, and the chair was too low, so I knew I had to ask for help to stand. I took a nervous breath and asked her if she wouldn't mind helping me. I went to explain why, and she simply said, "Oh, it's not a problem! I help people all the time. Tell me how I can best help you."

Throughout the rest of the appointment, she checked in to make sure I was okay, asked if I needed help pouring my tea, and even went as far as to let the apprentice who was washing my hair know what I needed help with, so I didn't have to worry about anything. My worst case imaginary scenarios floated off into the mental paper shredder in an instant.

For the first time in my life, I could attend a hair appointment where I felt empowered to speak up and say what I needed help with, and people just got it. Even better yet, they understood to the point of making sure everyone working on me was aware, so I didn't need to explain myself. It was as close to an "abled" life as I could get.

There are other times when using your voice isn't just for advocating for what you need help with; it is also for speaking up when you desperately want to do something, such as having a solo holiday. Given the amount I need help with on any given day, I have really never been able to fully be alone 24/7. I am always dropping something, unable to reach something, or, yes, tripping over the dogs, which means someone needs to come home and rescue me.

However, the best part about finding my voice is becoming more confident in what I want to do and just doing it.

There was a time when I was desperate to have a holiday. However, given the fact that I can't drive, I needed to make a compromise. I booked a room in town, literally ten minutes away from my house, gave my parents the spare key, and then said exactly what needed to be changed in my room to make it as accessible as possible. I got straight to work, bossing my family around, going, "Can you move the microwave down onto the kitchen side?", "Can you stack the outside chairs so I can stand up if I want to sit out there?", and "Can you open the alcohol?"

Because I was able to speak up for what I needed, which was to get away and have some time to myself to reset, it meant I was able to truly experience living on my own and having my own holiday. Something that I thought I would truly never be able to experience.

For so long, I felt like a prisoner in my own body, and in my own home, as I didn't feel like asking for help all the time was a positive thing.

I simply reached a point in my life where feeling like a burden was getting me nowhere, which ended up in a revelation; I realised the level of freedom that comes from being able to say, "I need help with..." or "Can you please help me..."

I used to think that was shameful and that I was wasting people's time. However, you learn very quickly that the right people in your life won't bat an eye when you ask for help. Simply because everyone at some point in their day, or their life, will have to ask for help. No one is perfect at absolutely everything. We also grow old at some point, which means we then have no choice but to ask for a little extra helping hand.

Finding my voice has given me the freedom to live my life in the way I want. Make peace with the fact that everyone needs help, and there is nothing wrong with asking for that little extra help to enable you to get on with your day.

At the end of the day, regardless of the situation, we deserve to be able to advocate for what we need in life, without judgment. Equally, we deserve to receive help with dignity and respect.

I have learnt over time that my life instantly becomes harder when I lock the doors and shut off my voice. I become a closed-off shell, and ultimately do not give myself what I need—the ability to just live!

Everyone's life is different, and the mind is a fucking masterpiece; it all starts with using your vocal cords and feeling like you are worth having a life as stress-free as possible in between the chaos of disability life. Or even just life itself.

CHAPTER 8

WEATHERING TOGETHER: FAMILY IN THE STORM

Everyone in life needs a strong support system, regardless of whether they are disabled or not. Either way, we all go through some pretty shitty times. And when that happens, we need people around us.

Whenever we go through something life-altering, it's often not just ourselves that are directly impacted by it—it also takes a toll on those who provide us emotional support. They go to appointments with you, are with you when you receive your diagnosis, stay with you through surgery and rehab, and navigate the new version of life that is unavoidable. They are often there for every moment, unable to do anything to solve it other than just simply being there and providing emotional, and even sometimes, physical support when we can't do it for ourselves.

I have needed a support network my entire life, from family and friends to medical teams. Without them, I would be navigating this unknown world on my own. I don't know about you, but sometimes, it helps to navigate all that life throws at you — and the uncertainty that comes with it — with others rather than alone.

I am luckier than most. My family didn't for a second hesitate the day my diagnosis came; they didn't say it was too hard or too scary for them. They didn't tap out. My parents rallied together to ensure that I had a joyful childhood, despite the doctor visits. And when difficult times came, they were always there to support me in whatever way I needed. Whether that be an ear to listen, a shoulder to cry on, help me off the ground after I faceplant, take me to appointments, or yes, even wiping my butt; my family has been the one anchor in the entire journey. They ride the highs and the lows alongside me. Even when they had to see their daughter or sister go through all sorts of tests and they themselves had to hear some crappy news, they still did their best to uplift me when I was down.

To this day, I have no idea how they managed to handle the emotional weight of all of that, and yet, not let it define them or bog them down in any way. It takes a superhuman to be able to handle all of that, with all the required decorum and class that society often demands.

From as early as I can remember, I have never really been able to do things completely on my own. Sure, as a young child, you legally can't drive, so you are chauffeured around, which is exactly what happened in my childhood. But the little things, like getting ready for the day, were different.

Most people are usually able to dress themselves at a very early age. For me, even as an 8-year-old, I still needed help putting my shoes and socks on, tying my hair up away from my face, and getting out of wet togs after swimming. I also needed to be manhandled upstairs and off the floor, whereas every other 8-year-old was climbing stairs two by two at that point and were starting to master cartwheels.

As time has progressed, for the most part, the things that I have needed help with have remained the same, but in many ways, what I need help with is the same as almost every 26-year-old: opening the impossible jars and cans that feel like they are superglued from the supermarket, needing extra hands zipping up a dress and jeans, and an arm to hold getting to the car in heels and trying to make it look like you aren't one step away from falling flat on your face and rolling an ankle at the same time.

I do still need to get chauffeured around, especially if I want dinner from the best takeaway Toowoomba has to offer, Super Rooster (Toowoomba folks, you know what I am talking about), and to all my appointments. I also now need help navigating paddocks and really any sort of grass area, and grabbing the multitude of things that I drop daily.

To be honest, I would add needing help changing my sheets to the list, but I chalk that up to practicality more than disability. Instead of spending until next week engaged in battle with them, I choose to make my life easier and ask for help with the fitted sheet and doona. Okay, yes, my disability is a factor as to why I can't put fresh sheets on my bed, but really, don't we all age a decade each sheet wash day, regardless of disabled status?

The dedication my support network shows is mighty impressive, and often, what makes things a little less awkward in situations is a lot of laughter and a touch of crass humour. For example, if I go to a bathroom that isn't my own with my toilet frame, not only will I need a hand standing up, but I also need a hand with a few extra bits and pieces, if you catch my drift. Needing a hand with anything super personal is often awkward, so it is absolutely vital that the awkwardness is dispelled very quickly.

I am fortunate enough that my incredible mum is my primary caregiver, so given the fact that she changed all my nappies as a baby, it's not as awkward asking for extra help with the toileting side of life. Even though it has become second nature and normal for us at this point.

I, like so many other people, have days when things are just more mentally heavy, and the guilt of having my mum help me with something you usually do by yourself before you reach kindergarten still weighs on my mind. I often like to think her motherly intuition is off the charts, and she can immediately pick up on when I am struggling mentally on any given day.

I remember there was such a time when we had guests over for dinner. Whenever we do, I like to move my toilet frame out of the second bathroom and just use my parents' ensuite. On this particular night, like any human, I had to go to the bathroom, so I told my mum and asked her to give me about five minutes before she came to help me. When those five minutes were up, I saw the door slightly open, and an arm poke through the crack in the door with a bottle of either air freshener or perfume in hand. Like a robot, the hand snapped up sharply, directed the spray bottle in my direction, sprayed once before snapping back vertically, and the arm made a slow exit out of the crack in the door. Both my mum and I were in tears, given how hilarious the whole situation was, and the comedic genius she just displayed.

We also have other ways to find those situations less uncomfortable; instead of shouting bloody murder when I am ready for help, I will instead send my mum a GIF of either Forrest Gump waving in his boat with the captions, "hi", a cute puppy jumping to a sit, or a scraggly cat looking seriously hungover with a bold "help" underneath. My mum will return serve with a funny GIF, from *The Road Runner* to someone putting on a gas mask.

It's always fun seeing what we both come up with in the GIF department. There truly is never a dull moment.

It's times like these, when you are the most vulnerable, when you need to have people around you who don't even blink when you need help, who never make you feel uncomfortable for asking in the first place. Not to mention how crucial it is to find people who never make you feel like a burden.

So many of us with disabilities and illnesses often say the same thing: feeling like a burden can strike us at any moment. Even when we are feeling on top of the world, it's like something internally shifts, and we feel guilty for even asking if they can open a jar of mayo for us.

It's so easy to get consumed mentally and, as a result, almost feel like you are the only one in the world who ever needs any help. You don't see your sibling needing help moving furniture or figuring out what is wrong with their car. You don't see your dad needing help to move the firewood before it starts to rain. You don't see your mum needing help to bring down the Christmas decoration boxes. At some point in their lives, everyone will need help with something. So why is it that we can't see that, but our families and caregivers can?

I have been so blessed my entire life to have such a close relationship with my family. My mum, perhaps, more so. We have cried and laughed together more times than I can count. There have also been countless times when I have cried in frustration and heartbreak, with the feeling that I have held her and the rest of my family back, and that I am a burden.

Each time I have said that, she has practically grabbed me and said firmly, "You are not a burden, we all love you so much. It is an honour to be your mum, and to be able to still help you." There was a particular day when, right after she said this, with tears streaking down her face, the lightbulb went off in my head.

Most parents, while they never stop caring and worrying about their kids, and indeed helping them, my parents have had to help me with something every single day. In order to live my life to the best of my ability, I am dependent upon them and my brother to help me. I would say I am independent 90 percent of the time, especially when I am at home. That number rapidly goes down to about 60 percent when we are away.

So many people in the world are what I call independent. They can do practically whatever they want, whenever they want: go on trips alone, get in the car and just drive to nowhere just because they can, go get their hair cut and not worry about needing their parents to be there to help them at the wash basin, work in an office and not worry about needing their parents to turn up to help bring in a toilet frame, or lug office equipment back after a pandemic. For me, I am the opposite. I am largely dependent on those around me in order to practically live.

The bright side of all of that? I still live at home. And as a result, we spend a lot of time together, meaning my relationship with my family is, perhaps, a lot stronger than the average family.

Because of this close relationship, we can work together, live together and holiday together while, yes, also still being able to take the piss out of one another for running into closed doors or baking a cake with a whole can of condensed milk and forgetting to pull it out of the oven.

We all experience the highs and lows of life together. My family has been there at every doctor's appointment growing up as a kid, every surgery, every milestone, and graduation. They have also been with me when I have fallen and ended up in the hospital, been told that I may never be able to start a family naturally, and been told that Achilles surgery will most likely result in me never walking again. As a result of navigating the highs and lows, I believe we are a true team.

I remember one day in Grade 4, I tripped on a school bag strap and fell face first onto the concrete, ending up with a concussion. I was sent to the hospital via ambulance as there was concern for my neck. My brother was in Prep at the time, the step up from Kindy, and the year before you begin Grade 1, so he was only around five years old. As soon as he heard that I was in the hospital when dad went to pick him up at the end of the day, my brother ran to the car immediately, wanting to get to the hospital. Even when he was thirteen, he also didn't want to leave me after my gall bladder surgery, and slept on the couch in my parents' apartment instead of going back to Toowoomba with my grandparents.

Growing up, my brother never complained when I asked him to do things for me, like getting me a drink of water if I was eating lunch on the floor, or grabbing hot pans out of the oven. He never once complained about a day off school when we had to go to Brisbane for my appointments, and he never grumbled or protested about not being able to do things he wanted to do on holidays because I wouldn't have been able to join in.

For the most part, I feel like he was robbed of the typical sibling relationship. In saying that, though, we fought and wrestled like any other siblings. Of course, he would take it easy on me, making sure I never got hurt or fell over when we wrestled in front of the TV or in the pool, which would end up in tickle fights.

I often feel that siblings who have a disabled brother or sister end up playing second fiddle. They are exposed to some scary conversations, topics, and realisations when they should just be enjoying life. I feel that people focus so much on the disabled person, they overlook the mental and emotional, and yes, sometimes physical toll it has on those closest around them.

I knew one day it would be my turn to return the favour. That's why when we went on a big family cruise with my extended family in 2020, I was relieved that he was able to do the things that he truly wanted to do.

He decided to get a pass that allowed him to go on a flying fox over the boat, "walk the plank", abseil, and do a high rope course, and he was able to do it with our cousins and aunty.

Some people struggle with their fear of missing out (or FOMO), feeling sad while sitting on the sidelines watching everyone participate in activities they can't do or wish they could. And yes, while I desperately wanted to join in (although, you couldn't pay me to do the walking plank over the side of the boat), I was also excited to just sit and watch them all have the best time.

Did I feel FOMO? Yes. But I never felt sad for a second about my situation, or that I couldn't join in. Each time they had a new activity booked in, I would simply go and find a good vantage spot and take photos like a madwoman. I had as much fun watching them all laugh and, yes, borderline freak out as they stood on a plank over the side of the boat, almost as much as they did, actually, participating in the activities.

At one point, some of the people in our group went to grab a few drinks after watching my brother and the others on the flying fox. It was easier for me to give my mum my cruise card rather than try to be in line on my scooter.

As I waited, one of the people in our group came over to me and said they would wait with me for the others. They then asked me if I was okay and enjoying the trip so far. I immediately replied that I was having a great time and mentioned how amazing the accessibility on the ship was, to the point where I could go practically anywhere I wanted without having to wait for someone to accompany me. They said they were relieved, but asked again if I was okay, and if I wasn't sad. I reassured them again that I was fine and asked why they thought I might be sad. They said they thought I would feel that way, given that I was watching all my cousins, aunty, and especially my brother, have a great time doing all the adrenaline-filled activities that I wasn't able to.

I was immediately shocked by this, but at the same time, I tried to be grateful they were concerned. I simply responded, saying that I most certainly was having a great time, and for once, I could watch my brother do all the things we wanted to do for a change, as I often felt like he missed out. They simply said, " I am so glad you are still having a good time," and went to help grab the drinks.

I still get so much joy watching my brother live his life. Whether it's sitting on the sidelines watching him play AFL footy for eight years locally, to eventually making the local squad to compete at a state comp, and even this past year watching him party in the nightclub with our family friends, I love cheering him on. In a way, I am living vicariously through him.

I think it is important to mention that siblings also inadvertently take on a caregiving role to some extent. My parents, however, made a choice when they decided to have kids—that they would always be there and support their kids no matter what. A diagnosis of any sort would test even the strongest parents or couple. However, from the minute they were told about my diagnosis, and perhaps, even before then, they were in it for the long haul. If you asked my parents, they would say there was no choice.

I suppose siblings have a little more choice than parents do. I am so fortunate to have my brother in my life. He never bats an eyelid when I need any sort of help. He is the brawn and provides the comic relief I need in life. He will carry me across the sand effortlessly if I am too tired to walk over the uneven and soft terrain that beaches often have. He will drive me to get dinner or pick up our lunch if we want sushi on a Friday when he knocks off from work early. He will open jars and lift things that I will for sure drop if I even attempt to lift them. He manages our dog's zoomies when it is unsafe for me to do so, as I prefer to remain with my feet firmly on the ground — and out of the Emergency Room.

He does so all without complaining, and not to mention, he will go in to bat for me without a second thought, without me saying a word. He is perhaps my fiercest defender, and even though he didn't sign up for this life, I am so beyond grateful he is a part of it.

Our family has always been major supporters of each other. We cheer, laugh, and cry with each other. We also push each other to try new things and to simply do whatever it is in life that brings us joy. I have always pushed my mum, perhaps, more so than my brother or dad, to go on brunch dates with her friends, or to go to a yoga class. She isn't the biggest partier, and prefers a good book and a chocolate coffee with a *Nice* Biscuit; however, I have been desperate to see her let her hair down even for just a second. Given she has been my primary carer for twenty-six years, and the last few years have been difficult for her due to other reasons, I have seen her spark die out a fraction. I want nothing more than for my entire family to be truly happy and full of life.

So, you can imagine my surprise when, on cruise this year with Mum and Dad's friends from high school and their families, my mother didn't hesitate to join everyone on the dance floor in the nightclub! We hadn't even been there for five minutes before my brother, my godmother, her husband, their eldest, my mother, and our other friend and her eldest were all on the dance floor, all doing the textbook '90s hands-in-the-air dancing.

In between my fits of laughter and dancing my tail off on my scooter, because I always love a good boogie, I was simply just thrilled and beaming with pride and happiness to see my mum having the time of her life with the girls she went to high school with, who have also become family. It was like her spark returned, and she was laughing and jumping around like a 20-year-old all over again. Even my dad looked on with a big grin on his face.

We all know how much each of us has been through in our lives, whether it's because of the byproducts of the disability life, or from the standard difficult moments that come with simply being on this planet.

So, to see all of us enjoying life, having a boogie, or me and my brother singing along to "Sweet Caroline" when Charlie Cameron scores a goal for the Brisbane Lions at the footy, or enjoying a sunset walk to Froggies beach at Coolangatta; those are the most magical times that we all cherish. Those are the moments we don't have to think about the future, or really think about muscular dystrophy, and instead, can just enjoy the moment with each other.

One of my most cherished memories is the 2017 AFL Grand Final. Given that we are diehard AFL fans, the last Saturday in September is marked in each of our calendars. Nothing is booked on that day, other than sitting as a family in front of the TV.

To us, watching footy is an occasion and a moment to cherish between the four of us, especially on grand final day. The day starts early with a full breakfast usually of bacon, eggs, croissants, hash browns, and juice while the pregame show starts during mid-morning. Lunch soon rolls around, which is usually a roast with veg, as we watch the teams begin to arrive at the ground. When the game begins, no one moves a muscle, yet we scramble for extra snacks, drinks, and indeed, bathroom breaks, the minute each quarter ends.

The 2017 AFL Grand Final was no different. We had family that came over to watch the game. This Grand Final held extra significance as me and my dad's team, the Richmond Tigers, were playing in their first grand final in years, and hoped to end a 37-year premiership drought.

The week leading up to it, I was a bundle of nerves. The team we were playing against, the Adelaide Crows, were the dominant team all season, and we had lost by about 80 points the last time we played them in the season. The entire game, Dad and I sat next to each other, my mum and brother, as well as other family, equally huddled around the TV. We screamed, shouted, swore, at each call and goal scored, and poor umpiring decisions made.

Halfway through the final quarter, it became obvious we were going to win the premiership. Dad and I held each other's hands, and my brother and Mum came to sit next to us as the final seconds ticked down. With five seconds to go, I started tearing up as I heard Dad quietly repeat, "We've done it. We've done it." The final siren went, and we both yelled and started to cry, as those who were watching the game with us equally applauded and yelled. My brother marvelled over our star player, Dusty Martin, as Dad and I wrapped each other in a big hug as the team song blasted through the TV. Both of us shouting "Yellow and Black" at the top of our lungs, in time with the song.

That day and the subsequent premierships Richmond went on to win in the years following, and indeed, each Grand Final after that, are always among my favourite days. It's a moment where disability isn't involved, and where us as a family can enjoy each other's company and usually barrack for the same team for once! The days when we can put disability aside, and just be together as a family are the days that I hold so dear, and the memories created are equally special.

Family are the ones who stand by you during difficult times, who lift you up, cheer you on, and—metaphorically, of course—slap you over the head when you are being stupid, telling you to get your arse into gear. As you grow up, you begin to realise that the people you spend most of your time with are your family.

Family doesn't have to be people who you share DNA with. They are those you confide in, who you feel comfortable around, who make you feel seen, heard, and understood. More often than not, your chosen family becomes your ride or die.

For me, my chosen family is a blend of extended blood and immediate family, friends, friends of friends, godparents, and yes, I will even include my four-legged companions. They didn't all sign up for the disability life; to watch someone go through times that would make them question the fairness of life. They are the people whom I lean on when I feel like I can't lean on myself.

You may be scratching your head, wondering why on earth I consider my four-legged companions in the list of chosen family. To me, my dogs have become an integral part of my support network. Not only do they provide emotional support on the harder days, but they also lend an ear without judgment. If they do judge, thank goodness they don't speak human, so they can't tell me they are judging.

But over the years, when physical tasks have become too hard, they have been there to pick up the pieces, literally. I trained my beautiful late border collie, Milly, to take my socks off, pick up items off the floor, and hand them to me. From clothing to measuring cups, she was always within earshot to help me if I needed it. Our bond was unlike anything.

I believe that dogs choose their pack just as much as we choose them. She found me during Year 7 when I was at my lowest point in my confidence and self-esteem, and had just gone through losing our pomeranian, Maverick, to a brain tumour a few months prior. Yes, I believe he was named after Tom Cruise's character in *Top Gun*.

My uncle and his wife's border collies gave birth to puppies only about a week or so after Mav passed. When they came into town from

Tallwood to sell the puppies, we were invited to my grandmother's place for dinner and to say hi to the cute bundles of fluff.

Before we went for dinner, Mum sat both my brother and me down and said that no matter how much we love the puppies, we simply didn't have the space for a herding dog, given that we lived in the suburbs.

However, I think she was convincing herself more so than us because it became obvious the minute we laid eyes on the 7-week-old pups running around that one of them was coming home. Throughout the night, one little fur ball caught my attention. She was the runt of the litter, was by herself as her siblings didn't want to play with her, and each time I called the pups, she would be the first one to come to me. She stuck to me like glue the entire night, and I became smitten with her.

There was something there that I couldn't ignore, and I spent the rest of the night carrying her and showing my parents how much we had already bonded and begging to keep her. The answer was still no. I left the dinner a sobbing mess as she was being sent to the pet store owned by my other uncle and his wife at the time, to be sold the next morning.

The next morning came, and I did the immature thing: I scowled at my parents, behind their backs, of course, and still tried to drop not-so-subtle hints about this pup. When my brother woke up, he, too, was sad about leaving the puppies. Finally, Dad told us, "Will you help us look after her? You need to help train her, it can't be up to just Mum and I. And you do realise there will be a time when she will pass away. Are you sure you want to sign up for that?"

Without thinking, I said yes, and so did my brother. My parents both pretty much said, "Alright, let's go get her." I hoped that we weren't too late and that she was still available. It was just our luck that we pulled up to the shop at the same time my uncle turned up with the puppies. He knew immediately which one I wanted, and said, "Your parents couldn't say no, hey. I knew it! She is all yours; you may as well take her inside." I had never felt more relieved in my life.

That, then, started the twelve and a half years of companionship I had never felt before. Milly was my rock and my little helper. It was effortless to train her in what I needed help with, though taking my socks off proved to be a nerve-wracking experience, as it was always a gamble to see if you got a complimentary foot piercing in the process. She hated when I would use my grabby stick to pick anything up, and at the first squeak of the stick, she would come bolting around the corner. She gave me a level of independence that I didn't expect could come from a dog.

Perhaps my biggest regret is that I wasn't there for her when she crossed the rainbow bridge unexpectedly. The night before, something was wrong with her. I remember she and I just looked at each other, her in her bed, and I, by the door, as we had just turned on our Christmas tree lights, which she always loved.

I somehow knew, looking at her eyes, that she wasn't okay, but despite that, she still, for some reason, had the look of "It's okay." on her face.

The following night, when we had to say goodbye, I sat with her on the floor of the veterinarian's office, gave her plenty of cuddles and kisses, thanked her for being with me, and for choosing me and our family to be her pack. I told her she had been so brave and strong, and that it was okay—that we would be okay.

However, I couldn't bring myself to be in the room when she left this world. I mentally wouldn't have been able to take it, as at that time in my life, I was going through a lot of absences. The moment she needed a support network, I felt like I had betrayed her and let her down as I walked out of the room with Dad on the floor holding her. I sat in the car and just kept trying to send out to her that I was still here, that she was okay.

My parents stayed with her the entire time, never once leaving her side. They did what I couldn't. And I fear I will never forgive myself.

When I told Mum that, she said to me, "But honey, you were there. You got out of the car and willed yourself into that room. You were able to show her love and kept her calm, reassuring her that everything was okay. She wasn't alone. And she would have understood you not being there."

To this day, nearly two years later, I still ask Milly for forgiveness.

After her passing, my independence crashed. I felt lost, hopeless, and like life became even more difficult. I struggled to take off my socks, and trying to pick up a pair of jeans with my grabby stick felt like lifting 60 kilograms. I had to rely on my family more and more, and my version of independence that I had been used to for almost thirteen years was stripped from me, seemingly overnight.

I knew that when the time was right, I needed to find another dog. Not to replace Milly, as I believe you can never replace someone. But I knew I needed my support network to feel whole again. I needed a dog in my life that would help me feel my version of independence again. Sure, we have my brother's dog, a mini dachshund, but he is more of an emotional support dog rather than a physical labour support dog, even though he tries so hard to be.

I spoke to Hayley, my equine-assisted therapy coach, about finding a dog a few months after we lost Milly. At the time, I was looking at either a shepherd breed or a Labrador, as they were bigger and could help with mobility. However, there was something about the smartness of border collies that neither of us could overlook. Hayley mentioned a breeder who had a pup go on to be a trained assistance animal, and mentioned I should follow the breeder on social media.

As soon as I got into the car and looked up the breeder, to my shock, she had a litter of pups for sale. A few days passed, and the breeder put up yet another photo. There was something that made me look twice, and I felt I had to just ask the breeder if she had any pups left from that litter.

I didn't want a black and white pup purely because Milly was black and white, and I felt it would be too difficult to have another of the same colourings. As it turned out, the only pup available was this tiny female black and white ball of fluff.

And just like that, Lexi came into our lives. She arrived in rather dramatic fashion. She was about to go to another person who lived across the country, there were no suitable flights available, so at the last minute I put down a deposit, and this black and white fluff ball became part of the family.

She came into my life at a time when I desperately needed love and support that only an animal can provide. She took to training like a champ, and there were slight subtleties that made me convinced that Milly had spoken to her. The biggest thing was her food bowl. Milly would always pick up her bowl and walk around the house with it when she was hungry. One evening, little Lexi Luna came around the corner carrying her food bowl. That was the sign I needed that Milly was still with us and had well and truly given us her blessing.

Now at almost two years old, Lexi is a pocket rocket. She makes me laugh until my stomach hurts, has the most intense obsession with tennis balls, and simply just knows when I need something. She aced picking up things off the ground and passing them to me, long before she figured out what "stay" meant. She even lifts up her head to give me what I have dropped, so I don't have to reach as far down—another thing I taught Milly but never asked Lexi to do. She just did it on her own accord. Lexi even sleeps on my bed, something I have wanted my entire life. She will curl up pressed against me all night, barely leaving my side. When we wake up in the morning, she drowns me in kisses, before scratching the door down, as if saying, "It's breakfast time, Mum, let's go."

She found me at the perfect time, as did Milly, and how can I forget Levi the dachshund? These three dogs have put me together and found me at the exact time I needed them. They weathered multiple storms with me, the storms they were designed to be with me for.

Milly got me through a phase of life that was perhaps the hardest I had to endure. She was there for my surgeries, the bullying, the relationship breakups, the never-ending loss of ability. She was there when I was teetering on the edge, about to fall into an abyss. She carried me through it, as did the rest of my family. But she was always there with a gentle, caring eye and an eagerness to help me survive whatever it was I was going through.

Levi came and provided me with emotional comfort when we lost Milly. It used to be Levi, Milly, and myself—home alone, a few days a week. When she passed, it was just him and me. We would spend hours together, with him on my lap or on my bed — not that my brother needs to know that, since Levi is his dog — curled up together just enjoying each other's company.

Both of us needed love, support, and reassurance that we were okay. I don't know what I would have done without Levi, and I can't fathom the thought of being at home alone those first few weeks after Milly's passing. I truly believe he got me through those few months.

And then there is Lexi, my next chapter dog. Her confidence is infectious, as is her zest for life. I'm not sure what she is here to teach me, or exactly what chapter of my life she is here for. Lexi did more than just bring back my version of independence; she has shown me that healing, growth, and support can come in many forms.

Family isn't always born of blood. Sometimes, it's born of fur, instinct, and an unspoken understanding of one another.

Chapters close and others begin; that's the unique beat of life. And with each new chapter comes a different kind of support. The people in your corner for one season might not be the same ones who walk—or roll— beside you in the next. But that's okay. People and animals show up exactly when they're meant to, and often leave when it's time to make room for someone new.

I've been incredibly lucky in my life. My support network is made up of the most remarkable beings: coaches, parents, my brother, extended family, godparents, friends, friends of friends, allied health professionals, dogs, and even horses. Each one has shaped who I am and has weathered countless storms alongside me.

Life is a never-ending cycle of endings and beginnings. And knowing that I'm always surrounded by those who lift me, challenge me, and carry me through this unique journey, that's the part of living with a disability I'm most grateful for.

I have had a few people who have said to me, I would always be alone, for one reason or another. But I can confidently say: I'm not alone. I have never been alone and never will be. I've found my tribe. I welcome and bid farewell to those who are joining me for a season, knowing they're just as crucial to my story as those who stay for a lifetime.

SECTION 3
Rising Strong - Triumphs and Tenacity

Our job is not to deny the story, but to defy the ending—to rise strong, recognise our story, and rumble with the truth until we get to a place where we think, Yes.
This is what happened. This is my truth. And I will choose how the story ends.
—Brene Brown, *Rising Strong*

CHAPTER 9

THE LAW OF DETERMINATION

Like every child, I wanted to be many things growing up. From the clichéd ballerina and firefighter, to the more unique Paralympic swimmer and actress. My head was full of ideas of what I wanted to be when I grew up. Going to law school, however, wasn't even on my radar.

When I accepted my offer for my law degree a few months after graduating from Year 12, I was absolutely packing it. Even though, at the time, I was so sure that I had found the thing I was good at or thought I could be good at, the anxiety and fear of starting back at square one had me on the verge of a breakdown.

Could I finally use the bathrooms? Could I access my classrooms? What do I wear? Will I even make friends? Are we allowed to submit drafts for feedback? So many necessary and rather peculiar questions filled my head.

I was fortunate enough to meet with the staff who were in charge of disability inclusion at the university. Before starting my degree, we had to go through the standard 101 questions, such as how my disability works, how it impacts my everyday life, and how I think it could impact my degree.

While doing rounds of the university to make sure that I could access everything I needed, including the toilet, the person in charge of documenting everything I needed help with said that they knew that there were things on campus that needed improving to be more accessible, but they couldn't get anything done because the higher-ups refused to see a need for it, until someone who is actually disabled comes along and say it needs to be changed. Even then, it is a long, drawn-out process.

For example, the disabled bathroom near the main lecture hall didn't have automatic doors. The door itself was extremely heavy, and it was incredibly difficult to open for those sitting in a mobility scooter, or perhaps, even a wheelchair.

After many failed attempts at opening the door gently, I realised I needed more force. I didn't have that physically, however, my mobility scooter sure did. So, I lined my scooter up with the door, cranked up the speed, and rammed my way through the door in a way that would make Jason Bourne proud.

The staff member in charge of the disability services at the university jumped ten feet tall, and we both couldn't help but laugh at the ridiculousness of almost having to break my scooter just to go to the bathroom.

I had to, then, repeat the process so she could film it as evidence to show that the door finally needed to be automatic. Apparently, this was only one of the issues they had been trying to address for years, and the powers that be refused to listen until someone could show why a solid wooden door wasn't good enough. With that being said, the door still wasn't made automatic until my second semester at university.

Obtaining all the extra help I needed, however, was as simple as just asking. I was able to obtain extra time during exams, which were held in a separate room away from the main exam floor, and an ergonomic chair in lecture rooms that didn't already have them. I was fortunate that everything else around campus was completely accessible for me, at least, in some way.

Worrying about accessibility has always been a constant for me, just like worrying about what to wear to that dinner party you dread going to. So, it is always a major win for me whenever I can go somewhere without thinking about how I will get around. Having a place that I knew was accessible, meant I didn't have to waste energy worrying about not being able to access my classes, and I could simply focus on learning, just like everyone else.

Some of the more hilarious moments of being disabled come at the most serious times. In the moment, it's not funny at all, but eventually, down the line, it's something you can absolutely laugh about.

During Orientation Week, which is the week before university starts and all the first-years get acquainted with the campus, we had an introductory lecture by the Head of the Law Faculty. It was on the fourth floor, which didn't matter because, fortunately, for my sake, there was a lift. What I didn't anticipate was how quickly the lift doors shut. The lift was certainly on the smaller side, only big enough to fit me and two other people, and that was with all of us sucking in. Yes, I am fully aware no amount of sucking in would make me smaller given I was encased in my scooter!

That particular day, I was lucky enough to have even made some friends, which was an even greater surprise and one less thing I had to worry about when classes started. Everything seemed to be aligning well, that is, until the lift fiasco.

My newfound friends and I decided to head to the lecture together. They could have decided to climb the four flights of stairs. However, they opted to come with me. Not only was the lift convenient for them, too, but we were all afraid of getting lost, so we thought sticking together, and potentially getting lost together, was better than getting lost alone.

As we arrived on the fourth floor, I told them they could get out first as I needed a bit more room to reverse. As I went to reverse, the doors started closing on me. For some reason, though my friends stuck their hands through the door to activate the sensor to stop it from closing, the sensor didn't work.

As a result, I was stuck in the lift. My brain panicked for a moment because the lift wasn't going anywhere, and I knew I was going to end up being late for the lecture. Those who know me would know how much I despise being late to anything, and especially given the fact that I would be late to a lecture run by a solicitor who was all about punctuality. I was crumbling inside.

After sitting in the lift for a moment and getting my bearings, I verbally slapped myself. And that's when I realised; I could just press the button to the fourth floor again (what a dumb arse!).

I eventually made it to the lecture and received a scowl from the professor in the process. I didn't have the confidence to tell him I got stuck in a lift, so I just apologised profusely and sat next to my friends, who fortunately saved me a seat, which meant I didn't have to climb up the stairs to the back of the small auditorium. Had that been the case, I probably would have made some dumb excuse of "Wrong lecture. So sorry for the intrusion." and just left, because there was no way I was navigating those stairs. It was going to risk my dignity and pride regardless, whether it be falling on my face or leaving. And I would have chosen the latter.

Many people believe that disability is the sole factor that tests and forges determination. However, more often than not, external influences unrelated to one's birth significantly impact the development of determination and assess whether you are ready to endure in the long run.

My first official lecture the following week didn't go according to plan, which was the perfect test of that determination.

I immediately felt out of place. I was in a sea of people who seemed to know who they were. They were full of confidence, their lawyer ego already starting to grow. Unlike me, they came prepared. Pre-readings for the following week had all been done, and they certainly weren't intimidated by the lecturer, speaking with her almost like a long-time colleague.

On the other hand, I was a complete fish out of water. I was still very much a broken mess after my schooling years, and was lacking a serious backbone. Okay, not a physical backbone, but a backbone built on self-belief, self-worth, confidence, and the ability to stand up for oneself. I was still terrified to speak up for myself, so how on earth was I going to be able to stand up for others?

The gremlin in my head immediately started telling me that I was very much in the wrong place, asking what kind of lawyer I was going to be if I couldn't even have the confidence to raise my hand to ask a question in class? It took me forty-five minutes out of the entire hour-long class to muster the courage to ask, "Are we able to submit drafts for feedback before the final copies?" Spoken like a true school-leaver. My face burned up with embarrassment as soon as the question left my mouth. I was one of the youngest in the class, with the oldest being in their 60s.

My lecturer's reply was a simple, "No, here at uni, especially in the law degree, we prepare you for real-world scenarios. And in the real world, and especially in the courtroom, you only have one chance to get it right. So, you may be used to that in high school. But at this university, it is not the same."

At that moment, I felt very much as though my lifeline was ripped from me, and it was very much sink or swim.

I left that class and called my mum to tell her I was finished for the day and to pick me up. As soon as she asked how it went, I burst into tears. "Everyone here is much stronger than I am. They speak with such conviction and confidence. I asked the most stupid questions compared to everyone else. I don't know how I am going to be able to do this. I feel very much out of place."

I felt this way during the entirety of my first year. I was floundering all over the place. I couldn't keep up with the amount of readings we had to do each week, which was three to four chapters of the textbooks, plus, case law and extra journal readings. I felt like I couldn't learn anything and felt like a complete impostor. A lawyer who is disabled. The gremlin mocked me at the mere thought.

For the first time, this was a test of my mental fortitude. Not one of physical resilience and mind over matter. Academia was the one thing I had felt confident in. I loved studying and using my brain. It was the one thing in my life that my disability had no control over, nor could it ever take from me. It was completely up to me.

Only six months into my degree I still felt like a floundering fish, so I decided to walk away from law and booked a meeting with the careers officer. We spoke about why law didn't feel right, and what I would love to study instead. We had to be practical, and I wanted to at least gain something from studying law, even if only for six to twelve months. I said that I loved drama and acting, and wouldn't mind getting into performing arts.

However, it was going to be a little more complicated than sending an email and signing on the dotted line. I had no prerequisites that would meet the eligibility criteria.

The counsellor then asked if I had considered a career in teaching. I told her I had considered it for a brief moment in Grade 10, but that was all. She then pitched me a marvellous plan.

Given that I still enjoyed legal studies and loved drama, why not pursue a Bachelor of Secondary Education majoring in Legal Studies and minoring in Drama? This way I would get the best of both worlds, and the best part would be that I could exit my law degree with a graduate diploma of legal studies, which would satisfy the major specialisation of the teaching degree.

She made a few phone calls to make sure that it was possible, and after the go-ahead from the education and arts faculties, it was up to me to make a decision.

I have always been one to ponder over serious decisions, borderline overanalysing them, so I couldn't make a decision right then and there. I went home and slept on it for a few days. The pathway made complete sense in my mind, and so, with that, I drafted an email stating that I wished to transfer into secondary education.

But as I hovered over the send button, something stopped me. I had to get real with myself. Was I just leaving because it was hard, and I hadn't found a way to learn the material and find my feet? Or was I leaving because it simply just wasn't right for me?

After pondering for a few minutes and journalling, I realised that I simply felt like I hadn't found my feet yet, and I was leaving because it was too difficult. I also felt it was a three-year degree, and I was almost halfway through; It felt pointless to throw in the towel and not see it to the end. So, I decided to give it a little more time and kept the email in my drafts folder.

I realised that I needed to find my feet quickly, and what better way was there than to sign up for the first-year moot?

A moot is a mock court scenario with a defence and prosecution. Each side is given a set of facts of a fictional court case, based on which side you are on. The aim is to argue your case in court, just as if you were a proper practising solicitor in a real courtroom.

The thing with me is, once I realise I need to flip the switch and change my outlook on things and get a grip, I certainly don't do it lightly. I will go in all guns blazing and rip the band-aid off. So, a moot was the perfect baptism by fire, and the perfect opportunity to see if I'd enjoy standing up in court. If I still hated it when it was over, then I would happily send that email and enter the world of teaching.

The entire process of preparing for the moot didn't do much to ease my crippling self-doubt. My moot partner was way more outgoing and knowledgeable, even as a first-year student. Not only did I not want to embarrass myself, but my severe case of people-pleasing meant I was more afraid of embarrassing him, more so.

My mind was conjuring up all sorts of scenarios, from calling the judge "mate'" or "buddy" passive aggressively, to forgetting what I was saying, losing my place in my notes, and saying "fuck me dead" out loud or falling on my face walking into the fake courtroom. I started to seriously doubt why on earth I had not only agreed to do the moot competition, but also why I decided law was a good idea in the first place.

I was fortunate in that my partner didn't see my lack of confidence, or the fact that I couldn't retain anything we learnt in class to save my life, as an issue. Instead, he rallied with me and really guided me through the entire process with a lot of patience.

In the end, we formed a great team, and despite my tendency to overthink, I was still able to come up with several strong points that we could include in our submissions. I felt relieved that I was able to contribute and not have it all be up to him to come up with the arguments.

If I was to be completely honest, I did enjoy the entire preparation for the moot. I love problem-solving, writing, and research. So the competition, and indeed the degree itself, utilised all my strongest skill sets.

The day of the moot rolled around, and I was grateful the bathroom was around the corner, because I did not need to be also worrying about having a *Bring It On* moment and vomiting all over either my partner or the judge.

I was able to draw on the lessons from my drama training as well as the handful of speeches I had given at functions years prior, and apply them to calm myself enough when the time came for me to speak. I remembered to address the "court" properly, as well as the judge, and didn't flub any of the points that I had to make. And my face remained firmly away from the floor, which was a much welcomed bonus.

In the end, we won both of our moots convincingly and tied for first. The judge was actually a solicitor posing as a judge for our moot, and the winners were awarded work experience with his firm.

We thought that, maybe, just maybe, they would give all four of us work experience. I was shocked first that we had won both moots, and second that there was a chance I was about to walk away with work experience from a top law firm in town.

Unfortunately, they decided to offer the experience to the team who were in their 40s, and who really took a risk in their arguments which impressed the pants off the judge, or should I say solicitor, as even they mentioned they wouldn't have been game enough to take the risks she did if it were a real case.

I was caught off guard when I felt a twinge of anger and disappointment that my partner and I didn't also score work experience. My competitive streak wanted to lash out and throw a tantrum worthy of trashy reality TV. However, this exercise was intended to be a test to determine whether I was suited to study law or pursue a career as a solicitor.

To be brutally honest, I was desperate for it to be my confirmation that it wasn't for me, so that I could walk away and at least be able to say to people that I didn't just walk away, and I gave it a red hot crack. See again? Worrying about what everyone else thought, except for what felt right for me?

But I didn't expect to absolutely love the entire process when it was all said and done. It felt amazing to stand up and speak on behalf of someone who needed help, even if it was a completely made-up person. It sparked a glimmer of belief in me that, maybe, I did have what it took to not only finish my degree but also go on to be a qualified solicitor and excel at it too.

The one thing I loved most was that I was treated the same as everyone else. I was spoken to like everyone else, not spoken down to. There was a mutual respect shown by everyone the minute you walked in the door.

Everyone knew how hard we all had worked to get to that point, and it didn't matter if you were disabled or abled, young or old; everyone was there for a common purpose. To learn, to argue, and to start building their legal careers.

I was seen, heard, understood, and respected. All the things I was desperate to find and desperate to feel in my life up to that point. That was the moment I realised I had actually found my place, and if I was to bail out because the study was "too hard" or the lecturers were too "intimidating", I would be doing myself a major disservice. I had never bailed out of a physical challenge with my disability before, because I legitimately wasn't able to. So, why should I bail out of a mental challenge? Especially when I realised I wanted that degree and a career in law after all?

Failing that Contracts Law class a few weeks later was another complete test in discovering what I was made of mentally. Not only did I fail my entire subject, for my end-of-semester exam, I ended up getting like 13/70. I failed in spectacular fashion.

Throughout my entire life, I felt that academia was the only thing I was good at. I wasn't good at anything to do with sports or numbers. Studying English and remembering lines in a movie or script was about it.

As a result, I attached my self-worth and the value I had as a person to academics. So, when I failed that class dismally, I was shattered, and I was embarrassed. I was also worried that I would be a disappointment to my family, and at a time when I was still struggling with feeling like I had let them down by being disabled, failing felt like the icing on the cake. This is despite my parents not showing an ounce of anger or disappointment. They were more shocked at how badly I had failed, but also comforted me when I started sobbing like someone had just run over my dog.

I immediately knew that my flight mode had been activated, and my brain was trying to convince me to pack it all in. I was then furious at myself for failing, and deep down, I knew that I hadn't put in nearly enough effort to learn the content, knowing it was a challenging class for me. Instead, I had put all my effort into that moot.

The one strange thing about me is that when I am angry and need to sort shit out in my head, I need to move. What I didn't know back then was that it was because all these emotions were stored in my body, and I needed to release them from my system. The only way I knew how was to exercise and almost punish myself physically with a workout. So, I grabbed my shoes, asked my parents to chuck them on my feet, grabbed my headphones, and told my family I was going for a walk down the street to clear my head.

Despite their concern about me going by myself due to obvious reasons of ending up with my nose splattered over my face, I assured them quickly that I would be fine before waddling out the door.

As I walked, I was seething. How could I have failed so badly? What went wrong? How can I fix it? Why did you think you could do this? How stupid can you be? My thoughts were racing faster than I could walk, which lets be honest, who is surprised by that?

At some point in time, if we want to be able to improve our lives, jobs, relationships, or whatever it may be, we need to get real with ourselves rather quickly.

So, while the gremlin in my head was in major self-loathing territory, I was desperately trying to get real with myself and do some serious problem-solving. I knew that I couldn't just throw in the towel because I failed. That wasn't in my nature; if I was going to walk away, it had to be because it just wasn't the right fit, not because I barely made it past the start line with my results. So throwing in the towel was not the solution.

What I did realise was that my note-taking system was dismal. Since exams in my degree were open-book, I realised that I needed to be able to locate sections in my notes quickly. I also realised that I barely did any tutorial questions for either exam prep or to consolidate what I learned in class.

In short, I was lazy, and perhaps, slightly cocky, thinking that since it was an open-book exam, I could just coast through it. That's what happens when you are an 18-year-old university student who didn't take a gap year and was still very emotionally immature in a lot of ways.

I ended up doing two laps on the street before going home, so I had time to calm down and problem-solve the entire degree, and just short of solving the world's problems.

When I eventually came home, I was eager to retake the class, but I had to wait twelve months before I could retake it, as the class was only offered in the second semester each year. That didn't mean I couldn't implement my study comeback straight away.

I started having conversations with one of my friends, who was a straight-A student. She was in her late 40s, incredibly intelligent, and was cut out to be a lawyer. I asked her what she did to study for exams and class. I, then, decided, based on her advice, that typing my notes instead of handwriting them and doing the tutorial questions as if I were answering them in an exam was also just as crucial. These changes would mean that I could easily read my notes, and if any questions were similar to the tutorials, I would already have half-written answers done.

Over time, I continued to tweak my methods and introduced table of contents pages for each class, which made my organisational heart sing.

I simply refused to give up and call it quits. I was so used to having to hang in there when I would have bad days physically, so I had to find a way to adapt what I learnt from experiencing the physical discomfort and apply it to the mental discomfort.

The main reason at the time for refusing to quit was because of my "why." Everyone has times when things get hard and they become uncertain. For most, it takes really understanding the "why" behind what they are doing to continue pushing through. Mine was to be able to help people like me who were scared to speak up, who didn't have a voice. But I also had another "why"—to help myself grow stronger mentally, stand up for myself, and enforce boundaries when the time arose.

I was desperate to be seen as an adult, and not be constantly spoken down to or treated with kid gloves. These were compelling enough for me not to give in.

As time went on, through my degree, I started to turn a page. My grades picked up exponentially, and I was starting to feel less timid and more confident in my ability to have tough conversations. I was starting to morph into the strong, confident woman I had wanted to be for a very long time.

What I had learnt within myself and my newfound confidence was put to the test in my third-year Constitutional Law class. That class was one of the few that allowed us to select what assessment we wanted to do, either an essay or participate in a moot. For those of us serious about pursuing a career as a solicitor, the moot was another perfect opportunity to gain hands-on experience of what our careers could look like.

I immediately sought out my friend who had helped me become a better law student. Given her knowledge and confidence, I wanted to have the opportunity to work with her and learn from her further. There was almost an unspoken agreement amongst the cohort that if there was anyone you didn't want to go up against in a moot, it was her, so I wanted to make sure I was working with her, not against her.

The stakes were raised even higher when we found out that the moot wasn't going to be in the mock courtroom on campus; it was, in fact, in the District Courthouse in Ipswich, in front of a practising and well-known judge.

As soon as I heard that, my stomach was immediately on the floor. It was one thing to practice being a solicitor in a mock court set up, but it was another thing to do it in an actual courtroom in front of a legitimate judge.

I was sweating bullets arriving at the courthouse on the day of the moot. I felt like I was nowhere near prepared enough, and I knew my flaws would be obvious, especially given that I was following a woman who could effortlessly command respect and attention the minute she started to speak.

The self-doubt returned, and the performance anxiety hit an all-time high.

It didn't help that the environment was as intimidating as it was stunning: floor-to-ceiling glass windows overlooking well-maintained gardens, with tall ceilings and wooden finishes in the main lobby. The courtroom itself could easily fit a two-story house in it, given how tall and wide it was. The judge's bench towered over the rest of the courtroom, making a statement of respect and superiority without having anyone sitting on it.

Driving my scooter into the room, I was grateful I didn't have to walk in, as I was convinced all the blood had vanished from my legs.

Performance anxiety has always been a pre-game thing. I will get so incredibly nervous and on the verge of throwing up before speaking. But the minute I stand up, I am instantly calm.

This particular day, I couldn't focus on what my moot partner was saying; all I could pick up was her tone, her energy. It screamed, "I know my shit, I know I am good, and you will listen to me," without a hint of arrogance or ego about it. She effortlessly held the attention of everyone in that courtroom, and when the judge stopped her to ask questions, she didn't miss a beat. I was in awe of her, yet it did nothing to stop my nerves.

I was doubting if I could even have a pinch of the confidence and presence she had when it was suddenly my turn to speak. I blinked, and next thing I knew, she was wrapping up her submissions and handing the lectern over to me.

I was sitting in an ergonomic chair that we could raise slightly, but even then, I had to essentially lay myself over the table to stand up. I was immediately mortified that everyone's eyes were on me, watching me struggle to stand. I was desperate for the ground to swallow me up right then and there. Alas, even though I tried so hard to manifest it, it didn't happen, and I had to try to play it cool. I hoped my makeup was heavy enough to hide the red colouration spreading across my face and blotches across my chest.

I was immediately grateful for the ten years of drama classes I took, which allowed me to make it look like I was doing the most mundane thing in the world, as if I simply didn't care. Even though, deep down, I was dying of sheer mortification. I was able to act focused and like I deserved to be representing our fictional client. In reality, I was far from focused and felt like a fraud.

I shakily began reading my submissions, hoping the judge couldn't see my shaking hands and that they couldn't detect the wobble in my voice. I slowly and surely made my way through, speaking with as much authority as I could muster without it sounding like I was disciplining my dog for digging another hole in the backyard. I was doing well and had just started thinking my submissions were on the money, as they hadn't interrupted me to ask any questions, until I heard, "Excuse me, Miss Anderson, I want to stop you there for a moment."

Instead of panicking and passing out, something in my head said, "Right. Game on." I immediately felt my shoulders becoming square, and my posture became more strong and steady.

My nerves that hadn't yet disappeared during submissions finally vanished like someone snapping a rubber band. I was incredibly present, and I was adamant that I was going to confidently answer any question they had to ask, but I didn't anticipate that the question was going to question my morals and ethics as a human.

The case centred around our client being potentially sentenced to life in prison as he refused to answer questions at his preliminary hearing. We were arguing that the law (made up for the case) that allowed them to lock our client up, on the grounds that his silence implied guilt, was unconstitutional.

The question I was asked was along the lines of, if someone allegedly committed a serious crime, and everyone believed they were guilty, shouldn't it be in the best interest of the community if they were automatically locked up if they refused to answer questions?

It was a long time ago, so I have probably got the question wrong, but I do remember that at the time, the question was asked in a way that my head immediately said, "Oh, good point, you have backed me into a corner."

I knew if I answered it as any regular person would, it would automatically mean I lost our case, and my (fake) client would end up going to jail even though they were innocent. Allegedly.

I had two seconds to contemplate and answer the question. I simply said that everyone deserves a fair trial, and simply throwing someone in jail without due process was still unconstitutional, especially since there is the "innocent until proven guilty" element that everyone deserves.

As I was giving my answer, the judge peeked over the top of his glasses. I knew it was a pure intimidation tactic, and I willed myself to keep standing and not allow my knees to dead-leg themselves and split my chin open on the wooden lectern on the way down. I finished answering the question, and he grinned slightly and told me to continue.

I still had one last crucial point to make, but I only had two minutes to argue that last element and wrap up not only my submission but also my mooting partner's, as well as request that the court dismiss the charges under constitutional grounds and release our client. I decided quickly that I felt our case was strong enough without the last element being argued, and so I wrapped up our case and thanked the judge for their time.

The sense of accomplishment I felt at that moment was indescribable. I had stood up for someone even though they weren't real, when they had no one else believing them. And I refused to allow my head, or the environment I was in, to control me. It was as if a part of me had not only helped our "client" but also helped me heal that little girl still inside of me who was hurt and felt alone.

I had done what I wish someone would have done for me all those years ago in primary school.

I was just grateful to have been able to survive giving submissions in a real courtroom; surprisingly, the thought never crossed my mind about potentially winning the entire thing, until the opposing side began giving their submissions against our client. Two sentences in, and they were already stopped for questioning.

My heart skipped a beat. They had prepared their submissions as if they were arguing for our client, not for the opposing side. They used the exact same case law and legislation provisions as we did. It became obvious to them as well that they had majorly stuffed up in front of a District Court Judge.

I was immediately conflicted. I knew right then that we had won our moot, and I was so happy and relieved. But then, at the same time, I felt so sorry and heartbroken for the guys who were imploding right before my eyes.

I was getting big time second-hand embarrassment watching them stumble and try to put together a compelling argument, which was impossible to do considering they had prepped for the wrong side. The opposing team stood there, shaking and stuttering, and I swear I could see beads of sweat starting to form on their faces. They were desperate for the moot to finish, just as I was for them.

No one likes seeing someone implode or stumble, especially in front of people they will potentially one day work closely with. I can say that despite all of this, one of the team members has gone on to be a rather successful solicitor in the civil and family law circuit. It just goes to show that failing a moot or assessment, doesn't mean you aren't cut out for your chosen industry. You always learn more from your failures than your wins.

In the end, the judge declared us winners and thanked us all for our time officially, before our lecturer, who was also judging, spoke to us and passed on personal remarks from the judge.

If winning and surviving a moot wasn't the best thing of all, the judge had personally said that he was impressed that I was able to stay level-headed and think rationally, and professionally, about the question that was purposely designed to trick me.

If there was anything that being disabled taught me, it was the ability to problem-solve rather quickly, running through options A to Z in seconds, and acting on them straight away. Learning that skill set early on in life has paid off in so many ways, and the fact that it inadvertently helped me win a mock court case under pressure, and to be commended by a sitting judge, was something I didn't anticipate my disability would ever help me with.

Even though I was ecstatic to win, it was such a valuable experience, and I marvelled at my growth in only a year or so, I couldn't help but feel a twang. I saw a side to legal life that didn't really agree with me, yet I was still so focused on being a solicitor that I pushed the voice to the side and instead looked at it as more confirmation that I was in the right place.

I have found, though, that the universe has ways of making sure you are on the path you need to be on; one way or another, it will always bring you back to the path you were always meant to take.

It wasn't long after the moot that I ended up working in the legal industry.

I had a week's worth of work experience at a Legal Centre, which offered free legal advice and assistance to those who couldn't afford private lawyers. For my work experience, I was shadowing the civil and family lawyers. There was such an array of work we got to be involved in, from undertaking basic legal research to being allowed to sit in on client meetings and phone calls. Those of us who participated in the work experience were able to gain invaluable, firsthand insights into life as a solicitor, particularly, one who wasn't in it for the money that often comes with a career in law, but rather for serving the vulnerable, something that appealed to me greatly.

I thoroughly enjoyed my week there. However, this was yet another one of those times when life showed me that I wasn't on the right path.

My next sign was on a Wednesday. We were shadowing the family lawyer during "Duty Lawyer Day" at the local courthouse. Wednesdays were what I like to call 'toxic unsafe relationship' day, and we had to be there bright and early before the courts opened so the lawyer we were shadowing had proper time to set up in her interview room and receive the briefs for the day.

I have never been more uncomfortable and felt more unsafe in my entire life than that day, driving through the public waiting area outside the courtrooms. The lawyers and us law students turned up in suits, polished and looking professional. We stood out like a sore thumb. Everyone else was wearing everything from thongs (flip-flops for the Americans) and board shorts to people, at least, trying to make an effort with a T-shirt and jean shorts with holes in them.

As soon as we turned up, it was like pelicans to a chip. All eyes were on us, staring intently as if we were the problem that had just entered the room—the ones that were capable of ruining their lives. I was grateful that security was escorting us to our interview room, but being on my scooter, I immediately felt vulnerable.

Any one of the people in that room could have jumped up and grabbed me within seconds, given how close we were in proximity to them as we went by. I was an easy target, and it took every ounce of strength in me to keep my head up and not look like I was about to pee my pants. I was only nineteen at the time and still very much a nervous and anxious person, especially when it came to my disability and being in a situation where I knew I was physically powerless.

The minute the interview door shut, and it was just me, my fellow work buddy, and the lawyer we were shadowing, I released a breath I didn't realise I was holding.

There were moments where the lawyer had wanted us to venture out of the room to get a real sense of what we were signing up for, staying only in the lobby and waiting area outside the court rooms, as we were not permitted to enter the court rooms themselves. I knew she was wanting to get us comfortable being in those environments early on, but I felt safe in my little box of a room. There was no way I was venturing anywhere without her, or even without security.

Fortunately, it was a rather short day, and we were out of the courts by just a bit after lunch. I had never been so relieved to go and sit back at an office for the day.

When the end of the week rolled around, the staff came by our makeshift office to say thank you and goodbye. Two of the lawyers, one of whom we had shadowed to court, and another a civil law lawyer we had helped with his legislation research, said that they would love it if we considered hanging around and volunteering because they felt like we did an amazing job, and they could use an extra pair of hands.

It was one of the few times that I had felt welcomed in any space before. They didn't care that I was disabled; in fact, the civil lawyer begged me to let him drive my scooter around the office. Let's just say no one was hurt, and the walls remained intact. Minus maybe a few scratches. It gave everyone a good laugh, thinking that it was brilliant and that I was a tad stupid for allowing him to drive my scooter in the first place.

Because of my experience that week, and with how welcoming the environment was, I couldn't turn down the opportunity to stay on and volunteer. I started volunteering once a week in reception, and what I thought would be a walk in the park was anything but.

At the time, I suffered from major phone anxiety. I was a 19-year-old and still struggled to call to book my own haircuts and doctor's visits. I would even have a meltdown when my parents asked me to call and book a table at a restaurant, having to write out a script and psych myself up for almost half an hour before I even dared to make the phone call. So, you can imagine the dread and sinking feeling I felt when I realised that being out front at reception meant answering the phone.

At that time, the phone would ring almost continuously. I was paired up to work the front with one of the law graduates who was working as a receptionist while finishing up the practical experience portion of his Graduate Diploma, which is the last study requirement needed to become a lawyer here in Australia.

I was so humiliated and embarrassed to tell him that I struggled to make phone calls and answer the phone. Instead of mocking or giving me a hard time about it, especially at my age, he reassured me that he had my back and that I could answer the phones when I felt ready, and that the answering machine would pick up the ones that I missed that he couldn't get to.

I put the headset on and got to work on what the other receptionists out back needed me to do, but sure enough, not too long after, when my colleague was busy on the phone, the phone finally rang for me.

My heart started beating out of my chest; my hands got cold and clammy, and my brain went into a mix of meltdowns and trying to hype myself up to answer the thing. By the time I got the confidence to press answer, the answering machine picked it up. I gave myself some grace; it was the first phone call, it was fine, I would get the next one. The next call came through, and again I missed it. And the third call.

I was starting to get frustrated with myself; it was just a bloody phone call. Why couldn't I just answer it?

What I realised later in therapy was that, being disabled, the fear of the unknown is exponentially heightened for me. I was desperately looking for predictability in my life, and part of that was being able to control the outcome. If I couldn't do that, avoidance was my coping mechanism.

So, for me, I couldn't control a phone call, I couldn't predict what they were going to say. I also didn't have faith in myself to know what to do with the information they gave me. Do I send it off to be booked in or refer them to a different organisation? What if I messed up? What if we could have helped them, but I sent them somewhere else? What happens if I upset them? What if my centre says, "You stuffed up. We no longer require your help. Please leave."?

In my mind, there were so many variables that could have gone wrong. Anxiety and perfectionism egg each other on like siblings trying to prank their parents.

My colleague noticed my frustration, and he kept reassuring me that it was okay and not to worry. He was on the phone once more when, again, you guessed it, my phone rang. His pep talk went in one ear and out the other, and I was at risk of not answering again. He looked over my screen to see whose number it was. He then clicked at me and pointed to my phone, mouthing, "Answer it, answer it!"

I thought he was setting me up, but I answered the call professionally and calmly. For someone who has struggled with trust most of her life, which is ironic considering I have no choice but to trust people in my personal space, it was odd how quickly I trusted him. As a result, I answered the phone so quickly at his insistence. I took down all the details from the call, as I was trained to do.

When I got off the phone, my colleague asked how it went, and I relayed all the information to him. Which it turned out I didn't need to take down as much info as I needed to for various reasons that I found out later. He grinned briefly before he burst out laughing.

I looked at my colleague, stunned, and said, "You knew who it was!"

He simply shrugged and said, "I knew they were going to be perfect for your first call. I knew you wouldn't have any problem."

I was immediately so grateful that he convinced me to answer that call. It gave me the confidence to answer calls throughout the rest of the day. Did I miss a few because the anxiety was still very much there? Of course. However, there is definitely something about exposure therapy that just works.

Within the next fortnight, I was answering calls left, right, and centre. There was even a day when I answered just shy of 100 calls from 8:30 a.m. to 4:00 p.m. For someone who struggled to answer phones and nearly had mental breakdowns before dialing a number, to confidently answer almost 100 calls in a day was a significant change.

I even had to deal with people who were frustrated and hurling verbal abuse at me over the phone. Usually, I would have just crumbled and started crying. Instead, I remained calm and firm in my tone and tried my best to help them. I got off that call so proud of myself. Even if I was slightly shaking.

I had excuses to throw in the towel, tell my supervisor that I couldn't volunteer, or use my university as an excuse to quit, but I didn't. Instead, I hung in there, simply because this was my first ever job that wasn't football-related volunteering, and I took it seriously as if I was getting paid. I loved my position and the people I was working with. I was determined to stick around for a long time.

It was a breath of fresh air to feel welcomed and a part of a group in such a short space of time. There were no egos; only people dedicating their lives to helping those whom the legal system had let slip through the cracks in terms of support.

It especially caught me off guard when I told one of my fellow receptionists that I went home for lunch every day to use the bathroom at home, because the disabled bathroom at work was impossible for me to use due to the low toilet seat.

The following week, I was called to my supervisor's office. I thought I had done something wrong and that they were going to send me on my merry way. Instead, she said she was saddened that I didn't come to her and say that the disabled bathroom wasn't working for me. I was tasked with finding a toilet frame I could keep at work, and they would pay for it. She also said if there was anything else around the premises that wasn't working, please let her know, and that I didn't have to be ashamed about a thing.

I knew immediately who had told her, and instead of yelling at her and asking why she told our boss, I thanked her. I thanked her because I didn't have the courage yet to advocate for what I needed, as I was too worried about being judged or being told I was too much.

My school wounds were still ever present, and advocating for myself was still a slow work in progress. I was so grateful that I had someone who wanted me not to worry about going to the bathroom, even though we had known each other for less than a year. She told me asking for help wasn't too much, and going to the bathroom is a necessity, and I deserved some dignity.

No amount of words can begin to describe how grateful I was to the entire team at the centre. They even pushed me to apply for a job in the intake department when the opportunity arose. I ended up being given the job on a part-time basis, working a 5-day fortnight alongside the person who helped me find my feet in admin and get over my phone fears.

My job was to call up the clients who had called in needing help, make sure they were eligible for our services, and either book them in with the relevant lawyer or refer them to someone who could better help them.

There was nothing I hated about that job. I loved every minute of it.

One afternoon, while I was having lunch, I couldn't help but let my mind wander and process just how far I had come. From the scared, timid 18-year-old who was one email away from giving it all up to pursue teaching because she felt she didn't belong in the legal world, to feeling like she had a place at the table, who was starting to really find her confidence, and finally grow a backbone.

Then, the honeymoon period was over. I had my review just past the six-month mark of being in that paid role when I was told that they weren't renewing my contract, and that I would be finishing up before my 12-month contract was over.

I asked if it was because of my output, or the accident of falling out of my car and taking three weeks off due to blood loss, or if the major mistake that we were all spoken to about was my fault. I was told that the mistake was mine. I asked why they didn't tell me, so I could have learned from it or even become aware of it. They told me the mistake wasn't the reason, nor were there any other reasons on my part. I was told that they didn't want me to completely leave the organisation as I was a valued and hard worker, and that there was a casual position back out the front in reception, mainly as a fill-in if people were away. They told me there were five weeks of work straight up, as one of the receptionists was going on leave.

I was desperate to stay in the organisation, so I said I would take the role. That didn't mean I didn't feel slightly rejected, my mind obviously started coming up with all sorts of reasons as to why I was demoted. I worked essentially full-time those five weeks, and after that, I had only two or so days before I was no longer called in.

After several weeks of receiving no work, I eventually received an email where they thanked me for my time and said that they would be in touch if they needed me. I was in the middle of the first day of a 5-day virtual seminar with Tony Robbins when I got that email. It almost felt fitting that I received the email then because the next five days of the seminar were about reclaiming the fire, the confidence to live the life you want, and releasing all the things holding us back.

The first day after the seminar, I went to the centre to hand my office key back. My supervisor informed me that I didn't have to leave and that I could instead volunteer in the same receptionist position for which I was originally being paid. I simply said, "Thank you for the offer, but I need to focus on finishing up my degree. I have a few big months ahead to dedicate my time to that. Thank you for everything."

I handed her my key and went to say goodbye to my colleagues, who made me feel like part of the family and went above and beyond to ensure I was a part of the occasional night out or bar hopping. They commented, saying how different I had looked, like I was refreshed and super happy. They asked if I had met someone. I laughed and said no.

My younger self would have had conniptions over the fact that I left that place with my head held high and so proud and grateful of the fact that I turned down volunteering in the same role I was being paid initially for, and I was equally so proud of the growth that I was able to find in my two or so years there.

Everyone you talk to will say that the person they are when they graduate university isn't the same person who arrived on campus the very first time. Goals change, personalities change, and you grow and evolve. Naturally, what you hope to do with your degree and your career aspirations may also change.

I am no different. When I began my degree, I was determined to pursue a career as a lawyer. My overactive imagination had big, ambitious goals. So much so that in Grade 12, I had figured that by the time I was around twenty-six, I would either become a partner of a law firm or be about to open my own firm.

However, by the completion of my degree, I realised that becoming a lawyer and owning my own firm wasn't for me. The combined safety and hours of the job simply didn't work for me. I started taking my health more seriously in 2019 and realised that working in a job that has to be put first on your priority list wasn't going to work with my disability.

After working in the industry for a couple of years, I also came to realise that what I thought the industry was like wasn't at all what it was, and that it wasn't something that I agreed with. The idea of treating the courtroom like a game and essentially treating your client's life like a roulette wheel in order to separate the emotions from the job was something I found hard to comprehend.

Given the nature of being a lawyer mixed with my deeply ingrained way of caring, perhaps too much, I wouldn't be able to sleep at night if I were ever to lose a case because I would feel like I had let my client down. The cons outweighed the pros, and ultimately, the dream that my naïve 17-year-old self held drifted away for good.

Having said that, though, studying law was perhaps one of the best things that happened to me. The person who left that degree was more confident in herself, found her voice and, indeed, her backbone, and no longer felt intimidated in having tough conversations. Gone was the timid little mouse who waddled into class and cried on her first day.

Studying law helped me find some of the pieces that I needed to step into adulthood. Even though I didn't go on to practice, it reconfirmed to me the fact that I desperately want to continue to raise awareness and speak about disabled life and the human rights issues faced by those in the community, and be able to call out legislation and programs that are failing in meeting the needs of disabled people—all things I couldn't do as a lawyer, and certainly something I wouldn't have had the guts to be able to do without my degree either.

I am a big believer that nothing you ever do is a waste of time. That includes spending a small fortune on a degree that may never be used in a professional capacity. If you learn something about yourself, grow as a human being, or also realise what you don't want in life, then spending that small fortune is just as worth it.

There is a line from one of my all-time favourite TV shows that says, "No Apologies, No Regrets." Living with no regrets is perhaps one of the most important things in the world. There is almost no worse feeling than the "should have, could have, would have" when the opportunity passes you by, and you will forever have questions about what could have been if you just took the leap.

For me, I have absolutely no regrets in finishing my Law Degree and even going on to do honours. I never hated my degree. Okay, yes, at the beginning, I most certainly detested it. However, as I continued into the later years, I fell in love with it. I fell in love with the kind of confidence it gave me, and how it elevated my passion for speaking up and making the world a better place. I simply realised that I can do that on a larger scale outside the legal industry and outside the courtroom.

In today's world, the concept of having one career for your entire life is no longer as popular as it was around thirty years ago. Having said that, so many people end up with a career that they hate, but don't feel like it is an option to leave, simply because it means having to start over as a rookie. That must be a daunting concept, especially having to be the "rookie" at thirty, forty, or even fifty years old. We always want to play it safe. Our brains are hard-wired that way. Our brains protect us, or so it thinks, from danger, including the threat of embarrassment and permanent cringe sessions at 2:00 a.m.

I personally feel that when we are ruled by our fear of danger, or in other words, letting our brains have their way with little resistance from the owners, we lose our determination and our drive to constantly be curious about the world around us. We lose the curiosity of what else life could hold for us if we were just brave enough to take that first step out of the box that we are kept in, or feel that we are kept in, either by outside perceptions, concepts, or our own opinions on our life and career.

The saying is true that we spend most of our adult lives working. For most of us, our daily routine is straightforward. Wake up, go to work, come home, go to sleep. Rinse and repeat. If you are lucky, you reach retirement and can then enjoy probably only ten, or maybe, twenty years of it before either pushing up daisies or moving to a nursing home.

My point is: Why not explore what life truly has to offer?

I am in a unique position where having a terminal illness over my head and the grim reaper sitting in the shadows means that the outlook I have on life is rather different. I want to be able to experience everything life has to offer. I want to try everything that interests me, and truly have no regrets when it comes time to leave this world. I also know, though, that not everyone is fortunate to be in the same boat as me. Due to finances or other reasons, they can't afford to leave a career on a whim because it isn't "who they are" any more.

Having said that, why completely stop living and be a slave to a job? Our lives are given to us only once. It is up to us to make the most of it. Finding our sense of self and adventure is, to me, what life is about. When you find these things, you begin to discover determination—to explore more, be who you are more, and simply live more!

Studying law, while a test of mental determination as opposed to the physical like I am used to, showed me what kind of life I want to lead. I want to love what I do and have the courage to stand up and admit when I have fallen short, or be brave enough to say that what I am doing isn't what I want to do for the rest of my life.

You may be wondering, "Rhi, if you loved studying law so much, why aren't you going to practice or even use your degree?"

I know that I want to do something within the legal space, whether it is working as a paralegal at some point in time, or even pursuing a PhD in Human Rights and becoming a doctor and lecturer at a university.

I am beyond grateful for the lessons and the opportunities that studying Law, and working in the industry albeit briefly, has given me. It challenged me and pushed me in more ways than I can count. Because I left no stone unturned and realised that it wasn't for me, I was able to recognise what I really wanted to do and how I wanted my life to be.

I want to be curious, passionate, feisty, and confident enough to pursue and try everything that life has to offer me. And when times get tough, I know I am built like a brick shithouse with a level of determination that comes with going toe to toe with a judge in a district courtroom, while standing on legs that could give way at any moment.

I know I can handle anything that comes my way. All thanks, in part, to a law degree with a major HECS Debt. Who would have thought?

CHAPTER 10

SETBACKS AND COMEBACKS: PUSHING THROUGH THE PAIN

Living with muscular dystrophy is like being on one big roller coaster. You are completely at its mercy; you are tossed around, flipped upside down, and shaken like a rag doll. If you are lucky, you have moments of calm when things are as "normal" as they could possibly ever be. Over the years, I have become really good at enjoying the little things: sunsets, sunrises, birds chirping, hooves crunching in the frost-bitten grass, and heading to a footy game with my family.

I have also become used to the setbacks of living with a progressive disease. I know that nothing I can ever do will make me completely disease-free on my own steam, unless a cure magically comes along in my lifetime. So, I have had to find a way to dig deep through the harder moments, to continue enjoying all of life's little joys.

Perhaps the most important thing I have learnt in my short time here on this earth is never allowing myself to be dictated by the label of being disabled. With that comes discovering what it means to live my own life. That also means enjoying life when it is beautiful and fighting like hell when the setbacks come.

There is nothing more frustrating to me than being treated with kid gloves, which, it appears, so many of us are treated with when we are either ill or disabled. People freak out big time when we mention all the mundane, and sometimes, daredevil things we want to do. It's often believed that we are fragile, like the finest China sitting in a cabinet. It's believed that we should be stored somewhere, safely, waiting for our time on earth to run out.

However, the one thing that living with a progressive and terminal disease comes with is an all-consuming appreciation for life. I don't want to be sitting on the couch, waiting for my number to be called. I love nothing more than experiencing life and pushing the boundaries of what I think I am capable of, like climbing Mount Everest—surely, a stark contrast to what everyone else thinks I am capable of. I simply refuse to be dictated by the outside voices.

Part of pushing the boundaries means dealing with injuries and the times when your body needs a minute to catch its breath. To live, you need to learn to push through pain.

Don't get me wrong, do I always push through pain and discomfort? No. I have seasons when I am in the right headspace to handle the physical discomfort of regular exercise, working with my condition, and not letting it work against me. But there are other seasons when my body will do a U-turn, and I am constantly dealing with lower back tension. My legs feel like they have become cinder blocks, and it becomes about how I am going to get to the kitchen without being barrelled by my dogs, rather than the HIIT workout I am going to do. And that is okay; life is also just as much about learning what your body needs and what your soul needs at that moment.

Injuries and setbacks, I feel, are a way of testing you. It's like the universe is seeing just how willing you are to keep moving forward. At some point, we all have to get up, dust ourselves off, and keep going eventually. When you have a terminal disease hanging over your head, you can only afford to be knocked down for a short while; if you stay down, fear will consume you.

My need to always try to outdo myself is almost like an addiction. I am always looking for the next physical challenge. I find that a physical challenge also tests your mental resilience just as much as your physical resilience. From doing a 5-kilometre walk, speaking at functions and panels, to riding horses. I'm always looking for something outlandish to try.

With that, though, come setbacks. One of my many setbacks happened in 2023, when I fell off a horse. I had been riding for about two years, and aside from a minor adductor tear that healed within a week, I had been mostly injury-free. I knew that falling was always a possibility, but when it finally happened, it still caught me completely off guard.

Around the time the horse accident happened, I felt like I was living a pretty perfect life. I had met someone. I was working out six times a week and was arguably in the best physical shape I had ever been in. I was living out my dream of riding horses each Saturday. It felt as though everything was aligning, and I was so happy. It felt almost too good, and I was just waiting for everything to crumble. I didn't have to wait long.

The day the accident happened was the first ride back in weeks after some pretty horrid weather and halted sessions. As I was saying bye to my dog, there was a tiny voice saying that I wouldn't be home that day, but I just shook it off, thinking it was my anxiety talking to me.

I was nervous on the way to the centre because of how long I had been out of the saddle, and the wind had picked up, which is usually a nerve-wracking combo with horses because, generally, it makes them even more prone to freaking out since they can't hear as well.

My nerves went out the window as soon as I got in the saddle. It was the first ride where I felt absolutely no nerves. Looking back now, I should've heeded the saying, "The minute you feel no nerves doing something even remotely dangerous is when you need to stop." When I felt no nerves, I should have said I wanted to get off my horse. But I had been on her so many times before, and it felt like clockwork, so I was relieved to feel a sense of confidence in the saddle. Not only confidence in my ability to ride, but confidence in our partnership and that she would keep me safe.

What happened was a series of unfortunate mistakes on the part of another that resulted in my horse, who was asleep in the middle of the arena while we were waiting for further instructions, being spooked and raring up.

I wasn't ready for it, and down I fell a metre and a half to the group below. It wasn't a fast fall. I felt the thud of my horse being kicked by another horse, I felt her rear up slightly, and then closed my eyes in preparation for the fall. I engaged my legs and my core as tightly as I could to try and hold on to her side as long as I could, buying time for someone to try and catch me. I felt a hand grab my left ankle, but by that point, I was completely out of the saddle and heading to the floor. For some reason, I, then, completely relaxed. I fell with my head, shoulders, hips, and legs all hitting the ground at the exact same time.

It immediately knocked the wind out of me, and all I could hear was my gasping, moaning breaths. I was waiting for my horse to freak out that I was on the ground next to her and, in her panic, stand on me. But she didn't. She simply moved out of the way, in the opposite direction I had gone. Whether she did it on her own or someone else did it, I still do not know.

Being winded for anyone is terrifying, but being winded for someone with 40 percent lung capacity is even scarier. I felt like I was suffocating, and what aided in that feeling more was the fact that I didn't want to inhale. Each time I took a breath, I had a shooting pain near my back in the middle of my ribs.

My first thought was that I had snapped the titanium rods in my spine. After I recognised I didn't have pins and needles in my arms or legs, I knew my back was fine. My second thought immediately was, "Is my horse okay?" As everyone rushed to me, all fretting, I kept asking about my horse's wellbeing, until someone finally answered that she was, indeed, fine.

The next thing out of my mouth was, "Okay, someone help me get back on. I need to get back on." The thing that everyone tells you about riding horses is that the minute you fall off, it is a terrifying come-to-Jesus moment. If you don't get back on ASAP, you will develop a fear of riding because your brain and body recognise that the last time you rode, you almost died. So, I was desperate to get back on straight away.

I heard my mum then say to me, "Honey, you can't even move without practically screaming in pain. You need to go to the hospital, and we have to call an ambulance." I fought her and the trainer tooth and nail. Like hell was I going to the hospital, I needed to be with my horse.

As you can imagine, complaining of shooting pain in your back makes everyone nervous, so I had to concede defeat and allow them to call an ambulance. Fortunately, I only had a bruised lung and later found a hairline fracture in my knee from when it bent over the saddle while someone tried to grab my foot.

I did end up having to stay overnight in the hospital, not because of my injuries, but because the hospital gave me too much pain medication, and my blood pressure dropped. I, then, struggled with feeling like I had the world's largest hangover; each time I closed my eyes, I would feel sick and then end up vomiting. Anyone with abdominal pain, or pain in the ribs or back knows just how painful it is to be sick.

I got barely any sleep that night. However, being sick every time I closed my eyes wasn't the only reason for the lack of sleep. I recognised how fortunate I was that the accident wasn't worse. Because it truly could have been. I could have landed directly on my head and broken my neck; my horse could have trampled on me, and I could have died.

When you're living with a disability that you know will kill you, you aren't a stranger to contemplating your mortality. But after a while, you just get on with life, and you don't allow yourself to think about death.

Lying there in that hospital bed, with my lung hurting each time I moved, or breathed, the accident replaying in my head over and over like a broken record, I truly felt mortal for the first time in years. It simply terrified me.

There was a stage when I lay there crying, and the ER nurse on duty stood there and ran her fingers through my hair to try to comfort me. She thought it was from the physical pain. But it was the emotional and mental pain of falling over a metre, while doing something I loved, and the thought that it could have been lights out for me.

The following day, I got home, and things continued unravelling. The guy I had met suddenly said that driving an hour from Brisbane to see me was too much and that it was best if we no longer pursued each other, when only twelve hours beforehand, he had told me he was interested in going out again and potentially being exclusive. I was hurt, confused, and angry.

I, then, had other external issues pop up a few months later that destroyed me even more. If I had been knocked down to my knees with the accident, it was now like someone had flipped me over and pushed my face down into the ground with their boot.

I felt completely vulnerable and shattered. Even though in the grand scheme of things, having to take six to eight weeks off riding wasn't such a big deal. But because of the level of freedom it gave me, which we will get into later, it felt like such an important part of my life was ripped from me. It was as though my disability had found a way to take my hobby, something I loved so dearly, away from me. There were days when I couldn't stop thinking about the accident, and I hated feeling so fragile and vulnerable.

Throughout my entire life, my main caregiver has been my mum. No one else. I consider myself so fortunate in that I have never had to rely on any outside help. However, a couple of days after my accident, Mum was called in to work, and she couldn't say no. So, we called in my grandparents to come over around lunchtime and make sure I was okay.

That morning, I ever so slowly baked a cake to share with them. I needed to keep my movement up somehow, and this felt like the safest option. However, at about mid-morning, I needed to go to the bathroom. On a good day, struggling to put my toilet frame over the toilet, pull my pants down, standing back up, and then pulling my pants back on can take a good five minutes. With a bruised lung, I struggled to even get my hand behind me to pull off my pants.

I was stranded. I knew what I had to do, and it broke my heart to have to ask. I held on for another two hours, until my grandparents arrived. As they walked in the door, I turned to my grandmother and said, "Nanna, I need to go to the toilet, but I can't pull my pants down. Are you okay if—" I didn't even get to finish my sentence before she said, "Yes, oh my goodness, yes, of course. You just tell me what you need me to do."

I sobbed as she stood there and helped me go to the bathroom. I kept apologising because, in my mind, no grandparent should have to help their 23-year-old granddaughter use the bathroom. It made me feel like a little kid, which is my pet peeve. However, my grandmother showed no signs of discomfort and continued to reassure me that it was okay. That I was okay. I then remembered she had been my great-grandmother's primary carer for years when she was sick with dementia. That should have brought me comfort, but given my emotional state, it made me remember my great-grandmother, which just made me cry even more. Safe to say, I was an absolute fall apart mess.

At some point though, life continues, and whether you like it or not, you have to get on with things even if you are experiencing some pain or discomfort. For the most part, I have learnt how to almost switch my brain off to pain, resulting in a decent pain tolerance. To this day, all the physiologists I have worked with have mentioned that I can handle a lot of pain before saying something.

I experienced a 10/10 want-to-jam-my-head-into-a-door-to-make-it-stop level of pain in Grade 11. The pain wasn't constant, and at the time, given its location in the middle of my Torso, I thought it was either heartburn or pockets of air. I quickly realised that the indigestion chews were not helping the pain at all, so it was certainly not heartburn or reflux. Because the pain wasn't constant, and in the early days, I would go weeks or even a month or two without any intense pain episodes, it didn't worry me much. Perhaps because I was still stupidly thinking that it was just pockets of air, because the pain would gradually move. Or it felt as though it did anyway.

As time went on, the frequency between the episodes and the level of pain exponentially increased. The pain was like something stabbing me with ten filleting knives mixed with a blow torch. Being a woman who experiences cramps and PMS, I am pretty good at just breathing through pain and carrying on with my day. However, this was another level altogether.

There were nights I found myself slowly pacing the house, and when the pain picked up momentarily, I would bend over the kitchen side and just swaying from side to side, making deep noises to try and just survive through the pain. To anyone on the outside, you would think that I was in labour.

The pain would, at times, then expand and wrap itself around my lower back. I felt like I could picture big hands snaking around my back and then squeezing the living daylights out of me. I always described it as having a reticulated python wrapping around me.

Eventually, the pain continued for so long one evening that I ended up in the emergency room. That's when I was told that it was gallstones, and I would have to look at either surgery to remove my gall bladder or remove the stones. We decided early on that removing the stones wouldn't fix the problem forever, as they will just continue to come back. So, removing the gall bladder it was.

It was the first time that I had something wrong with me that wasn't disability-related. For some reason, I had assumed that because the major powers decided to give me the cards of disability, I was spared from dealing with any other major problem. Anyone who has lived long enough will tell you that is the biggest load of crap. Just because you have a difficult hand doesn't make you immune to other struggles, regardless of whether that is mental, physical, emotional, or spiritual. If anything, living with a disability and being exposed to pain, trauma, and difficult times early on in life, in a way, teaches you tools and a mindset to handle the pain when it comes, even if it does knock you around for a brief moment. You just learn to get up, brush yourself off, and carry on.

Of course, there have been more times that my disability has resulted in major setbacks, from falling and ending with a hairline fracture in my foot, to falling in my room and splitting my head open a week out from Christmas.

My personal favourite, however, was falling out of my car heading to work. I was wearing a form-fitting corporate dress that ended just above my knees. I went to get in the car, but didn't pull up my dress enough, so when I stepped into the car, the hem of the dress dead-legged me. Instead of leaning forward and falling into the car, I ended up falling backwards and hitting my head on the concrete. This resulted in around three weeks off work because I lost a surprising amount of blood and was dealing with fatigue and dizziness for a while.

Perhaps the scariest setback that I have faced in my life, believe it or not, hasn't been disability-related.

In September 2024, I was woken up in the night as I felt something rock hard on my chest. My half-unconscious brain thought, "Is that a lump?", but I knew I was very much not with it and fell back asleep. I woke up the next morning thinking, "My word, that was so strange. I need to double-check that I wasn't just imagining things."

Sure enough, there was a small, pea-sized lump on my left breast. I just stood there in my room in shock. I went and told my mum, casually, about the lump. Even though I was shocked at first, I was still just thinking it was probably nothing. However, Mum and I both agreed that calling my doctor was the right thing to do, rather than waiting until the following week, or doing the "I will just keep an eye on it." thing that almost all of us do.

My doctor made an appointment available for me that exact same afternoon. When she felt the lump, she said to me that because I was so young, it was probably only a cyst, but to go and get an ultrasound just to make sure. Usually, booking an ultrasound takes time, and it's super uncommon to get an appointment the same week you get the referral. However, as I sat out the front of my doctor's building, I called the hospital, and to my surprise, they could get me within the hour.

Driving to the hospital, filling in all the regular forms, and even lying on the examination table, I was calm. I have completed this process a million and one times before, just not for something like this. I also thought it would just be a cyst, no problem at all. However, the sonographer, who turned out to be a distant acquaintance, scanned over the lump. What started as light, conversational banter changed, and her voice then dropped, becoming slow and clear. "Okay, so it's round and solid. It's not a cyst. I don't like the look of it, so we are going to have to get a biopsy done now, saving you having to come back during the week."

It was like a pin scratching over a record. My heart skipped a beat, and it was like time slowed down. I was only twenty-five years old, relatively healthy. There was simply no way in hell. There couldn't be.

Everything then happened so quickly. The doctor entered the room accompanied by an extra nurse. I signed the paperwork consenting to the biopsy, and then the next thing I knew, I was being jabbed with local anaesthetic.

They told me that it may hurt a bit, and not to jump when they took the samples. I didn't even flinch. Instead, I lay there quietly crying. Despite my best efforts to compose myself and shield my face from the others, the sonographer saw the tears and quietly handed me a tissue and placed a reassuring hand on my arm. I heard sniffles behind me, and I knew Mum was also crying with me.

Heading home, we remained silent, trying to comprehend what had just happened and desperately trying not to jump too far ahead to conclusions.

As my dad and brother arrived home that night, they knew that I had gone to the doctors and was sent for scans, but they didn't know what for. I said, "I found a lump this morning, and the doctor thought it was a cyst, but it isn't, and they had to do a biopsy. We should get results tomorrow or the following day."

Dad just looked at me, stunned, and my brother simply said, "Hmm. That's not good. We will just have to wait and see what the results come back with." The one thing I love about my brother (and also find annoying) is his ability to remain calm in any circumstance. When we are panicking or fretting, he will be the complete opposite, almost like a Zen master.

I lay awake almost all night, thinking, "You could have breast cancer. You could have cancer. Oh my God, what are you going to do if you need chemo or radiation?"

I have always felt confident in my body's ability to handle anything I throw at it. Setbacks, injuries, surgeries. I am constantly amazed at how my body is able to respond. I am also often perplexed by my ability to mentally soldier on once I comprehend the situation. I am like a dog with a bone; I simply will not give up.

However, lying there that night, it was the first time I was worried my body wouldn't be up to the task of fighting cancer. I wasn't as strong as I was before my horse accident, as I was in a major workout dry spell, and my family had just bought a business, so we were all living on junk food due to being consumed by work. I even remember saying to Mum on the examination table after the doctor left the room, "How can I do this? I'm not strong enough to deal with cancer. I can't do this."

It was the first time in my life that I ever muttered those words.

Mum's response to me as she held me was, "Yes, you can. You are strong. You are not alone in this. We are with you every step of the way. Whatever it is."

I called my doctor the following afternoon because I couldn't wait any longer. As I waited for the receptionist to pick up, I knew that if the doctor said I needed to come in, I was screwed. I kept hoping and praying that she wouldn't say those words.

When my doctor answered the phone, she told me the results had literally just turned up. There was silence for a moment while she read the results. The next sentence came out of nowhere, "It's all good. You have fibroadenoma. It's a common lump for someone your age. There is practically no chance it will turn cancerous. But we will just monitor it, and if it becomes bigger or uncomfortable, we will just remove it."

It was like breath returned to my body again. I sobbed with joy, not out of fear. My entire family was relieved.

However, it took me a good while to get over the events surrounding that day. I was back to feeling incredibly vulnerable and mortal. It made me aware even more that just because I was disabled, it didn't mean I was immune to cancer or cancer scares. What also scared me more was that despite all my experience dealing with setbacks and bad news, I had doubted my body's ability to handle potential cancer.

The thing is, though, that even though on the outside, people with disabilities seem bulletproof mentally, we still do have setbacks. It's a part of being human—a part of life. Life is about the highs and the lows. It can't always be up, and it can't always be down. Life is a yo-yo, so it is so important to continue to work the mental muscles and ensure that your rebound time is quicker after each setback.

Fast-forward, and the pea sized lump became more of a small rock, and surgery was a recommended option. Despite the positive biopsy result, my surgeon had placed just a few question marks. Which ,when speaking to an overanalyser, whose entire life is in fight-or-flight mode 24/7, is perhaps not the best thing in the world. He mentioned the growth rate, and some words within the original report that made him strongly feel removal was the best option.

Suddenly yet again, there is an air of slight concern that maybe, just maybe, it wasn't benign. Fortunately, surgery was straightforward, with a night in ICU at the anaesthetist's request due to my lung function. The lump, which I had affectionately named "Boobra" to add a touch of humour to the emotionally heavy situation, ended up measuring 3.3 cm x 2.4 cm x 1.8 cm and weighed 7.3 grams. A breast reduction I most certainly did not need! But all jokes aside, that week waiting for either the phone to ring or the pathology report to become visible in my health portal was another long week of my life.

I had support from so many people, so many women who had gone through lumpectomies, mastectomies, cancer treatment—you name it. What was perhaps the most touching out of the entire experience was there was no judgement.

One woman had even invited me to join a breast cancer group, regardless of the pathology. She told me, "In my opinion, as soon as you have had a lumpectomy, you are part of the team regardless of what the result is". She also told me that my fears, concerns and thoughts about the entire experience were valid, as all of those who have had surgery or go through the terrifying wait for results have experienced the same thoughts and feelings.

There is perhaps nothing more important than feeling validated. You suddenly don't feel like you are crazy for thinking, or indeed feeling, the way you are about any given situation. Just by this woman reaching out to me and personally, saying that even if my results were benign that everyone regardless of diagnosis feels and thinks all the same things, especially in those early stages, made me feel so seen, heard, understood, and most importantly felt. Which is all you can ask for when going through any scary or uncertain times.

Fortunately, the pathology results were officially ruled benign, and after another scan in six months time to make sure my tattas are all clear, I will be discharged from the specialist's care. Thank goodness for that!

However, as relieved as I am, I can't help but feel guilty. There are so many people in the world going through the same thing, and not receiving positive news. It almost doesn't feel fair that I am fine, and their journey is either just beginning, or are in the middle of their greatest challenge and setback yet. What I have to keep reminding myself, as the lady on social media so beautifully pointed out to me, I am a part of a club regardless of diagnosis, and I can do my part now to make sure I use each setback I have, including this hiccup of sorts, to keep moulding and shaping who I am. Yes, even physically. Thanks again Boobra for the unwanted breast reduction.

Setbacks build a level of resilience, though you still need to be able to tap into it. That day on the ultrasound table, I was experiencing something that wasn't related to my disability, so it was foreign territory, and I didn't think what I had been through could help me get through potential cancer. However, almost a year later, I have realised that resilience can be applied to any situation. All it comes down to is how you will show up when the going gets tough.

How will you show up when things are stacked against you? Do you just roll over and accept defeat? Or do you allow yourself to feel the pain and then get back into the saddle?

That's the thing about enduring pain and setbacks. So often, in the disabled community, and even at times in the wider community, you are often told you aren't allowed to feel emotions. You aren't allowed to feel angry, scared, confused, frustrated, or sad. You are only allowed to feel happy and confident. What happens when you don't allow yourself to feel all the negative emotions is that they just bottle up within you, and at some point, you will explode.

Part of dealing with setbacks is allowing yourself to admit that life is hard and things are unfair, and learning that you shouldn't feel bad for feeling that way.

However, you also can't stay in those feelings forever. You need to find a way to get back on your feet and keep living. Pushing through pain then becomes a way of life. Sometimes, the pain is front and centre, and other days it's just sitting in the background. Using negative emotions can be beneficial; harness your anger and use it to fuel your confidence and self-belief.

Oftentimes in my life, when I am in pain, in a hospital bed, or uncertain and scared, I find myself saying, "Fuck you. Watch me. Watch what I can pull off. You will not beat me. This will not beat me. I don't care if I have to crawl on my face, I will do what I set out to do."

Saying that to yourself isn't a bad thing. It's an empowering thing. Being quiet simply doesn't work for me; I will eventually die. My condition will eventually kill me if nothing else does. However, that doesn't mean it gets to decide when I do. It can continue to rob me of the ability to live independently, the ability to breathe, and kill me, but what I refuse to allow it to do is dictate how I will live my life, and when I will die.

That's on my terms.

Pushing through pain and setbacks is a matter of self-worth. When you realise that, suddenly, the iconic Patrick Swayze quote in Roadhouse, "Pain don't hurt," will make sense, and you will push yourself harder than anybody else. Because life is worth it, and I am worthy of living a good life.

CHAPTER 11

DARING TO BE BOLD: THE POWER OF DEFIANCE

What does a five-kilometre walk, raising money for charity, a five-week deadline, and a case of plantar fasciitis all have in common?

Defiance.

If you've learned anything about me from reading this book, it's that I love a good defiance moment. But even I might have bitten off more than I could chew when I signed up for a charity walk to raise money for Muscular Dystrophy Australia in 2022.

I was scrolling one evening, as one does, and came upon an ad for a fundraising walk for MDA. It was simple; five kilometres to raise awareness and funds for a cause that hits very close to home. My first thought? "How hard could it be?" My second thought? "Maybe I should've stopped at the first thought".

In 2022, I had been incredibly consistent with working out. I was the strongest I had been in a long while, or so I thought. I had been working out six times a week, doing various weight and resistance training. I felt strong and confident in my feet. I felt as light as a feather, and for the first time in years, I felt like I was working on my disability instead of it working me. Things felt easy. So I thought why couldn't I give this a shot?

There were only a couple of speed bumps. One, I hadn't walked more than two kilometres in one hit, and that was back in high school around 2016, which was around six years prior. The second was that the walk was less than five weeks away, and I had done absolutely zero endurance or walk training in the two years I had been regularly working out. Because honestly, who enjoys cardio?

You can imagine the look on my parents' faces when I told them that I was going to sign up for the walk. Could you blame them? Their disabled daughter just told them she was going to sign up for a 5-kilometre walk with barely a month to train.

To put it in a way that you can understand how big of a deal this was, to the 'average' person, five kilometres isn't really that major, and most moderately fit people can run that distance in forty minutes to an hour. For me, two kilometres was a struggle, so five kilometres was my version of a marathon.

Usually, when you train for a marathon, you spend months training, gradually working your way up to running a half-marathon, about halfway through your prep or so, and eventually running your marathon.

I am sure people spend a good year or, at least, six months training for a marathon, while I was only giving myself five weeks to train for mine.

Five weeks to train my body to do what it had been told for twenty-two years it shouldn't be able to do—walk.

Due to my ego and major naivety, this tiny detail didn't bother me as much as it did my family. Usually, seeing their hesitation would automatically make me go, "Yeah, you are right, I won't do it," because I had a shocking habit of wanting validation and approval from those around me before doing something.

Not this time, it was time to flip the script. So, with concerned and shocked eyes on me, I signed up for the 5-kilometre fundraiser.

The next step was to get a plan together. I had been working with my physiologist and exercise physiologist for about two years at that point, and I had all the confidence in the world they would help me finish the walk, hopefully in one piece. They never treated me with kid gloves; they both threw the 'rulebook' of MD out the window and were always treating me based on how my body responded. They were always in my corner, supporting and cheering me on, along for the ride of trying to make me the strongest and healthiest they could. However, I think I was perhaps pushing the support just a fraction when I waddled in that Tuesday morning, and told them what I had done.

After we all took a moment to digest this new challenge, we started arranging my training. I would walk alternating days, starting at around one kilometre and gradually increasing to around four kilometres two days before the event. That was our plan for the cardio portion and endurance training. In the gym, it was total-body exercises, still with an emphasis on strengthening the legs and ankles, and working the abs to help alleviate my lower back discomfort.

The first few walks were absolutely like torture, and a real wake-up call. You can do all the work in the gym, but if you do no cardio or functional training for endurance, and go to train for something like a distance run or walk, you will be humbled real quickly.

I thought I was pretty fit, and not to mention strong. I couldn't even manage half a lap around the local park, which was about one kilometre per lap of the oval, before I was bent over a park bench because my lower back was shorting out. It was like all the strength in my lower back was gone, my legs were like moving dead weight.

I hadn't felt this level of discomfort and heaviness in my legs since my rehab from scoliosis surgery. Just the mere thought that I would have to do about five laps of that oval in a month sent my brain spiralling, and I broke down in tears as Mum trigger-pointed my back, trying to get it to relax. Along with the weakness, it also felt incredibly tight, which was restricting the movement in my legs.

I honestly thought I had, perhaps, bitten off more than I could chew. However, Mum kept me focused, and after talking about the mammoth task that lay ahead of me, she simply said, "We just need to finish this lap today. That's all we have to focus on."

So, I pulled myself together, put my music in my ears, and tried to zone out. I eventually got the lap done in about forty minutes to an hour. I was so beyond relieved as I rounded the last turn and saw the car only a few meters away. My back slightly relaxed and became less uncomfortable, but my legs had become jelly instead of dead weights, and as relieved as I was, I used my last remaining mental energy to force myself to stay upright instead of falling face-first onto the concrete.

I naively thought that you just have to get through the first session, and everything after that becomes easier. Oh, how wrong I was. The next few weeks were almost exactly the same as the first. I was stopping at benches, in pain and contemplating my life choices. I was desperately trying to figure out what was wrong with my legs, and why couldn't they just get through a simple walk when I could do fifty modified squats in a workout at home.

I was frustrated with my body, and even though it was screaming at me that it was too hard, and I could just pull out, telling everyone on social media that I pulled a hamstring or my Achilles, or something stupid like being too busy with university as my excuse. However, my parents didn't raise a quitter, and I couldn't handle not finishing something that I started.

So, I persevered through the discomfort on that walk and the four walks after that. I had to prove that I could do this, because every fibre of me said I could do it, and the couch was painfree; I just needed to push past that initial mental roadblock. Gradually things started getting easier, my back could tolerate the distance and my legs had more energy.

So, sticking with the training plan, we upped the distance to one and a half kilometres. Once we figured that the problem with my back was that I was, for some silly reason, starting the walk on the incline part of the park, not the flat ground, we changed direction. Things became significantly easier. The back end of the walk, when I was the most tired, was then downhill, and my body was appreciating the change.

However, by Week 3, I hit a wall. I stalled on 2-kilometres. With any sort of exercise, I have to tread a very fine line to not overdo because of the reduced rebuilding capacity of my muscles. I have to pay extra close attention to my body and recognise when it is just exercise discomfort or if my body needs a break, because if I ignore that, the chances of me smooshing my nose all over my face exponentially increase.

I chose to listen to my body. I didn't know what it was, but I felt like I had hit a dead end; instead of progressing, I had to go backwards. At the advice of my physiologist, I reduced my distance for a couple of walks before trying to load up again.

I knew that if I wanted to complete this challenge successfully, what would ultimately stop me was my mindset. If I didn't have my brain on right, then I would for sure give in at the first sign of it being way 'too hard', or for any other reason it may be. I had to approach the challenge differently.

So, one day, when I was aiming to complete my 2-kilometres without a stop in between, I decided to put on a motivational speech called "Why do we fall" by a YouTuber called Mateusz M, which included the speech from Rocky that got me through high school. After the first lap I said to myself, "Okay, now we just start again. 1 lap, that is it."

The concept of breaking down the distance into laps and the concept of 'just one more' and starting from square one seemed to unlock something in my brain that I desperately needed. I was learning to take things a moment at a time, not get so carried away with the overall picture. I wasn't even thinking about how on earth I was going to manage five kilometres when I was still somewhat struggling with two; I was just thinking "one more".

Although my mind was firing on all cylinders, my body decided that it was not happy with the disability-sized significant hurdle it was presenting me with, and instead upped the ante. My feet felt like I was walking on sharpened filleting knives and needles. Every step was pure agony, plus the fact that my back still couldn't hold out for two and a half kilometres.

I thought I knew what pain and discomfort were, but the minute my physio lightly pressed his thumbs into the soles of my feet, I practically jumped off the table. In the two years or so that he had been my physiologist, I never once swore over the pain that everyone knows about when you are worked on by one. I never swore at the glute work, releasing the traps or quads, even though I barely made it through the calf work. I would suffer in silence, the only way to tell that I was in discomfort was by looking at my face or that I wouldn't hold a conversation, which my physiologist pointed out to me one day. But not even two minutes into working through the plantar fasciitis, I screamed,

"FUCK ME!", nearly kicking him in the face from the pain he found in the arch of my right foot.

My physio burst out laughing and said, "I was wondering if you would ever swear. We finally got there. But in all seriousness, are you okay? Clearly, your plantar is not happy, but we have to keep working through it. So swear away."

I immediately apologised for swearing. Even though I am known to swear like a sailor, out in public, I try my hardest to have a filter in my brain. He, again, chuckled and said to me not to worry about it; he had heard worse and even casually dropped an F-bomb. Clearly trying to make me feel better.

Even though the pain of the treatment was intense, when I stood up, the relief was almost instant. Aside from the surface of my arches being tender, my feet felt relaxed. And my physiologist and I both knew that the following weeks would be spent not only recovering the quads and lower back but also trying to fix the plantar flare-up.

I, again, began to doubt whether I could complete the 5-kilometre walk. My original plan was to finish the entire thing in one go, because, simply, that is what everyone else does when they do a marathon, right? They may stop running, but they don't stop to take a seat, catch their breath, stretch out their legs, and then go again on their merry little way. I have always been an 'all or nothing' kind of person, which also feeds into my long-standing battle with perfectionism. If I can't do something the way I want to do it or even how I think it should be done, then I won't do it.

In one of my walks the last week before D-Day, I pulled up just shy of doing three laps, so three kilometres without stopping. I broke down in tears, not only from the searing pain in my feet, but because, once again, I got sucked into my head. It was screaming at me that it wasn't possible, that everyone who quietly doubted me was right, and I should have just listened to them in the first place. Why did I believe it? Because I knew I wasn't going to be able to complete the walk as I wanted and believed it should be done.

Mum swiftly reminded me that just showing up in the first place was already an achievement, when I easily could have left it up to those without MD to raise money to help people like me. I decided to use my legs because my friends couldn't. She also told me that I was doing more than enough, and that just because I might not be able to complete the 5-kilometre in the way I had hoped, it wouldn't mean I had failed.

She floated the idea of perhaps spreading the 5-kilometre over the course of two days. Doing three kilometres on one day and then doing the last two kilometres either the following day or the weekend.

I immediately responded, saying "hell no," that I had people who said they wanted to come and walk it with me, and I would be letting them down if I did that.

Of course, Mum, as mums do, said that I wouldn't be letting anyone down, and that my health and safety come first above everyone, and that it wasn't worth injuring myself if my body couldn't handle it.

I shrugged her statement off, still desperately clinging to the original 'one hit' plan, and continued on to complete my walk.

That night, lying in bed, I had to get real with myself really quickly. I was desperately searching for ways to make the walk easier on my body. I felt that if my back just cooperated and didn't decide to tighten up and become weak, making me work ten times harder to move and stay upright, I could just maybe get through it in one go.

I reached out to my friend, Amy, from the US, who would regularly ask me how my training was going. I told her about my back and feet problems and she had the best idea I had ever heard; taping up your back almost like you are a mummy to provide extra stability.

I went and spoke to my physiologist about that theory. He said there was no harm in giving it a go, and that he also recommended strapping both of my ankles on the day to help stop my ankles from rolling out. Because I walk on my toes thanks to contractures (shortening of the tendons) in my Achilles, my feet tend to roll out as I walk, so having something like strapping tape provide support to my ankle should help it to not roll out as much.

These two methods combined, in theory, should provide my body with a little more assistance, and as it didn't have to work so hard, it would reserve some energy, and I wouldn't get fatigued as quickly. The result: finishing this 5-kilometre in one day, or even finishing it in 'one hit' like I wanted.

Suddenly, it was like I could see the light at the end of the tunnel, and this challenge that I set for myself, which was becoming increasingly impossible, was suddenly possible again. We just had to hold our breaths and give it a test run first.

I managed to get through my 3-kilometre walk well enough with just my ankles strapped, which helped slow the time at which my back would start having issues. My back had improved over the last five weeks of training, because I could manage 2-kilometres easily before it started giving me grief. This was a significant improvement, as during my first week of walking 1-kilometre, my back would have issues at 500 meters in.

I knew, though, that if I wanted to give completing the walk without stopping a red hot go, I had to try strapping my back. We didn't have enough tape for the last three training walks as well as the event itself, so we left strapping my back to the very last training session. I still don't know how Mum did it; she strapped my lower back in rigid tape, and then wrapped my lower torso in a lighter and wider tape to hold the strapping in place.

With my back strapped, reminiscent of the nurse who told my dad about other scoliosis patients' bandages, and both my ankles strapped, I set out on my last 3-kilometre walk.

To my surprise, the back strapping held out amazingly, and I was shocked at how easy walking was with a little extra support. It meant my legs didn't have to overwork, and my core didn't have to try to pick up the slack. I managed the 3-kilometre without any problem, stopping only once, and in record time. I left the track that afternoon fully optimistic and ready to smash the 5-kilometre out of the park in two days' time.

The morning of the walk, I woke up fresh and fully recovered, having been to my physio the day before for a quick recovery session. I spent the morning on my yoga mat doing some light warmups and using my massage gun to help loosen up my adductors, calves, and quads. I had prepared over the last five weeks like I was competing in an event, because, in all honesty, I was competing against my body.

As I sat there on my yoga mat in my bedroom, I looked over the last five weeks, how close I was to pulling out, to saying it was too hard. I hadn't even completed the event yet, but I felt a sense of accomplishment and pride that I didn't let my head defeat me. Even the most stubborn fools will have a tiny voice in their head telling them they can't do things and to listen to what others tell them. I was glad, however, that I told that voice to shut the hell up, and as a result, I was putting the final touches on getting my body as ready as it could be to complete my marathon.

That is when I had my lightbulb moment.

Why was I putting expectations on myself to be like 'everyone else' when the fact of the matter is I just simply am not? Why not just go and do better than my last walk? I had simply forgotten my reason for doing the 5-kilometre in the first place. My reason was that after being told "you can't" long enough, I owed it to myself to throw the middle finger and a big 'fuck You', and prove to myself, and them, that I sure as hell could do whatever it is they felt I couldn't while saying, "Watch me do this."

At twenty-two years old, I should have been dead, and I for sure should have been in a wheelchair for four years. Instead, I was still on my two feet and breathing. I owed it to myself to remove the fear of the inevitable and to show myself that I am still here and very much capable of doing the things I set out to achieve.

Suddenly, finishing in one go was irrelevant. Finishing was the important thing.

So, I made a plan. I knew I could do the first three kilometres without stopping—I had done that two weeks in a row, so I knew that I could do it. The last two kilometres were going to be my personal bests, and the plan was to take just one kilometre at a time after the third. If I felt my body was still as good as gold, then I would just keep walking.

For the last time, Mum turned me into a mummy. Strapping my ankles and tapping up my back, almost in silence, allowing me to just focus on getting my mindset in the right place. I knew it was going to be a grind, with all the niggles on top of my disability. But I had people in my corner who were going to see it through to the end with me.

The first 2 kilometres went according to plan; my body felt good, spirits were high, the weather was incredible, and those who joined me engaged in chitchat about all sorts of random things. I got back around to start my third lap, and my feet suddenly began causing issues. The pain started to increase, and I immediately thought, "Oh no, please don't do this." I knew my feet were going to cause problems, but I was hoping to at least make it halfway through the fourth kilometre before the pain started.

Instead of talking to those around me, I knew I had to get into the mindset and go somewhere else mentally. I had to stop chatting, put in my headphones, and crank up my music and motivational tracks. It certainly helps, somewhat, having Sly Stallone screaming in your ear when you are on the verge of questioning your sanity. I lowered my eyes and found a second gear to get through that third kilometre.

I gingerly made it back to our base camp, set up at our version of a start line, and I had never been so grateful to see a chair in my life. My feet felt like they were walking on knives and tensing up, almost like one major cramp. I told my mum she had to take off my shoes and dig her thumb as hard as she could into the bottom of my feet. That was the only way to find some relief when I eventually started walking again. The plan was to take a half-hour break before starting the fourth lap. I spent probably about forty-five minutes sitting, trying to get some life back into my legs and feet.

As soon as I stood up, the pain shot back through my feet, and I knew the last few kilometres were going to be arguably one of the hardest things I had perhaps ever done. I said to myself, "Right, we have matched out PB, everything after this is gravy. We are just starting our first lap. Just one lap, that's all we are doing." I repeated this to myself over and over, like a broken record.

I completed the fourth lap—the fourth kilometre in about an hour. My feet surprisingly relaxed somewhat halfway through. I felt I had found a second wind and was eager to get the last kilometre done and out of the way. I only took a break for a short amount of time to stretch out my feet and legs. Surprisingly, the tape on my back was working wonders, to the point where I honestly thought if I didn't have that extra support, I wouldn't have even made it to the final lap.

That last lap was a pure mental game. I was so happy to be almost done and counting down the steps to when I could sit in a nice bath and down a big bowl of pasta, revelling in a fantasy where my body wasn't in pain any more. However, despite my happiness, I was in so much discomfort. My legs were finally turning to jelly, each step feeling like I was walking on pillows without the comfort that pillows provide.

As I walked, my knees started to buckle, and I could feel my body starting to break down, finally fatigued. I was only about 300 metres from home. I kept repeating to myself, "One step. We are doing this. We will do this."

I started remembering all the testing I did as a little kid, and the times when doctors doubted me, not really caring I had been able to stand up off the floor by myself for the first time in years, telling me so many times I would be in a wheelchair at an early age.

Suddenly, this walk became more than just walking for my friends and what I thought was my present self. I was walking for the little girl who had been told so many times and led to believe that there was nothing she could do to help herself, that she was essentially a lost cause. I was walking for the little girl who was bullied relentlessly and mocked for being different. Each step I walked, my knees buckling, my back finally tiring out, I made peace with my past, showing that little girl, "I got us now."

Just when I was about to break down crying, my uncle put on the Rocky soundtrack, which nearly made me laugh so hard I had to tell him to stop because it was making my legs weaker, and I was going to fall over.

Crossing that line, I was overwhelmed with gratitude and pride. I love nothing more than defying odds and pushing myself harder than people think is possible, or reasonable, for that matter. I sat down and put my head between my knees, exhausted but happy. I completed my marathon, in one piece, my body screaming, "What did you just do to us ?!"

I pushed through and defied even my own thoughts about what I was capable of, and dug deeper to prove to myself I was worth continuing to challenge the odds, and to challenge my body. Once again, working my disability, not it working me, completing something without it being the perfect ending, but the necessary beginning.

CHAPTER 12

UNLEARNING PERFECT: FINDING TRUE VALUE

A show of hands, how many of us struggle with perfectionism? I am talking about it coming to the point where you will put off writing that project or book, signing up for that class, starting that business, or having that conversation because, unless everything is absolutely perfect, like all the planets lining up (which only happen once in a millennia), then there is no way on earth you can do the thing?

Recently, I have discovered that perfectionism and disability, in fact, work hand in hand with each other. This is particularly true when you place your value in the external world and your achievements. When you are disabled, I find that the value in the external is heightened even more.

Society expects us to excel and work harder than any of our 'able-bodied' counterparts if we want to fit in and 'belong'. Just being average is a non-starter. You have to be incredible. You also usually have two career paths. Either you have to be an athlete and represent your country, or you have to be a motivational speaker and inspire the masses. If you are neither of those things, then you are considered a waste of space 'dole bludger', or whatever else you choose to do, you need to be the best. Like Tom Cruise, he just had to take a flight on the *outside* of a plane — he couldn't just sit in economy like the rest of us mere mortals?!

In my opinion, being born 'abled' automatically gives one a level of privilege and position by simply just existing. This privilege and position are something people with disability have to work hard for, to even just prove that they have the right to take a seat at the table in that office that 'could', and perhaps, 'should' have been taken by someone without a disability.

Let me be clear—when I say privilege, I mean accessibility. The ability to enter a building without planning in advance or missing out on things because you can't get past the front door. To go out without fearing whether the bathroom is usable. That is what I mean by privilege. Okay, well, maybe you do fear about whether the bathroom isn't clogged with who knows what, when you have had one too many Espresso Martinis. But you get my point.

People born with perfectly strong limbs can access whatever they want in town, they can go to restaurants without having to check if it is accessible, they can go to the bathroom and not worry about how to stand up afterwards, or if they can even get in the bathroom to begin with. They can go to a nightclub and not worry about how they will navigate the flights of stairs regardless of the level of intoxication they reach, and they can go for a run on the sand at the beach and not worry about how far back they have parked the car or how firm the sand will be.

Many people I have spoken to over the years have been horrified to learn just how much pre-planning goes into simply leaving the house for those like me. They have never had to really consider all the extra steps it takes for us to go out and about. That, in my eyes, is privilege.

Now, add on 'position'.

Everyone, of course, has a different concept as to what the meaning of position is in life. In a lot of ways, no one is ever really handed things on a silver platter. They have to work hard for everything they have in life. Everyone starts at a starting point, especially in a career sense, and has to work their way up the chain as their experience and knowledge increase.

There is, however, a level of position that is also automatically granted to people who aren't disabled. It has often been said that able-bodied people are held to be 'above' those with disabilities. There is a level of subtle, or not subtle, depending on the situation, superiority that is also assumed, and automatically given towards non-disabled people. You see it in the school yard and even in adult life. For example, no one wants you on their sports team. Okay, that one, we can argue that a lot of us, regardless of whether we are disabled, will, for some reason, still be picked last.

In adult life, not having a disability is almost a subconscious prerequisite when deciding on successful job applicants. That specifically happened to me when applying for a paralegal job. One minute, the company loved my resume and was clear on what they were after and the job position. They felt like I fit the bill, and simply wanted to meet me in person and finalise things. I turned up on my scooter, and immediately, they weren't sure what the job description was. They took me on a 'tour' of the office via the narrowest walkways and said that I would just have to go outside to access the staff room due to the stairs. They also mentioned that even though they didn't have a disabled bathroom, they could just change the direction the door opened, which would 'surely make it a disabled bathroom'.

That was the first job I had applied for where the word 'disability' wasn't included in my resume or cover letter. After that lovely experience, I found myself once again begging the Big Man upstairs to magically remove 'disabled' from my life and my body. I was able to just press 'backspace' and remove it from my resume — surely He could do the same and 'backspace' it from my body, right?

According to the experiences of many people with a disability, they say they are often viewed as workplace health and safety risks due to falling or being stuck in the building if there is a fire, and as a result, employers would prefer to hire nondisabled individuals. When you think about it, everyone falls over and is capable of being unable to get out of a building in the event of a fire. So, technically, everyone is a workplace health and safety risk. Anyway, to save you from the wicked witch, I will move on swiftly!

It is my humble opinion that there is a level of privilege and position automatically afforded to non-disabled people, and therefore, being average as a disabled person is a non-starter. We constantly have to prove ourselves that we can do the job, or simply just deserve to exist.

That is where perfectionism, I feel, is born.

Growing up in such a relatively small town like Toowoomba, I hardly saw anyone like me in town. It was even more of a rarity to see someone who looked like me in TV shows or movies. And when I did, it was always someone who appeared to be depressed and lonely, and ugly, until they became the superstar athlete, or a world-leading motivational speaker, or, even better yet, the character who was in the wheelchair would get up and walk or dance without a problem.

I distinctly remember falling in love with *Glee* when it was airing. I was immediately captivated by the character in the wheelchair. I felt seen, and his worries mimicked my own. I felt as if I wasn't alone in the world after all, and there were people like me doing things that I wanted to do. Like acting, for example. My young heart shattered watching the episode when he had a major dance number and stood up and danced across the shopping centre. It felt as though I had a carrot of visibility and acceptance dangled in front of my face, and then, the creators yelled "sike" as they yanked it away. Which is ironic given the fact I use a wheelchair and walk. Safe to say it took my brain a minute to work through that slight contradiction.

I don't really want to go into a whole debate about whether only people who are disabled should play disabled roles, purely because that then opens up a major can of worms for other arguments in terms of representation in film and television that is best left for another day. However, while I believe in the best person for the role, it was also a little painful for my young self to watch that episode.

Regardless of the lack of TV and film representation, when I realised that even though I loved swimming and could talk anyone's ears off for days, these weren't going to become career paths for me. I became very much aware of the fact that whatever I chose to do, I had to not just be good, but great in order to simply have a seat at the table called 'society'.

The thing about lack of representation and the expectations that society has over people with disabilities is, when you grow up in a world that tries to put you in a box, and usually that box is "be disabled but not too disabled", you don't question the system that creates those boxes and opinions—you question yourself. It warps into an internalised ableism that breeds self-hatred towards not only yourself, but the people who brought you into this world.

That is exactly what happened to me.

When I was at my lowest point as a teenager, I was so angry with my body and my family. I would cry myself to sleep most nights. Not only because I was being bullied, or because I was confused and grieving over the death of my grandfather, but also because I was angry at my body, at God, and at my parents for me being disabled.

I didn't want to admit it or use that word to describe myself. I would force myself to endure climbing stairs, try to walk in heeled boots, and refuse to use my mobility scooter or wheelchair out of fear of being looked down on, judged, or treated as less than.

Because of the lack of representation not only in my own community but in the entertainment space, I didn't see myself. I thought I was an outsider, an outcast, and when I heard the horror stories of segregation and assaults towards people with disabilities, I became afraid. My fear heightened when I began to learn that my disability would eventually kill me, perhaps way before I truly had a chance to live a life I was desperate to live.

That version of life for me was one of immense freedom, experiencing the ease of navigating life without having to worry about whether the pavement was uneven or how I would get into a classroom. A life where I wasn't disabled. To me, that was the perfect life. It was perfect because people in society made me believe that to be disabled was to have something wrong with you, that you were taking up space, and that you would always be looked down upon. That is what internalised ableism does.

There is also, perhaps, another side to trying to find your own value, especially if you are in a wheelchair, or simply are disabled by any means. I grew to learn that when I was out shopping or at functions, and I was either on my scooter or wheelchair, everyone's eyeline was above me. Unless you are all having coffee and eating that second muffin you knew you shouldn't have ordered, most of the population will be standing. When they stand, and you are sitting, their eyeline will naturally be a metre above your own head. Unless they look down at you, you may as well be wearing an invisibility cloak.

Even though my family was always championing me and insisted that there was nothing wrong with me, I couldn't help but mentally call bullshit. If there was truly nothing wrong with me, then why weren't people like me on TV, finding meaningful employment, gaining access to any bar, club, restaurant, shop, or cinema without any worry of the presence of a lift, spoken to like an actual human and not a puppy? Why weren't we valued as human beings who had a right to be in this world?

To me, being disabled meant you were at the bottom of the food chain, never taken seriously, and just there to inspire people to do more with their lives because life 'ends' when you are disabled.

Remember how I mentioned earlier in this book that I disliked being surrounded by people in wheelchairs? I said it was a denial of my own condition. That denial stemmed from not wanting to feel as though I, too, would be considered 'nothing' to society. I desperately wanted to be 'abled' and part of that meant not interacting or being seen around people like me.

Those internalised standards and viewpoints attached me to a level of external value, which then also created a permanent attachment to perfectionism—constantly having to prove that I wasn't 'nothing', that I was human. Abled. Perfect.

I realised that I held next to no value. Nothing I did—or could ever do— would truly be good enough. I had also reached the point where I was done competing with people and trying to prove that I was worthy of a seat at the table. I was turning into someone I didn't like. Everything I was doing was based on hoping that I would finally feel more valued and taken seriously.

And yet, the outside world, combined with the gremlins living rent-free in my head, only amplified the storm of perfectionism. Surviving that storm is as intense as it is exhausting. Constantly feeling like you must prove that there is nothing 'wrong' with you, that you have the right to exist, and you can have a seat at society's table. To feel like you belong.

It's safe to say there is never a dull moment living with a disability, with the amount of drama and difficulties that could easily make for a great *Days of Our Lives* rerun. Add being a young woman, and the storm becomes a cyclone, and the sitcom becomes an Academy Award-winning feature. Now don't worry, I have no intention of rambling about feminism, so we shall swiftly move forward. You can now let go of that breath you were holding.

Trying to handle all of those difficulties of life, disability shenanigans, and being a woman quickly becomes murky territory. If you don't have a strong sense of self, and you have attached your value to external validation, then it can be said that your self-worth is probably at an all-time low. I can say that because I have been there.

Soon enough, placing value in the external and the viewpoints of others begins to feel exhausting, almost as if you are drowning.

I reached a point where I knew I just couldn't keep being angry, exhausted, and with an extreme dose of resentment in my system. I was tired of fighting with myself, and trying to reach a level of 'perfection' that I knew that no amount of wishing or working out would ever change. My disability isn't going anywhere; it isn't like a cold, after all.

And why was I trying so hard to have a seat at a table that was painstakingly obvious I shouldn't and couldn't be at? Why was I taking on board the opinions of a world that would only accept me with 'conditions' attached?

That is when it dawned on me that being perfect was keeping me stuck. I needed to stop orbiting around others' expectations and fall in love with who I was as a person. I needed to accept that my disability wasn't going anywhere. I had to stop hating it and start utilising it and making my life easier by not giving a fuck what anyone else thought.

That was when I used the disabled toilet in public for the first time. For years, Mum and I would struggle to use the ladies' bathroom, both of us crammed into the tiny stall with her trying to help me off the toilet. We soon realised that we were on the verge of becoming stuck in the bathroom due to the lack of wiggle room, and that using the disabled bathroom was now going to have to be an option.

For years, I hated that idea, because again, it meant something was 'wrong' with me. I fought not to use the disabled bathroom. When it officially became too challenging, I was so adamant that I simply refused to go to the bathroom all day. There were day trips to the coast where I would nearly be in tears when I got home because my bladder was so full. My parents tried so hard to get me to just go to the bathroom and kept reassuring me that there was nothing wrong with the disabled bathroom. I simply wasn't in the right mental space to believe it.

One day, we were out shopping, and I had already been desperate to go to the bathroom for a while. We weren't going to be home for another few hours, and I just knew that I would die more of embarrassment peeing my pants than going to the disabled bathroom. I told my parents I needed to go, and my mum said, "How about we just check out the disabled bathroom then, if you still don't like it, we will manage with the other bathroom next time?"

Dad also mentioned how could I possibly have known the disabled bathroom was the worst thing in the world if I didn't at least just give it a go?

So, I swallowed down my internalised ableism-fuelled ego and went to the bathroom. Going into that large bathroom, seeing the rails on the wall, the lowered sink, and the large blue wheelchair symbol on the door set off all the voices inside my head.

However, it didn't take me long to realise that this was perhaps the best decision I had made. Mum and I had triple the amount of space, she could help me up without worrying about hitting a wall or tripping over my feet, and I could go to the bathroom not really worrying about the judgemental looks from people when they saw two women leave a single stall. Although you could bet your bottom dollar that I still was worried about the looks from people when it came time to leave the disabled bathroom.

I left with my head lowered, trying to avoid the gaze of anyone who went by me. When I looked up, however, I noticed anyone near the bathroom was too enthralled with where they were going to really even bother looking at me, and if they did, I decided to challenge myself even more by giving a slight smile back.

When I rejoined my dad and brother, feeling a few kilos lighter, they asked me if it was as bad as I thought. It turned out it wasn't. Dad gave me a high-five and said, "Well done, chook, I am proud of you," and my brother gave me a simple nod and a fist bump.

Sure, the disabled bathroom wasn't the 'perfect' that I wanted and what society deemed as perfect, but it enabled me to just get on with my day. Now, I am at the point where I am so judgemental of disabled bathroom layouts, and just as equally excited to see a brilliantly designed one.

As time passed, my relationship with my scooter and wheelchair changed. They were no longer the things that I despised, but rather the things that gave me freedom to shop hours on end and not faceplant after walking eight hours. They allowed me to get into the footy ground with my family and not worry about being pushed and shoved. They were the 'perfect' things that enabled me to live my life. If I get glances or double takes, given the fact that it would be rather strange seeing a 20-something-year-old in a mobility scooter, I simply smile and say, "Hi, how are you?" Their startlement is something that never gets old. She Speaks!!!!! Who knew??!

Gradually, I started redefining my version of 'perfect'.

By starting to remove the expectations that society has over disability life, I have been able to redefine what value means for me and my life. I simply just don't give a fuck what society wants from me. I don't have to fit their mold because I don't want a seat at their table anyway. My table is one where I am celebrated for who I am, accepted, not tolerated, and allowed to be myself, with no conditions attached.

My value is less placed on achievements, and more on how I show up for myself and the people in my life. Making sure I stand by my values and who I am as a person, and if I fuck up, let's face it: I am human. I will always do my best to correct it and learn from it.

I have found a new appreciation for life, and now, I do things that I want to do, not to prove I am 'perfect' or to try and fit in, but because I want to do them. Whether that is starting a business, going back to university, or writing my blog. It is because I want to do what brings me fulfilment for myself, not what will make others 'accept me.'

I am a constant work in progress; I still have to challenge the internalised ableism inside me at times, and I still have moments where I am seeking outside approval or validation. But being more aware of it enables me to continue to work on it, challenge it, and make sure that what I deem as 'perfect' continues to be my definition, not others.

Turns out, I didn't need to wait for the planets to align and to wake up able-bodied magically—I just needed to stop orbiting everyone else's expectations and orbit around the freedom that I create from embracing my body, my flaws, and my wins to create a galaxy that I am proud to be a part of.

CHAPTER 13

LOCKED DOWN, POWERED UP: FINDING PURPOSE IN UNCERTAINTY

Ah, 2020. The year that is almost spoken about like Voldemort in *Harry Potter*. No one wants to talk about it because of what various people's opinions are on the subject. It is a topic that cost lives and relationships.

For me, even though it cost me so much, it also brought me a great deal. In many ways, I attribute everything I have in my life now to 2020.

Dealing with uncertainty is something that isn't a foreign concept for me. I don't know what my disability will throw at me next, I am constantly waiting and watching to see what will happen. It's like living in a horror movie, just without the gore and awful screams.

So, I should have been able to handle the events of 2020 like most people, without blinking an eye. However, that was far from what really happened.

As information came out regularly about this strange virus that primarily attacked respiratory systems in a way doctors and scientists hadn't seen before, it felt like I had just been issued my death certificate. When the new stations started saying, "It is targeting people with comorbidities, specifically the elderly and those with disabilities", my fear exponentially increased to almost uncontrollable levels.

The one big thing muscular dystrophy continues to take from me, apart from overall body strength, is the ability to have full, healthy lungs. My lung function continues to drop year in and year out. Currently sitting at just over 40 percent, one nasty chest infection could turn my lights out.

I have had pneumonia once before in my life when I was a child. It was honestly one of the scariest times I've experienced. I couldn't breathe without coughing up green, thick phlegm. I had to blow bubbles into a milk container with detergent in it to try to bring up all the gunk in my lungs. My mum had to even beat my ribs, (Okay, that sounds evil.), but more like, firmly pat my ribs to disrupt all the gunk from the walls of my lungs and make it easier for me to cough them up.

Having a weak diaphragm also makes coughing and clearing the lungs a bit more challenging compared to someone who doesn't have MD. This wasn't a massive issue at the time of my first bout of pneumonia. However, I can still hear my mum firmly telling me to 'cough' each time I went to cough. Clearly, my muscles were growing tired of the continuous hacking. My saving grace back then was my age and the fact that I was regularly swimming, so my lungs were basically as strong as they could be.

I knew that this time around, given the fact that I don't swim any more, my lung function has significantly decreased compared to when I was younger. If I were to catch Covid, I was pretty much sure that it would kill me.

Knowing this not so tiny detail, sent my mental health crashing. I told the place where I was volunteering that I was going to stay home and enter a voluntary lockdown. About a week or two later, the entire country was placed in lockdown. My family and I did a major disinfection of our house, as my brother and dad were still working and attending school right up until the lockdown was enforced. We scrubbed the door handles and light fixtures and kept windows in the house open for as long as possible before it got too cold as winter set in.

Staying at home, particularly in winter, should have been something I enjoyed, but it just sent me further down the dark road of mental health issues.

The thing about being stripped of living, basically, is that you get to spend a lot of time with yourself and your thoughts. My head at the time was dark, lonely, and scary. I was convinced that I wasn't going to survive the year. I had never been more terrified in my life. I would look forward to sleeping each night because I knew it was the only place I could seek refuge from the screaming voices in my head. Each morning, I would wake up calm, but just as soon as I regained full consciousness, it was like I was thrown into a mosh pit at a death metal concert.

The first time we were able to leave the house over a month into all the lockdowns and restrictions, I watched as my dad masked up and went into the grocery store to pick up a few things. I, of course, stayed in the car and watched everyone walking around outside in their masks. It felt as though I was in an episode of *The Walking Dead*. I viewed everyone outside as a walking virus who could easily kill me.

I was desperate to find relief from my brain, my thoughts, and the world spiralling into chaos and uncertainty. I felt a strong sense of fear for my own mortality, more than I had ever had before, perhaps, because it was something that used to linger in the shadows of life, but now, it was up front and centre stage. As soon as we could attend appointments again, I made an appointment to see my psychologist.

I told her I was really struggling and had contemplated things that I hadn't contemplated in years. I told her I wanted to sleep all day, eat junk, and my personal hygiene was slipping fast. I was scared and just wanted my brain to shut up and go quiet. I looked forward to going to bed each night because sleep was the only time when I was completely at peace, when my head wasn't screaming at me.

That is when she asked me if I was ever a creative person. I told her about my love for writing as a child and being a film nerd. She suggested that I find a creative outlet to channel all this negative energy into something more productive. She said that perhaps I should try writing something. Suddenly, a lightbulb went off in my head.

For a good two years prior, I had considered starting a blog, writing about living with a disability, and educating people about disabled life with the hopes of reducing the stigma. However, I allowed the gremlin that lived rent-free in my head to convince me it was a dumb idea, that no one would listen to me, that I was too busy with university. So, I never really pursued it.

I told my psychologist about my consideration of blogging years prior, and she practically jumped out of her chair. She suggested that, perhaps, I should revisit blogging as my creative outlet. I was hesitant because I didn't think I was that good of a writer, and, to be honest, I thought it was going to be a waste of time. Having said that, I was desperate to find a way to quiet my mind and to stop losing weight from the intense anxiety, so I reluctantly said, "Yeah, okay, I guess I will give it a try." With that, she set homework for me to go and investigate blogging, and even try writing my first post.

The desperation to quiet the screaming in my head led me to open my laptop as I curled up on the couch that same night. I thought, perhaps, if I could just come up with a name, that may just start to get at least some excitement going, and maybe, just maybe, start to drown out the anxiety. After writing out a few different names in a Word document, the name at the top of the list kept flickering a tiny spark within me.

Living Abled.

I liked that it was easy to remember, and the message behind it was simple. As a disabled person, you are just as entitled to live independently and 'able' like anyone else, and by 'living abled' in your own way, that is when you start to reclaim your life back. It was almost as if that name had aligned somehow with what I was desperate to feel in my own life. A reclaiming of my body, and, almost more importantly at that point in time, my mind.

I asked my family what they thought of the name, and of course, they thought it was brilliant. Equally, they were completely on board with the blogging idea, as they all knew how much I loved to write in school growing up. So, within two hours or so, I had my name for the blog.

As I had hoped, finding the name then sent me on a wild goose chase, researching just exactly how to start a blog. I had to learn what domain names were, hosting platforms, website builders, if I needed a business name, how to register a business name, trademarking, and whether that was a good idea, and how to build a logo.

I was grateful that all of this research gave me something to do, and it seemed to begin to quiet down my head, even just a fraction. I, then, realised how expensive blogging was going to be. It was certainly a costly way to achieve mental clarity in the midst of a global pandemic that could kill me at any given time.

It took me another few weeks of contemplating whether to hurt my bank account and my family's potential inheritance in the process. Alas, the need to just be busy and do something that I could enjoy, or try to enjoy, overruled the extra doomsday prepping my mind was somehow still able to accomplish.

I paid for the business name, even though I wasn't planning on starting a business; something in me just felt as though it needed to be done, just in case. I found my domain and web hosting, as well as my website builder site, within the month.

The next glitch was how on earth was I going to be able to build a website from scratch. I was a law student, not a tech nerd. I had googled how to create a website, but that seemed to confuse me even more. I knew I wanted a simple and minimalist design to avoid overwhelming people who may have vision impairments.

And after many failed attempts and my brain desperately wanting me to just admit defeat and tell my psychologist that there was no point, I found free templates that I could use. I found the easiest-to-navigate template that was minimalist and ticked all the boxes. My creative hobby came to life!

Writing that first blog post was, perhaps, the most panic-inducing part of the entire planning and set-up process. I knew I wanted to do a quick introduction post, and then the first actual post following it.

What to write specifically was my stumbling point. My head was swirling with ideas, but none of them seemed good enough. I tried to write, but would completely delete it one paragraph in.

I was still battling my head, as it still hadn't shut up, and despite my desperation to ignore the not-so-quiet voice saying, "It's no use, no one will even read it. What you want won't happen. Just drop it.", it felt like it was getting the upper hand. For another month, I went back and forth between concepts, with nothing seeming to be good enough.

I eventually grew frustrated with myself and was exhausted from months on end of fighting with myself. I needed to get something down on paper. I thought to myself, "Rhiannon, just write something. You can edit it later." So, I just started writing down a bunch of things about living with a disability. I wrote about the things I needed help with, from the mundane to the embarrassing, I wrote about the funny moments, the painful moments, and everything in between. It was like a mental purging that I didn't really want to stop.

Having said that, nothing really felt like it was good enough as a first post. My head finally flipped a switch and entered into truly creative mode. I started thinking about what people would want to read that wouldn't make them run for the hills due to discomfort.

I remembered that at the start of the year, I went on a cruise with my extended family. It was truly one of the best holidays I had been on. Not only was it fun, but it turned out to be the most accessible trip of my life. Remembering that holiday and all the fun, not to mention the mocktails and the nightclub, made me smile and feel lighter. It felt good to think of something happy, not depressing.

With that, the first *Living Abled* blog post was born, talking all about cruising and how accessible it was.

Posting about your life, especially to the entire world, is a daunting prospect even when you are mentally okay. Sure, I had spoken to countless people about my story, and it had almost become second nature to me. So many thought it would be confronting to talk about my life, but in actual fact, I had spoken about my life so many times that it was like recounting what I ate for dinner the night before.

However, I had never posted my story for the world to read. I wondered if anyone would read it, and particularly what the disability community would think. There are so many conflicting opinions within the community. A lot of people feel as though we don't owe anyone an explanation of why we are the way we are, and that it is up to the 'non-disabled' community to do their own educating on disability. Some are angry and think that anyone who speaks about disability should be positive, not negative. If you are negative, and by that, I mean simply admit that disability life is hard at times, then you are seen as ableist.

In so many ways, I feel that the disability community is a great place to feel like you aren't alone in what you are going through. But at the same time, it can also be a place of great division. That thought alone almost completely made me abandon my blogging venture.

Basically, I was looking for any way out that meant I didn't have to be vulnerable. It was a time when I didn't need to feel any more vulnerable than I was already feeling. My psychologist asked me at my next visit how the blogging was going, and I shared with her that I had set up the blog almost entirely, but I just couldn't press the post button.

Half my fear, too, was that once I pressed post, I would then have to continue writing and start building something that I was worried I wasn't capable of doing. Which is ironic, considering many thought I wasn't capable of the whole 'having a life' thing.

My psychologist reminded me that I was looking at the big picture, which I had a rather bad habit of doing, and should just look at it as a way to simply be creative. If people were to read my work, then that's great, and if not, that is still more than fine. The initial goal was never to reach people; it was a way to simply survive the uncertainty and fear that a global pandemic mixed with a terminal disability brings.

After throwing caution to the wind on the 14th and 15th of June 2020, the first two blog posts for *Living Abled* were posted. Apart from my friends and family, no one really read my work, and that was fine by me. I eventually started to enjoy writing each week. As the psychologist had predicted, it gave me something to focus on. I had even gone and unfollowed all the news channels, even turning the TV off during the day. I had to tune out and be in denial that the world was starting to feel like something out of *Stranger Things* meets *The Shining*.

Writing each week was a way for me to start dissecting parts of disability life I hadn't really focused on before. Growing up disabled, modifying and adapting was out of necessity, which then became second nature. Everyone around me was amazed at how fast I could adapt or problem-solve in any given situation, but to me, it was just what I did. I never stopped for a moment to take stock and pay attention to how I went about life. That was until I was writing each week. Having the blog also enabled me to pour my heart out about wider disability topics like discrimination in sport or in the wider community.

Living Abled seemed to also tie in to my advocacy aspirations.

Within a few months, I started to get the occasional 'stranger' who read my posts. My Instagram and Facebook accounts slowly started growing, and my voice and confidence in topics started to become louder.

Before I knew it, 2020 was done, and I had somehow survived the year from hell.

Did blogging magically solve my mental health issues? Not on its own, it didn't. But what it did give me was something I had never predicted when I started blogging. It gave me a platform to be able to advocate and talk about muscular dystrophy, which ultimately led to making new friendships, appearing on podcasts such as the *Listenable Podcast, Mystic Dog Mama, Challenges That Change Us* and the *Mindful Men Podcast*.

I had always wanted to use my voice to help others, and I honestly thought law was my answer. As I write this, I am coming up to the 5-year mark of *Living Abled*, and I can honestly say that it has given me the voice I needed to lift and educate others, as well as help me make sense of this thing we call life.

Uncertainty can be a blessing if you lean into it, despite the fear and the anxiety. We humans are hard-wired to run from fear; our brains are in constant fight-or-flight mode. For most of us, we prefer what is 'known' and predictable in life, and when there is anything that disrupts the known, we go into full meltdown mode, which can spiral if we aren't careful.

Living with a disability, especially one that is progressive, is all about uncertainty. You don't know what is coming next, what will be taken from you. So, sooner or later, you have to harness and learn from uncertainty. You have to learn to find the lessons, the mystery, and the adventure surrounding it.

I am not saying leaning into uncertainty isn't a scary thing. It's absolutely fucking terrifying! It's like being barrelled by waves in the ocean, you don't know which way is up, and you don't know if you will ever be able to find a way to calmer waters, but eventually your feet will push off the bottom, and you will break through the waves. Even if only for a moment.

I feel that uncertainty is trying to teach us all something about ourselves and about life. Those who have mastered riding the waves that uncertainty brings have a level of determination and steel grit to power through even when it appears that there is no hope. Because it is uncertain, that means that there is still reason to hope, so why give up? It may just be the best thing that has ever happened in your life.

I know that for me, finding a way through it, doing what I could to survive the mental war, has given me more gifts than I had ever expected. I saw more purpose in writing, and what *Living Abled* has evolved into—not just a blog, but now a coaching business that helps others reclaim their lives after grief/loss in whatever form that comes. I feel that *Living Abled* has given me more than a career in law ever could.

And for that, I can honestly say, hand on my heart, that I am grateful for the struggle that 2020 was. Without that, I don't know where I would be today. All I know is that I wouldn't be happy, I would still be lost in a world that wasn't built for someone like me.

2020, thank you, but good riddance!

SECTION 4
Roots of Resilience: Redefining Healing

So now again I look to my horses to heal me, to reassemble the broken parts. To steady my thoughts, which drift and spiral like wandering planets, just outside their proper orbit. That sweet horsey smell, the familiar cadence of a canter, the sound of hooves in the aisleway- these are the things that keep me sane.

—**Paige Cade**

CHAPTER 14

THE SADDLE AND THE SOUL

I have always been your cliché horse-crazy girl.

Growing up, for whatever reason, I was immediately drawn to horses. Perhaps it was their calm nature and seemingly carefree attitude that appealed to me when I was little.

My aunt was, and still is, horse-crazy and would often go for horse-riding lessons, and at one particular occasion, when I was about five, I was able to join her.

It was a miserable, cold, rainy day. Not the sort of weather that makes you want to go and sit on a horse and trot around in the mud and rain. But five-year-old me couldn't care less. And as soon as we pulled up to the property, I was amazed at how quiet it was. Despite the rain hitting the tin roof of the barn and the slight breeze whistling in my ears, it was so calm. Peaceful.

Suddenly, the rain became irrelevant. My aunt had her lesson first and got to decide on her horse. As we walked through the dark barn, you could hear the hooves on the floor, the slight sigh from one that would reverberate off the walls. I remember walking over to a stall and seeing this black mass staring back at me. I was immediately intimidated, given the fact that I was knee-high to a grasshopper.

The riding instructor saw me looking and said he was a beautiful horse, but one for more experienced riders. She led me over to the horse that she felt was perfect for both my aunt and me. An older, grey mare named Trixie. She was a beautiful, quiet old girl.

I sat and watched as she got tacked up, her eyes so calm, both of us having an epic staring contest. I waited in the barn and looked out the window as my aunt trotted around on Trixie, full of confidence, like she had been doing it forever. I was excited about my turn and imagined trotting around, wondering what that would feel like.

As my turn approached, the instructor said she didn't have any stirrups for my height. Of course, why would she? My legs barely draped over either side of the horse's back! As she lifted me and sat me in the saddle, suddenly, I wasn't so sure. I felt like I was ten feet in the air, even though I was only around a meter off the ground.

As soon as Trixie took one step, I felt off balance, like I needed to hold onto something or someone. Because I was so little, and it was my first time on a horse, my aunt led Trixie around the round pen, with the instructor next to me.

From memory, they didn't have a lead rope, so my aunt had to lead the horse around by the reins. I was left to try and hold on to Trixie's mane, as the saddle was an English saddle, so there was no horn to grab on to.

Despite feeling off balance, I was still enjoying being led around. That was until Trixie went to shake the water from her mane and body. The simple act of her shaking was enough to send me off to the side and hurtling towards the mud below. The instructor caught me before I had a chance to leave the saddle completely. However, it was enough for me to become terrified and want to get off as soon as possible.

My second time on a horse, I was around nine, at the opening of my uncle's and his wife's pet store. They had mini ponies for people to come and ride, and, of course, being the horse-crazy nut, I wanted to have a go.

I thought the last time went wrong because I was so small, and that this time, being older and taller, I would be able to simply ride a pony. The strength such a small horse possessed made me immediately feel nervous, and again, the slight side-to-side sway as the pony lifted each hoof as it walked made me feel off balance. There was no mud to land in this time, so I asked to get off, as falling wasn't on my agenda.

I thought that riding a horse was something not made for someone like me. So I parked that dream and moved on.

I was still a horse-crazy girl; however, I would watch equestrian events, read books, and watch movies. Anything horsey, I was in for.

The first time I attended the Australian Outback Spectacular show on the Gold Coast, I was treated to a dinner and show setup full of livestock, with horses as part of the performance, doing all sorts of tricks from barrel racing to liberty work. The show had it all.

The performance detailed the light horse brigade in World War II. I was mesmerised by the performers and the relationships they shared with their horses, as well as the patriotism, seeing the riders dressed in Army uniforms holding flagpoles with the Aussie flag flying behind them as they galloped on their steeds.

Everything about that performance and the venue made me feel at home. The smell of the livestock, the Border Collies sitting on hay bales for photos, and the country music. Everything about it was like a warm embrace.

It had been about three years since I had been on a farm. After my grandfather passed, my grandmother sold the farm shortly after, and I hadn't been near farm animals since. Being at that show sparked something in me that felt like I had found something I had been craving. However, eleven years old is a bit too young to really figure out what that is.

The second time I went to see a production at the Outback Spectacular was around eight years ago. I was about eighteen years old, and just like the previous experience, I was struck by how familiar and warm it felt.

As we waited in the main lobby, which had country bands playing music, the bars full of people ordering beers, I looked to the opposite side of the lobby, and there were two or three horses in stables for people to go and have photos with. As soon as I saw them, my eyes started welling up. I was shocked at how overcome I was just by seeing their faces over the stable door. My parents and aunt told me to get a photo with one of the horses, but I knew if I went any closer, I would embarrass myself and cry. I was also worried that my wheelchair would spook them, and I didn't want to risk causing mayhem or injury to the horses. So I opted not to.

I thought I had pulled myself together. But the opening scene of the show slapped me in the face.

The doors to the arena opened, and the room was dark except for one small spotlight. The music started, and one lone horse came galloping out from the open door, silhouetted by the spotlight.

Out of nowhere, I broke down completely in tears. I wasn't sure why that sequence moved me so much, but looking back on it now, that lone horse galloping around the Olympic-sized sand arena, silhouetted, represented the epitome of freedom that just broke me.

Looking back, I was so desperate to experience that level of carefree, present, freedom that that horse represented, the majestic nature of it galloping, bringing home those feelings all the more powerfully.

I knew then that I was somehow linked with horses. I felt pulled in a way that I had never felt towards anything in my life, even drama and acting. The pull towards horses was magnetic, almost like the universe telling me that they needed to be in my life. I just didn't know how.

After the events of 2020, I had reached a real YOLO stage. I was over feeling like I needed to please everyone and worry about what people would think about my life choices.

So, one day, while I was on a staycation in town by myself, I looked into disabled horse-riding lessons in town. I felt like my two previous unnerving attempts to ride a horse were because I was vertically challenged and not because of my disability.

I had seen Amberley Snyder's film on Netflix detailing how she got back into barrel racing after a car accident left her paralysed, which made me realise that, perhaps, riding could be something I could do, even with weak legs. Or, basically, weak everything. But if she could still ride, and there were Para-dressage riders riding without limbs, then why couldn't I?

The only riding place that did riding lessons for people like me was appropriately named 'Riding for the Disabled'. I emailed them straight away and asked if they had any availability.

I was shocked that I did this on my own accord. Usually, when making any big decisions, I would always consult my parents. Even though I was twenty-two years old and no longer needed my parents' permission or approval, a major part of me still felt like a little girl and needed to make sure my parents were on board with my decisions. Deciding to go ahead and email a riding school without talking to my family first was a pretty big deal. Not to mention, I also didn't spend an entire month over-analysing my decisions before sending the email. I felt like, especially after the previous couple of years, that there was a new chapter on the horizon, and it was one that I was excited for.

I eventually heard back from RDA, who said I had to be placed on the waitlist because there were so many disabled people wanting to sign up.

This was a blessing because it meant I could start training to be able to sit in the saddle, and also talk to my family about the decision I had just made.

My parents are completely opposites when it comes to fears and concerns. My dad is more easygoing and laid back, always excited for whatever venture my brother and I wanted to try. I have no doubt that if either my brother or I went and told our dad that we wanted to jump out of planes, he would say, "What about me?! Can I come?!"

Our mum is a little different; she is a little more reserved and measured, looking at every side of the coin, weighing up both the pros and the cons. If I told her about jumping out of planes, she would probably say, "First, good luck with that, you won't get me anywhere near doing that. Second, have you thought about whether you will be able to hold your head up? Or how you will land because I am sure you have to land with your legs up."

Often, her reservation is enough to really make you second-guess, naturally, because at a young age, we don't really do risk assessments, so it is always a good thing to at least have one person who worries about the worst-case scenario or logistics in the family.

You can imagine how my mum reacted when I told her that I had gone ahead and emailed RDA about horse riding lessons. She was completely stunned. I could see the flash of emotions across her face, ranging from shock to surprise to amazement, to contemplation, and, finally, to worry.

Naturally, she was shocked I had done something without asking first, which was something she had been desperately trying to get me to do since I had turned eighteen. Next, the risk factor associated with riding horses became the focus of her concern.

"If you really want to do it, then I can't stop you. However, you will fall off eventually. It's not a matter of *if*, but *when*. What happens when you fall off? You could break a hip, your leg, or your neck. What will you do then? I am just concerned because of one bad injury, and that's it. This could easily lead you to being in a wheelchair permanently. I just want to make sure you know what you are signing up for."

I am always grateful to receive feedback. Luckily, this feedback was something I had already considered long before I sent the email.

Everything we do in life carries risk. Even just going to the grocery store poses a risk. You can slip on a banana dropped on the floor and end up with a broken hip. For me, even just walking poses a risk—one awkward fall and a bad landing, that could be it.

I told my mum that I had weighed the pros and cons, did a risk assessment, and realised that I was at a stage in life where I didn't want to just sit around any more. The 5-kilometre walk ignited something in me, a fire to see what else I was capable of and give things a go because life is simply too short. I said that I would inevitably end up in a wheelchair one day. *That* is not a matter of if, but when.

It's just how muscular dystrophy works. I would much rather end up in a wheelchair doing something I love or trying something for the first time, rather than do nothing out of fear of 'what if', still end up in a wheelchair, and have regrets for the rest of my life about not trying or doing the things I really wanted to do.

There is nothing worse in life than having regrets. I felt attached to horses, and I wanted to explore why.

My explanation about preferring to end up in a wheelchair doing something I loved made sense to Mum, and she understood my reasoning for giving riding a go. However, for the first time ever, it didn't matter to me whether she understood my reasons; I felt with every fibre in my being that this was the right call for me and my life.

Still, I decided not to invest in my own riding gear just yet, in case riding truly wasn't for me.

The day I had my first ride, I was a bundle of nerves. I had spent ages YouTube-ing tips on riding, so I knew somewhat what to do, but one of the things the videos all had in common was about controlling the nerves, as the horses would also be anxious, given they are flight animals.

I also had to sign a bunch of forms saying that I understood the risk posed by riding horses and that I was aware that injury or even, yes, death could happen. Signing those papers made reality set in that what I was signing up for was incredibly dangerous already, without adding mobility issues to the equation.

On the car ride to the property, I tried my hardest to control my head and, in turn, my nerves. The thing about anxiety or nerves is you can't control it; the only way for it to disappear is to let it move through you and notice it. However, I didn't know that at the time, so my desperation to try and control it and stop the nerves just increased them and my anxiety more.

My brain started conjuring up all sorts of worst-case scenarios, from falling off the minute the horse takes a step, to my horse spooking and me falling off, hitting my head, and getting trampled.

I believed that my horse would somehow be a mind reader, which didn't help my anxiety at all. I was also worried about how my body would cope with sitting in a saddle. Having muscular dystrophy means that your muscles and tendons are short due to not being used, so trying to straddle a horse when you have tight adductors and hips that don't move could easily pose a lot of logistical issues.

As my head started spiralling about tearing muscles off the bone to ending with a traumatic brain injury or dying, I tried to go back to what I knew worked with my walk prep—taking one lap at a time. Or, in this case, taking one hoof at a time.

Arriving at RDA, I didn't know what to expect. It was a simple setup, outdoor stables for the horses with a tin roof, an arena, and acres of lush green paddocks with slight rolling hills, filled with gum trees and other flora.

Getting out of the car, hearing the birds chirping, and the breeze did help with my nerves until I looked over and saw the horses all tacked up, waiting to be led to the mounting ramp.

It took every ounce of me not to listen to the gremlin in my head and tell my parents to get back in the car and take me home. I was aware enough to know that my head was lying to me, but also trying to protect me. I had to reassure the gremlin that I was in a safe space and that I could ask for spotters on either side of me if I wanted. I knew that this experience would test me to use my voice, advocate for what I needed, and be okay with asking for help. However, the first step—getting out of the car—was done.

The walk to the shed, where we would all wait to mount up, was like my legs had officially turned to jelly. I felt as though I was going to turn into a puddle on the ground, like a jellyfish on sand. It was so bad that I worried how I would be able to walk up the long mounting ramp to even get on my horse, let alone get to the shed to hand over my papers and sign in.

My head continued to scream at me, "You are going to die. What the hell are you doing?! I don't like this," as my mum put the hairnet over my hair. Dad chucked the helmet on me, giving it a loud and hard tap and asking, "Did that hurt?", as if to try and take my mind off the fact I had stupidly signed up to sit on the back of a half ton flight animal that kills more humans than sharks on average.

I felt I was doing a relatively good job of hiding my nerves, but clearly, I can't play poker to save my life. The volunteers and riding instructors must have seen that I was pretty nervous and decided that I should be one of the first to mount up.

I could hear my horse approaching before I could see her. Her hooves in a rhythmic time, almost like a trance on the soul. Then she appeared, a stunning, 15.2 hands high, bay thoroughbred mare called Gelly, with the softest eyes that showed a hint of mischievousness. I would be lying if I said I wasn't taken aback by her height, especially being eye to eye with her. The instructors gave me a moment to say hi to her before jumping on her back, and it was intimidating how tall she was, considering that I am barely five feet on a good day. I walked up the mounting ramp as she walked beside it.

The one thing we hadn't thought through was how I was actually going to get on her. Traditionally, you put one foot in a stirrup, hold the saddle as you push up and swing the other leg around before sitting in the saddle, or you use a block to stand on before putting a foot in the stirrup.

Neither option was a possibility for me. I didn't have the strength or flexibility to be able to put a foot in the stirrup and swing a leg over, nor did I have the strength to stand on a block either, as steps were too difficult for me, given my lack of quad and general leg strength.

The mounting ramp provided the first answer to the equation. It gave me the height I needed, and I could use gravity to sit down onto the saddle rather than up into it. But given the height of the ramp, the horse was lower than me, and I didn't have the upper body strength to grab her mane and bend before swinging a leg over. If I tried that, my arms would give out, and I would end up falling off the ramp and landing between me and Gelly.

After a bit of trial and error for a few minutes, we figured Dad would help me sit side-saddle, before holding me upright and helping me swing a leg over Gelly's head, ultimately getting me into the saddle. Throughout the entire process, Gelly stood patiently and quietly, not moving an inch. It was as if she just knew she had to be extra gentle and steady.

Sitting in that saddle, I became immediately aware of two things. One, how bloody high up I was. I didn't take into consideration my height sitting on top of her. What seemed to be a comfy height on the ground, looking at Gelly, turned out to be an extra metre or so on top of her. Second, my adductors were immediately on fire, and my thighs were stretched as far as I could go. The discomfort was almost to the point that it gave me an excuse to say I couldn't do it, and get off, saying, "Been there, tried that, not going to work."

But I promised myself I had to do just one ride before I threw the dream in the bin, so I took a breath and just hoped I would get used to the height and that my adductors would release enough for the pain to go away.

The next part was adjusting the stirrups, and the only way they could do that was by moving Gelly away from the ramp. Immediately, the memories of being on a moving horse without having stirrups to help balance me came flooding back, and my anxiety returned with a vengeance.

All I could do as they moved Gelly away from the ramp was hold the strap that was on the horn of the saddle, and trust that my body had enough strength to at least handle a few steps. The sway from side to side felt as though I was on a boat in calm waves. It felt familiar, and yet foreign at the same time. I felt unbalanced and thought I could fall at any moment.

Fortunately, before I could panic further, the instructors stopped Gelly with the lead rope and gradually adjusted my stirrups. I was sure she would freak out and start bucking. Instead, she just stood there, playing with the bit in her mouth. As they fixed the length of the stirrups, they handed me the reins, and with that, the equation was complete. The only thing left to do was go riding.

Given that I was one of the first in the group to mount up, it afforded me time to just sit on my horse and take in the farm and get used to being on a horse. As I engaged in small talk with one of the volunteers, I became aware of the fact that I was completely fine with the fact that I wasn't steering my horse on my own, and that having spotters on either side was definitely a good thing, and nothing to be ashamed of.

I was in a riding group full of disabled people, of all kinds and severity, who were just excited to be on a horse in the first place. We weren't trying to show off or prove a point. We were simply just existing and doing something that brought us joy. Disabled or not, our horses and the instructors couldn't care—we were seen as human. Something that is often overlooked in mainstream society.

Soon enough, with a spotter on either side and the volunteer leading my horse, we set out for the arena, followed by a short trail ride around the property.

The feeling of riding a horse is something I cannot describe. The power, the grace, the fluidity. As someone who hasn't been able to feel strong their entire life, feeling the power in simply just walking took my breath away. There was no effort to it, just merely moving through the paddocks with a quiet and leisurely pace. Gelly was doing all the work, and I was just a passenger.

What struck me next was the freedom that being on a horse provides. On my own two feet, I can't go through paddocks—the uneven ground and being a toe walker with weak muscles were a combination that would surely end badly.

The last time I was able to walk around a paddock with relative ease was when I was around eight years old. I haven't been able to just experience walking through grass, through trees, and just enjoy the peace of being surrounded by nature on my own two feet in seventeen years.

Any time I have to go over uneven ground, I am always in a wheelchair, at the mercy of whoever is pushing me, and I am simply not in control. Or I will be on the sidelines, and let everyone go off and explore, while I sit and read and watch them have the time of their lives.

Being on horseback provided me with an opportunity I thought I would never have again: the ability to go wherever I wanted, whenever I wanted. I didn't have to worry about how my body would cope with the uneven terrain, and whether I could participate in the first place.

Being on Gelly, my brain could completely switch off, and I could be free from my disability, from life. Even if for only an hour. She gave me more than I could have asked for at that moment. Her power gave me confidence and the ability to just sink into how mesmerising the world around me was. Something I have never been afforded previously, because my brain would work overtime to keep me safe and in one piece.

As the ride came to an end, and we found a way to get me out of the saddle, essentially the same way I got on just in reverse, I had a chance to completely marinate in what I had just experienced. I sat in the car and just cried. I finally found something that I didn't have to overexert myself over, the rods in my spine from scoliosis surgery assisting and keeping me upright as Gelly moved. It meant I could just let go and, for a moment, feel 'normal'.

My confidence grew each week, and I was afforded the ability to really ride her, as the person holding the lead rope was asked to walk by my side, to give the illusion to the horse that I was the one in control.

Gelly thought she would test me by throwing her head down and pushing through the bit, ignoring my directions. As much as I loved her, her stubbornness was too hard to handle, and the instructors correcting her made me feel bad for her, because it was my fault that, even though I felt some level of confidence, I wasn't confident enough to fix the issue myself in the way I wanted to. She and I just weren't the perfect fit.

I was moved on to a different horse, who proved to be the most magical horse.

Hazel was a grey, 15 hands high thoroughbred mare, and, like Gelly, had come from the racing industry. However, Hazel had raced not as long as Gelly, and it showed in her demeanour. She preferred to just fall asleep rather than pay attention to what was going on around her. This was perfect for me because I felt safer with her than I did with Gelly.

I had been singled out by Will, one of the coaches at RDA, who mentioned that he wanted to separate me from the main group and help me develop my riding abilities and confidence. He saw something in me that I couldn't see in myself just yet. He got me riding around bales in the arena, first with his guidance with the lead rope, and then shortly after he removed the rope, it was up to me to direct Hazel in the direction I wanted her to go.

This proved to be a challenge, as she too decided that she would ignore me and go wherever she wanted. I couldn't even get her to walk straight.

I started to really doubt my strength, but one conversation with Will changed everything. He told me, "Hazel is testing you. She is seeing if you will woman up and be the boss. She wants and needs you to be the boss in the relationship, so show her."

I was nervous about hurting her, even though my full strength on the reins would have been like a soft breeze to her. Will assured me I couldn't hurt her. I was 46 kilograms, she was half a ton. I had to find my confidence and believe that, despite being disabled, I was capable of steering half a ton.

I whispered to her, "You have to work with me, please. We need to be a team."

As if by magic, the next walk through the barrels, she was perfect. I had no lead walkers, no spotters. It was truly just me, my horse, and the barrels. This was the moment I knew I had found the missing link in my life.

I found something I knew I could do, and I was surrounded by people who were willing to invest their time in me and wanted to see me succeed.

During my time at RDA, I also rode Kegs after an unlucky fall off Hazel, which saw me hospitalised for a night, not due to injury but a reaction to the pain medication. I spent six weeks off with a hairline fracture in my knee and a bruised lung.

When I returned to riding, I was told that in the weeks since the accident, Hazel had started showing signs that something wasn't right. The vets found that she was beginning to go blind. Mind you, this wasn't a contributing factor to my accident. She got kicked by another horse, and she spooked, reared, and off I went. Nothing more than a freak accident.

Riding Kegs was like being on a completely different machine. I thought Hazel and I worked well, but Kegs and I were a team. The gelding was bombproof. You could tell if something concerned him, but he stayed rock solid, as if he knew he had precious cargo on board. Each time I rode him, my confidence in riding and myself was regained in the saddle.

I never took one ride for granted. It was my happy place, my safe haven. I cherished the feeling of freedom, the power of the horse beneath me, never getting old.

With something as simple as riding a horse, I found the piece that had just completed my complex Rubik's cube of life. I was able to be myself without any apology. On the land and horseback, I was finally free.

CHAPTER 15

BACK TO THE LAND

Growing up, my grandparents on my father's side (my grandma and her second husband, Bert, whom I still call Grandpa) owned several hobby farms in my young life. When I was a toddler, they had a property just down the Great Dividing Range, shortly after they moved to acreage just out past Toowoomba. They had several heads of Dexter cattle, chickens, a duck called Mildred, a goose called George, a white Persian cat called Kahlua (yes, like the alcohol), and a dingo-cross called Wal. Their farm was bustling with life, full of energy, and there was never a dull moment.

The farm was like a sanctuary for my grandfather, a Vietnam veteran dealing with the beast of PTSD. However, he made sure never to show his struggles to us grandkids. If there were days when his PTSD was bad he would stay in bed, Grandma would just say that he was sleeping in from baling hay into the evening the day before, before grabbing a bowl and his muesli from out of the cupboard, ready for when he came out.

I never thought much of it at all; I was just happy to be at their farm, eager to explore and cattle watch.

Because my condition was super slow to progress in those early years, it meant that I could run around the farm and climb through the green cattle crush. It didn't matter to me that I couldn't climb to the top of the crush, like my cousins; I just loved being out in the paddocks.

I was also a sook and precious about getting new clothes ruined. When I was about two or three years old, I was given gumboots and was excited to wear them out to the farm. As soon as my grandfather saw them, he immediately said, "Oh, let's go find manure and christen them! Standing in cow manure will make you grow." I was horrified at the thought of 'ruining' my new boots, and I sure kicked and screamed when he picked me up and stood me right in the middle of a fresh batch. I still have a photo of that moment that, looking back, makes me laugh.

There were times when we would all be busy, pitching in as an entire family to bale hay. When my brother and I would stay over, we would help with feeding the cattle or putting scraps together for the chickens. Then there were the moments that were still and peaceful. At 5:00 p.m. precisely, it would be smoko time, and my brother and I would be given a can of Coke to share and a small handful of plain chips each while watching ABC Kids downstairs. Meanwhile, Grandma and Bert would have a glass of wine with some nuts while watching the evening news.

There were times when I would slowly waddle out through the backyard and to the gate leading into the first paddock. On the right was Grandma's pride and joy, what we kids affectionately called the 'Fairy Garden'. She had and still has a big green thumb, and her garden is like her sanctuary. The fairy garden was full of different plants, flowers, and trees of all sizes. The flora was expertly placed around a gravel pathway throughout the garden, and in the middle was a small wooden table and chairs with an umbrella in the middle. We didn't really need the umbrella, as the gumtrees provided a green canopy over the table, almost giving the garden a magical quality to it, hence why it's called the Fairy Garden.

To the left, you would look up to the main shed and the chicken coop, with a mulberry tree in the pen. My brother and cousins would regularly pick fruit from it with Grandma when it was in season, with Bert nearby with a shovel in case of a snake.

The entire property was peaceful, the road nearby was quiet, the only sounds being the cattle gently mooing to each other, the birds in the birdbath chirping and splashing about, the hens silently milling about with the occasional cluck, and the breeze filling the void or carrying my grandfather's booming voice though the air when it was windy enough.

The thing about being on the land I cherished the most was that even though I was too little and physically challenged to do all the heavy work, I was never encased in bubble wrap. If I wanted to go to the cattle crush with my cousins, I could, and if I wanted to sit and play *Tomb Raider* on the original PlayStation next to my grandfather, I could.

I was treated like the rest of my cousins, and out on the farm, I was treated no differently. To this day, I am not sure whose insistence that was. Whether it was my grandfather's, grandmother's, or parents'.

Just like everyone else, I was prone to scoring a few injuries, mainly from being run over by my cousins when they decided to turn the garage or patio into a racetrack with the toy Jon Deer tractors. Or when I tried to get up a step, thinking I could be clever and not hold onto anything for balance, and fell backwards. I was also allowed to sit on my grandfather's lap on the odd occasion, and drive the slasher, with the blades not working, of course, much to the dismay of my mother.

There was something about being on the land that felt comforting, like being wrapped in a peaceful hug. I felt at home, and the smell of cattle was like a bottle of the finest perfume to me. Each time we would go on school trips and drive past cattle yards, or cattle trucks, everyone would be gagging at the smell, but not me. I would be inhaling it like I was smelling potpourri.

I also strangely felt the most seen on that farm. My thoughts and feelings were taken seriously by my grandfather, even at only six or seven years of age. There was a time when a calf was born, and everyone was naming him 'Yum Yum'. When I asked why, being on a cattle farm, there was only one clear answer. Bear in mind, the cattle weren't raised for meat; they were raised to provide my grandfather with a sort of comfort and to keep him busy. But they were used as meat on the odd occasion (twice that I can recall).

It sounded brutal to my little ears; I was heartbroken and ran outside crying. I didn't know whether to believe them or not.

As I sat silently crying on the patio overlooking the paddocks and seeing little 'Yum Yum' happily walking around, I heard the back door creak open, and long, striding, calm steps behind me. My grandfather quietly sat down on the chair next to me and asked me what was wrong. I told him I didn't like the name Yum Yum, and that he was too cute to be eaten. He asked me what name I thought would be better for the tiny, jet black calf. I looked at him and simply said that I didn't know, but anything was better than Yum Yum.

It felt like, for the longest while, both of us sat in silence, watching the sun set. My grandfather broke the silence by apologising to me, and saying he didn't mean to make me upset, and that, while he couldn't promise me that the calf wouldn't eventually become dinner, he promised me that he wouldn't call the calf, Yum Yum. He said that it was a beautiful thing that I cared so much and that he was proud of me. With that, he stood up, gave me a kiss on the head and a slight smile, and walked back inside.

There was something about him that was unlike anything else. He treated his step-grandkids as his own, never referring to us as his 'step grandies'. Always his 'grandies'.

While he had days when he struggled, and he was often cut and dry, he always treated us with a softness and a kindness that was the polar opposite of his tough exterior. Oftentimes, when he had a scratchie on the fridge, he would bring over a silver coin for me and him, and we would sit on his favourite chair in the living room and scratch it together.

Beneath the softness, there was a resilience and determination that I had never seen before in my younger years.

When he became sick with cancer, he never once complained, or, at least, never in front of us. He would get on with the job at hand, even if he had to take a minute to rest first. He always made sure Grandma was okay. I knew that, being an army veteran, there was already a fight and stubbornness instilled in him from when he couldn't refuse an order and had to show up even on the days he didn't want to. However, I didn't realise the depth of that fight and stubbornness until the last week or two of his life.

He had sold off his cattle before he got too sick, making sure that Grandma didn't have to worry about a thing. Their other farm animals had already passed over the rainbow bridge, apart from the grumpy white Persian.

I watched as he was helped from his chair for the last time, into a hospital bed in the middle of the living room. The view perfectly looked out onto this farm, exactly where he wanted to be. Not in a stale hospital room. He was adamant that he wanted to be at home. He didn't know that I was peeking around the corner, watching as my dad and grandma helped him up. I must have made a noise because Dad saw me and said, "Go downstairs, chook. We will call you back up in a minute."

Later, when I was allowed to return to the living room, I went straight over to him. He asked me about my day, the exhaustion of the short journey from the recliner to the bed in his eyes mixed with the slight yellow of jaundice. To all the adults in the room, they all knew time was definitely our enemy. To me, he was still the same person, joking, smiling, caring.

The last phone call was a few days before my birthday. At a certain point, I was no longer able to go out and see him, probably his way and my parents' way of making sure my memories of him were positive, and not to traumatise me for life.

We spoke about riding the tractor the next time I visited, and he said that he would help me climb to the top of the cattle crush. He ended the phone call, wishing me a happy birthday as it was two days away, telling me to be good for Grandma and my parents, and saying that he loved me very much. That was the last time I spoke to him.

The day of my eighth birthday, I was having a party as it was on a Sunday, and I remember being so excited because I felt like I was becoming a grown-up.

Before the party started, Mum and Dad raced out to the farm to see my grandfather. He couldn't speak, taking small breaths but very, very aware despite being exhausted. Clearly, both my parents, as well as he, knew that he didn't have much longer with us on the earth.

As Mum said goodbye and went to leave, she whispered to him, "It is okay. She will understand. She will be fine." She was saying that if he had to go on my birthday, that was okay, and that I would, in time, understand. He grabbed her hand, looked her in the eyes with a steel-like gaze, and slowly shook his head.

He made the decision months prior that he would make it through all of his grandkids' birthdays, that he wouldn't make his death our cross to bear as we were all so young—the oldest only ten years old. He got through every single one, and mine was the very last he had to get through. He was determined with every ounce of his being. He was not going anywhere until he got through my birthday.

So, for those twelve hours, like he did his entire cancer battle, he fought like a son of a bitch. There are simply no other phrases that would do that battle justice. The thing about my grandfather was that if he made a promise or decision, he saw it through, no matter how difficult it was. He lay there, with grandma by his side, using every single last bit of energy he had to just make it through. If he was going to go, it was going to be in his way, on his terms. No ifs, buts, or maybes. Cancer robbed him of so much, and he was damned if it took his last promise away.

On the 30th of July 2007 at 4:20 a.m., as the sun started rising, he became a guardian angel. Not only did he make it past my birthday, he made it an extra four hours just to be on the safe side. Like an extra 'fuck you' to cancer.

The farm after that was quiet, incomplete. Without the animals and him, it was just grass and some trees. A shell of its former glory.

My grandmother sold the property to her stepdaughter shortly after Christmas of 2007. That was the last time I had been on farm land.

In the years that followed, I was a mess.

As I explained earlier in this book, I was dealing with accepting and comprehending my own battle, bullies, and major self-worth issues. On top of it all, I was secretly dealing with anger and resentment like I had never felt before. I was angry at my grandfather for leaving when he did. Even though he didn't leave on my birthday, my birthday each year felt heavy, sombre, and bittersweet. It was tainted with an event I was desperate to forget, but was unable to. I would scream and curse at him, asking why he did this to me. As selfish as it was, I felt like he robbed me of happiness.

I was stuck in a grief spiral, unable to accept or find peace in his passing. That was until the day, a few years ago, when Mum pulled out the journal she had kept that year. She read out to me the entry she wrote the day of his passing. When she told me about the fight he endured to not leave on my birthday, and how poorly he was, I immediately felt so guilty. That night, I sobbed and begged for his forgiveness. What I thought was the most horrible thing in the world that he did, in one second, became the best gift anyone could have given me.

Even though I had that revelation, I still felt lost. There was a void within me that couldn't be filled. Regardless of what I did to fill it, nothing seemed to work. I was desperate to find peace; the weight of his passing, in combination with my own battle, was slowly drowning me. As much as I tried, I just couldn't reach the other side.

That was until I told my psychologist, one day, in 2022 about learning to ride horses. I told her I wanted to actually understand horses instead of just jumping on their backs for an hour each week. She had just received a brochure for an Equine and Animal Assisted therapy business that was just about to open outside of town, and it sounded just up my alley. I took a copy of the brochure and called the owner.

A couple of weeks later, and for the first time in over fourteen years, I was back on a farm, with rolling hills, and animals in abundance.

As soon as I opened that car door, something unlocked within me. The peace was familiar. The sounds were not cows this time around; instead, they were replaced with the sighing and neighing of horses, the birds in the trees gently singing along. The breeze, the gates with the same horseshoe locks—it was as if, in the blink of an eye, I was back to where I felt most comfortable. The thing I was desperately searching for.

Peace.

Working with horses has given me a sense of connection back to a time in my childhood that made me feel the safest. It has given me a connection back to my grandfather. Whenever I step foot in paddocks, hang out with cattle, and even feel the breeze, it is like he is with me at that moment. Immediately, I feel like everything is going to be okay. One conversation with my psychologist led me not only to find what makes me whole, but to find myself, and, perhaps, my grandpa in the fields once again.

CHAPTER 16

ROOTED IN NATURE: FINDING MYSELF AGAIN IN THE COUNTRYSIDE

Everyone has some level of baggage, trauma, skeletons, whatever you want to call it, in their closets that require some level of organisation and compartmentalisation, especially if they are unwilling to work on their seasonal closet clear out.

When I first arrived at equine-assisted therapy, my psychologist originally sold it to me as a place where I could learn more about horsemanship. At the time, I was interested in working in stables and just becoming more aware of the half-ton majestic animals that I was riding weekly.

Perhaps she mentioned the therapy part, but all I heard was horses, and I blanked out after that. My head was filled with possibilities, dreams of driving around stables in my mobility scooter at the crack of dawn in early winter, the deep, relaxing sounds of the horses breathing, the steam of their breath visible in the air. The thought of working so closely with them had me full of butterflies.

However, never in a million years did I expect the soul-searching journey that is embarked on once you decide to let horses become a part of your life.

I thought I had done a lot of work on my mental state in the past, especially after my near-suicide attempt. Looking back now, the work I had done was to build up walls to ensure no one, or thing, could ever hurt me again. I had moved on from my grandfather's passing, or so I had thought. In truth, I only buried the feelings of anger, hurt, resentment, and fear that came with life with a disability. In short, the only work I had done was put a band-aid over an open wound that actually required TLC, proper acknowledgment, and healing.

The thing about working with horses is that it isn't a matter of just showing up, smiling, and telling them what to do. If you think they will simply lower their heads and do what you want, then you're in for an awakening.

Horses require and demand much more respect and honesty. They don't tolerate bullshit and fakeness. They know when you are bullshitting yourself, and being fake with yourself. If you aren't real with yourself, or in other words, have not worked on the skeletons in your cupboard, they will know and won't have any interest in working with you.

Nobody told me that I had to almost become Yoda the first time I went out to equine therapy. To be honest, even if they had, I, again, would have ignored them.

In the first few sessions, I was with a group. We spent time with all sorts of animals, starting off with the smaller cuddly creatures: dogs, cats, and guinea pigs. Each week, we were asked what we wanted to work with, and being the older one in the group, I made the decision that I was going to just go with the flow. Or more so, I didn't want to upset anyone, so even though I desperately wanted to work with the horses because that is what I was there for, I let everyone else decide.

It wasn't until a good month or so later that we first worked with the horses. I spoke up a big game about how I rode horses, and when asked if I could handle the full-sized horses rather than the minis, I confidently replied, "Sure. No problem at all."

Being on their backs is one thing; being eye-to-eye with them is a completely different kettle of fish.

In this particular session, the aim was to teach a horse named Jatz Crackers to pick up a ball with a rope attached to it. I was lucky, in that he is a mouthy horse and will pick up practically anything, and he had already taken to picking up the ball. The exercise was more for us to get used to working with horses and the clicker training technique.

There is something intimidating about being on eye level with horses, especially the first few times you are around them. Their size, their strength, the hooves that could break your feet. For someone with mobility issues, who just needs a breeze of wind to pick up to be on the floor, being around a free-spirited brick of an animal immediately made me feel vulnerable and uneasy.

My big-talking game quickly flew out the window, and timid little mouse Rhi made her presence very well known. I realised that I needed to eat some humble pie and once again compromise on the reality that was in front of me, and not the perfect picture painted in my head of easily working and standing alongside these creatures I felt so attached to.

My coach, Hayley, said that I could easily stand under the threshold of one of the training rooms, and Jatz could poke his head in the door to get the treats from my hand. As much as he wanted to, there was no way he could fit through the door, so the room was my boundary, my safe space, and I could take a step back if I felt like he got too close.

Standing in the door meant I also had something to grab hold of for extra balance and a way to reassure my mind that I was going to be able to stay on my feet, even though my rational mind knew that, if he wanted to,

Jatz could still bump his nose in my chest and no amount of holding onto a door will help me. Luckily, I survived the session with both feet never becoming horizontal.

I hated feeling stupid or not knowing what I was doing, and I also wanted to contribute to any horse-related conversation, so I spent all my free time researching horse behaviour, riding tips, and anything equestrian I could get my hands on.

In one particular session, my coach was talking about a barrel racer named Amberly Snyder, who was paralysed, and how she managed to get back to riding after her accident. I had just seen the movie about her that week and jumped at the chance to geek out over her. Later, Hayley was speaking about other interesting things about horses, and instead of listening, I said, "Oh yeah, I have heard about that," and proceeded to word-vomit again.

In the car, after the session, Mum said to me, "You know you don't have to impress her. Or anyone here. Hayley wants to teach you and impart her knowledge. When you say you know, you are slightly coming across as perhaps a little arrogant. Just remember, you haven't been around horses all that long; she is expecting you not to know everything. And that is completely okay. Being teachable is a brilliant and valuable thing. My hope for you is that you will eventually feel comfortable enough that you feel like you can just be you, and not have to try and impress anyone."

At the time, I didn't realise what she was talking about. I was frustrated and, at the same time, embarrassed that I came across as arrogant or even maybe rude. As a major people pleaser, I couldn't stand the thought of someone being upset with me, or me being rude to them.

For the next week, I would wake up and cringe. However, something in me was struggling to comprehend why I was desperate to impress and why I struggled to be teachable. Every time I tried to figure it out, I immediately became frustrated and angry, and instead of wondering why I felt those things, I just closed the door and thought about something else. Avoidance in its finest form.

A few months later, what I came to know about myself and horses flipped on its axis.

Hayley recommended that, instead of group sessions, I move to individual sessions as she felt like I could benefit from them. That way, I could guarantee working with horses, as some people in my group hated them and preferred the smaller, cuddly creatures.

As you could expect, I was beyond excited at the prospect of being able to work so closely with the horses. However, I was equally shitting myself, as I was still getting used to being around them on the ground. Surprisingly, I was more comfortable on their back than eye to eye. Something I would discover later was for a reason that I didn't expect.

My first time lunging a horse was with a mini pony called Chicky. She is a full diva, and lets you know she thinks she is God's gift to the human world, but, my word, she is absolutely gorgeous. White, fringe for days, and the cutest little legs that move a mile a minute to keep up with you.

I had her on a long line and was trying to lunge in the sand, which, for me, was a sure way to end up with a sand burn on my forehead, so I opted to sit on a seat instead. Trying to move a horse that was connected to a long line around me, with my added poor range of mobility in my shoulders and arms, resulted in my getting caught up trying to bring the rope around the back of my head.

The feelings of embarrassment and anger were beginning to make themselves known. I didn't want to appear incompetent, even if I was a complete rookie. To me, being incompetent and a rookie were no-go zones. I was desperate to appear capable, in control.

A few weeks later, Hayley suggested going to the round yard in the bottom paddock. Whenever we would go to the round yard, I would be driven down to the paddock by my Mum, to save me trying to navigate the hilly and uneven terrain that the paddock became as horses walked on it. While we would make our way down to the round yard, Hayley would go and grab a horse for me to work with. They were her horses, and I trusted in her ability to pick whichever she felt I could and needed to work with.

On this particular day, as I waited by the pen, my heart leapt into my mouth, a mix of panic and awe. Down came a black and white Clydesdale mix. His broad frame and head morphed into one when looking at him head-on. The white feathering along his feet swayed gracefully with each step he took.

I knew immediately which horse this was. I would pet him through the open windows of the training room when we would be in there for group sessions. It was Larry. I couldn't believe that Hayley thought of all horses for me to work with, that a broad, incredibly strong Clydesdale Mix was a good idea.

She had thoroughbreds, quarter horses, mini horses and mini ponies, and yes, Clydesdale mixes. And out of all of those, she had to pick the largest horse of the herd. My legs turned to jelly, and I could barely stand upright, the uneven ground and the breeze not working in my favour.

The task was simple: stand in the middle of the arena, send energy, and the horse will walk around you. That is the basic definition of lunging.

However, it became quickly obvious that my mind was more focused on not falling over than trying to connect with Larry. Even with a large blue drum to hold on to as a barrier between me and him, it wasn't doing much to aid in calming my mind and my body.

Hayley never left my side, and even got Larry started for me. I just had to keep the momentum going, which, as you could expect, didn't go well.

Leaving the session, there was a heaviness on my chest, and I had to blink rapidly to fight away the tears. Lunging and working on the ground was something I had dreamt of doing for years, and my dream once again wasn't a walk in the park.

I thought that, after twenty-two years, I would be able to compromise and accept that I would have to go about things differently. As hard as I tried, I just couldn't shake it from my mind. The anger at my body and the world still lingered.

To this day, I am still unsure what it was that got me to compromise. Whether it was one of many firm conversations I had with myself or the gentle, encouraging conversations with Hayley, something flipped a switch in me to get me to approach lunging differently.

It ignited something in me that even during walking training, I still had to find and utilise. The sheer will, grit, and stubbornness to achieve the thing I was desperate to achieve, regardless of how I would have to go about it. I was going to do it one way or another.

I am a big believer in the universe presenting you with the same lessons until you learn from them, and can easily apply what you learn to any situation. Clearly, for me, my lesson was in letting go of perfection, of the aching desire to be like 'everyone else', and live my life in the way that it needed to be lived.

In other words, having the balls to stand up and say this is who I am, and there is nothing wrong with that. That was the day I decided to take my scooter into the round yard with me. And that was the best decision I had ever made.

Having my mobility scooter in that round yard meant two things. One, that I could sit down if I felt too uneasy on my feet, and two, that I could still stand up and hold on to something a bit more sturdy with a wider circumference than a water drum.

Ultimately, by having two ways to ensure my confidence in my body, I could really focus on building a connection with Larry and finally achieve something that I had been working towards for what seemed like months. I didn't realise at the time, but having my scooter next to me, and accepting its help, was a stepping stone into the land of finding acceptance and removing the shackles that muscular dystrophy had locked my brain in for over two decades.

As an extra step, I started to try to ease the pressure and expectations that I had on myself to ace lunging a half-ton horse on the second attempt. There was that little voice in my head saying to just 'let go'.

As I stood there in the yard, I was fumbling with the lunge whip, which isn't really a whip; it's really just used as an extension of your arm. I kept dropping it as it would get caught on my scooter, and as I would hit the ground to send energy out to Larry, it would wrap around itself, making me have to stop and unwrap it, meaning he would then stop and look at me, which felt as though he was silently mocking me.

I wanted the ground to swallow me up, the carefree thoughts I went in with were suddenly being overridden with the old thoughts of 'perfection' and embarrassing myself. I could feel myself getting worked up, tears threatening to spill over again.

Hayley noticed this and simply told me to just look at him, breathe, and even suggested I try sitting down. As if by magic, everything fell into place.

As I sat on my scooter in the middle of the yard, sweating from exertion, I was told to say, "Walk," in my head or out loud, and direct it to Larry. I had to picture in my head that he was walking around me, as clear as if it were happening right then. I closed my eyes, took a steadying breath, listened to him breathing two meters from me, his breath calming me, and imagined him moving. I opened my eyes and said, "Walk," as I hit the ground with the whip.

One hoof, two hooves, a shoulder turn, a shake of the head, and Larry was moving around me. It was as if time stood still. His hooves rhythmically hitting the ground, the tail swish cutting through the air.

I turned my scooter on and started to do circles in the middle of the arena, so I was facing him the entire time. I didn't have to think about where my feet were or if there were holes that I could accidentally step in. I didn't have to worry about Larry knocking me over or falling and getting stepped on.

For the first time in my life, I felt like I could just be. Be present in life—in my life.

I spent that entire ninety minutes existing just with him; it was like my mum and coach weren't in the corner—it was just him and I bonding, experiencing such a special moment together that not everyone gets to experience.

At the end, he walked over, stood over me, and lowered his head slightly, as if to wrap me up in a hug. I wrapped my arms around his giant neck as much as I could and was in awe of what had just happened. I did the thing that I had been desperate to do for years. All it required was letting go. My coach then handed me his lead rope and said, "You can walk him back to his yard." Larry and I then slowly made our way back to his yard in silence, taking stock of the setting sun and the quiet breeze.

Like I said before, lessons will repeat until you learn them.

The following time with Larry wasn't as smooth sailing. It is in those moments, however, when the work begins, not in the easy times when you don't have to try. This particular day, we were in a proper round yard, and for whatever reason, when I would ask him to walk, he would walk, but he would go straight at me instead of lunging around me.

No matter how hard I tried to get him to go, he just stood right in front of my scooter. I used the end of the lunge whip to put pressure on his chest to push him back and out of my space, but as soon as I asked him to lunge, he would just walk back into me. He did this time and time again.

I started to get worked up and frustrated. What happened next was something that no one told me would happen when working with horses.

Larry took a step back and looked me straight in the eyes.

My brain suddenly went into rapid fire. Images of my childhood started flashing in my head. My grandfather's death, watching him wither away into nothing, the phone call, the funeral, being physically bullied, having my stationary stolen, holding a knife to my wrist in front of my brother, lying on the hospital bed, screaming after my muscle biopsy, the times I couldn't stand up for myself, people whom I held dear walking away from me, the inability to run, jump, do my own hair, put on my shoes, wipe my own backside at times, everything my disability was robbing from me, the concept of dying young.

With that, the emotions came rapid fire too: fear, confusion, anger, sadness, anxiety, alienation, feeling subhuman, loneliness, and pain.

It was as if Larry took a key and opened the filing drawer in my head labelled 'do not open,' and everything I tried to bury fell out of the cabinet all at once. It was overwhelming; it was like I couldn't breathe. Larry blinked again and then turned his back, so his rear was facing me. It was like someone had just snapped something inside me, and I felt like I jerked forward.

Suddenly, I was back. Present. The birds chirping, the tall trees swaying, the noise of their leaves quiet, almost like wind chimes. I looked up into the paddocks, the place that felt like home. Then I felt him. I felt a presence that I had longed for. Everyone, at some point in time, when they lose someone dear in their life, will often have moments as though they could feel them, their energy.

That day, as I snapped back to reality and looked at the afternoon sun beginning to set on the golden long grass in the paddock over, it was as though I could see my grandfather standing in the distance. Looking at me as if to say, "I've got you, I am proud of you, sweetheart. It's time to move forward."

At that moment, I had unlocked the key to the grief spiral that had held me captive my entire life. I had been stuck in denial and anger for so long. I hadn't fully moved onto acceptance and peace. In that one moment, I felt as though it would be okay, I was okay. I could hear his voice reassuring me of that exact fact.

I also realised the truth of what has been keeping me stuck in needing to please, to impress, to be in denial: I didn't want to be alone. I felt like everyone in my life would eventually leave. My grandfather left me, my friends left me, those I loved left me, and my body was even leaving me. I feared being alone.

Then, Larry turned his back. I felt as though he was saying, "I don't want to deal with you any more." Horses have a way of mirroring how you feel about yourself. He was mirroring what I felt was happening in my life, but what I also came to realise was that he was also mirroring the fact that I, too, was turning away from myself and what was true to me.

I could hear myself say, "Don't turn your back on me, too." As soon as I heard myself say those words, I broke down in tears. My mind was still, and I was the most present I had ever been in my life. It was like the internal floodgates had finally been unlocked after years of being suppressed.

Hayley came over to me then and wrapped me up in a reassuring hug. I was in a safe space where I could just let it all out, without worrying about being judged.

When she went back to her seat to let me process everything, I realised that Larry had turned back around and was watching me. There is something about having a 500-kilogram animal staring at you with so much love, patience, and understanding that can reduce you to tears and trigger you to start realising the blockages that had stopped you from healing or moving forward after trauma. The rest of the session was spent just sitting with him, ugly crying at times, almost unable to breathe.

That session, however, was the catalyst to having some deep and necessary conversations, particularly with my mum, about how much I had struggled with my grandfather's passing and my own disability journey. I explained to her that it felt like everyone found it so simple to move on with life after his death, and I was left confused and scared. Confused because it was the first time someone died in my life, and I felt like I was drowning in all these emotions, and I didn't know how to handle it at eight years old.

I couldn't understand the concept that life still moves forward, even after losing someone so important to you. I felt like everyone wanted to forget about him altogether, and I couldn't comprehend that the most mundane things in life for everyone were the only things keeping them together. I explained I felt so lost and alone, and that, paired with the grief and confusion and being told I needed to move on by someone close to the situation, inadvertently made me trapped in a grief cycle that somehow could never seem to reach acceptance. I also explained that it triggered a fear of my own mortality, and it ultimately compounded my own disability journey, and that I often felt alone in my journey, even though my family was there the entire time.

It's safe to say that many tears were shed by both of us during this conversation, apologies were given, and a newfound understanding was reached.

That one lunging session with Larry kick-started my own healing journey, discovering what kind of person I wanted to be. Whenever I see Larry or work with him now, there is a bond that can only be created by going from hell and back. Each time we see each other, it's almost like a telepathic communication that simply says, "I see you, old friend." That feeling is something that I can't describe. It is truly incredible. That horse broke me, and started to fix me, all at the same time.

As time went on, Larry helped me develop my voice and enabled me to realise that having a voice is never a bad thing, nor is standing up for yourself. He made me become stronger in my sense of self, and made me less timid or eager to please. In order for me to work with him, I had to establish a level of self-awareness and self-belief, in that if I said something, it was with conviction and I meant it. If I asked him to move, I meant it, not, "Hey Larry, if you feel like it, and it's okay with you, can you please move for me?" Like it used to be.

Hayley explained it simply. Horses and people need boundaries; it's how we establish connection and an understanding of each other. Horses need to know we have their back, just as much as we need to know they have ours.

After weeks of work to unravel and unpack twenty years of crap that I kept buried, inclusive of tears that could make Niagara Falls look like a leaky tap, I began to turn a page into acceptance. I started realising that my scooter was never an obstacle in my life; it was an opportunity for me to be independent, for me to play and explore life in my own way.

My disability, while difficult, presented me with extraordinary gifts and an opportunity to live life on a deeper level and understand its meaning. I eventually arrived at a sense of gratitude for all the difficult times that may have broken me, but didn't; I was never meant to stay broken, I was meant to get up, dust myself off, and move forward.

These revelations transitioned into my work with Larry. What started as me being practically unable to make him move around me, resulted in getting him to canter around me, with me following him on my scooter. Both of us experienced unconditional trust in one another. Each time I would call 'woah' and bring him to a stop, he would turn in and walk to me, lowering his head, and looking me in the eyes. His eyes would be saying, "I see you." Something I needed to hear. It wasn't just him saying that to me with his eyes; it was me I was seeing in his eyes saying that to myself. For the first time, I saw myself.

When you embark on a journey of self-discovery, you eventually arrive at a place where you can put everything into practice and continue healing while also healing others. I was at a point where I was beginning to put all the puzzle pieces back in my life, when I was given the opportunity to work with a horse that had some level of trust issues due to horrible things that happened in his past. I was told that he was a very gentle-natured horse and was sensitive to a lot of energy. So, the energy that I required to move a stubborn horse like Larry was like a nuclear bomb to this horse.

I waited in the arena for yet another stunning jet-black horse with a white strip on his face and the cutest white socks. Riff Raf came into the arena with an unsure step as he approached me.

I said nothing to him; I simply sat on my scooter in the middle of the arena. I knew he wasn't sure of me, but I was sure that both he and I were in good hands. I trusted Hayley completely, and I knew he trusted her as well.

A few minutes went by, and I just started talking to him softly, still not moving. I said, "Hey, buddy. You are gorgeous. I heard what happened to you, and I am so, so sorry you went through that. It's not fair. I went through my own fair share of crap. It sucks, it hurts. I know. I know you felt like you were invisible. I felt that way, too. But I see you, you aren't alone. You are loved and valued. I see you." I kept repeating, "I see you," like a broken record. It was as if I was speaking to myself just as much as I was speaking to him.

Soon enough, I got an ear turn; he was listening to me. Then a look over. Then a slight drop of the head.

That's when I made my move, inching just a few centimetres closer to him, draping my torso slightly over the front of my scooter to make myself look smaller and non-threatening, to show him he could trust me. I, then, waited for him to make a move.

Sure enough, after continuing to talk to him some more, and extending my hand, he lowered his head further, turned his shoulder, and slowly and cautiously walked over to me.

Touching a horse is magic. But touching a horse who is just as mentally scarred as you are, who is desperate to be put back together, is another thing entirely, especially when the two of you are mirroring each other.

Within fifteen minutes, I had him playing follow the leader, him following me as I drove around on my scooter within the round yard. As each minute passed by, he eased up more and more, his eyes softened, and each time I stopped, he would immediately come over for a scratch on the nose.

As I sat there talking to Hayley, both of us in awe of how the session was going, Riff stood there resting on his back hoof, head lowered practically in my lap, half asleep.

Hayley then told me that he was a nervous nibbler, and the fact that he was just standing there, not mouthing or nibbling anything, was a victory not only for him but for me.

When Hayley asked me what had changed, I simply replied that I didn't have expectations. I just wanted to make him feel seen, have fun, and feel safe. All the things that I was desperate to feel in my own life. That day in the round pen, there was lightness in the air, my head was clear, and I felt like I could physically feel all the blocks falling into place.

Lunging Riff is always a dream. He wants to work for you, and if you get it right, the magic happens when he lengthens out his trot, lowers his nose to the ground, and inches his way closer to you with each circle he does around you.

There is a bond, a respect, both of us growing in our confidence each time. He also makes me aware (sure as hell) when I am not okay within myself or am struggling to regulate my emotions. He is a horse that is incredibly sensitive to energy, and even the slightest elevation in you can make him nibble like no tomorrow.

He has my back, and I have his. Both of us were finding ourselves in the process. He has made me fall in love with the freedom my scooter provides, and has made me feel less embarrassed about turning up to the shops in active wear while driving a scooter. He truly is my miracle horse.

Each horse I have had the pleasure of working with has come at the exact time that I need it. Larry came to me when I was afraid to confront the skeletons, and presented my wounds on a silver platter, and simultaneously started the journey to put me back together again. Riff turned up when I was beginning my healing journey, reflecting where I was and where I was going, putting into practice everything Larry taught me.

Then came Kandie, whom I have only worked with twice. She is a stunning grey mare, and she knows it. She is literally the polar opposite of who I am, or was, and the epitome of a strong woman. She is so sure of herself and carries herself with such poise, elegance, and a touch of a diva. She commands respect. She knows her boundaries and will tell you if you have crossed them. At the same time, she is so gentle in taking food from your hands and is incredibly protective of you.

There was a time when I was sitting on my scooter, of course, next to her, talking to one of the coaches. Kandie lowered her head, looked me in the eye as if to say, "You can pet me." I extended a slow, cautious hand out, as she is one whom you must ask permission before you touch her.

As my hand touched the spot between her eyes, she sighed, and her eyes softened. She even began to drool, something both the coach and I were shocked about! The coach said to me that in all the time she knew Kandie, she had never seen her be so willing to have someone give her a scratch, let alone start drooling in the process.

Immediately after my second session with her, Mum and I were talking in the car, and I said to her, the first horse comforted me when I was broken and taught me how to start healing; the second taught me how to trust and how to help others while showing him that in return, all while letting go and enjoying life without a plan... and the third? Kandie is teaching me how to be a strong, powerful, and confident woman. A woman who stands up for herself, her family, and her values, and is unapologetic about it, all while still having class. And a touch of diva certainly doesn't hurt.

Each of these horses has taught me so much and has healed me in ways I never thought a horse could do. They continue to teach me something new every single day.

When you are disabled, there is this ever-nagging feeling that just 'being' isn't enough to be seen, heard, or even respected. To be honest, every human being measures worth based on the external things one obtains in life. How much they have achieved, how much they earn, and what they do for a living. When society easily writes you off the minute you are sick or disabled, to try and prove you are worth a seat at the table, you often feel as though the measuring pole for every other person doesn't even begin to cut the mustard of the pole you are measured with. You can easily feel as though you are still a child. From the way people speak to you, unemployment, and internal triggers. They all result in you feeling undervalued, like a doormat, with a lack of self-belief and confidence. The perfect recipe for carrying so much emotional baggage and holding yourself prisoner inside your head and your body.

So everything I had done in life up until that point, working with horses, was trying to prove I was worthy of a seat at society's table, and the table I found myself at in my circle. My law degree was a mix of sheer desperation to never be mistreated again, to ensure others weren't silenced, and also to prove I was more than a being in a chair who walked funny.

Each decision I made in life was to prove to myself, just as much as the rest of the world, that I was more than just 'disabled'. As a result, it added fuel to the raging inferno that was anger, confusion, and grief inside of me. I lost who I was. I was becoming someone I didn't like when I looked in the mirror. The pressure I was placing on myself based on society's stigma and perceptions was suffocating me.

What I truly wanted was to be free mentally, physically, emotionally, and spiritually. I had to find my own definition of being physically free, but everything else was attainable. I wanted to feel at peace, calm, confident, and in love with my life. Instead, I was dreading it.

I am on borrowed time. Technically so is everyone else. No one is going to live forever. But for me, having something inside me that is slowly chewing away my ability to breathe, walk, talk, and eat is like a ticking time bomb that I am always aware of. So why on earth was I trying so hard to fit in and have a seat at a table that I didn't belong at? Why was I trying to even compete with those around me?

Heaven knows that competing against people will either inflate your ego to the point you can't fit it in a room, or it will destroy your self-worth. Both are just as soul-crushing as the other. For me, it just destroyed my self-worth even further. The desperation to be seen as on par with everyone in the room was exhausting. The need to prove that I wasn't a child, that being in a wheelchair doesn't make me five years old forever, was soul-destroying.

As a result, I built the walls that I thought would keep me safe. I was in my own bubble, trying to create defences that I could use to show I wasn't a child any more. A degree, nice clothes, possessions, and even writing my blog. Ultimately, what I realised while working with these stunning horses was that I was also trying to prove just as much to myself that I was a woman, an adult who needed to respect herself. The walls I put up weren't keeping me safe; they were keeping me hostage. I didn't allow myself to feel and be okay with feeling.

Without feeling, there is no healing. Without healing, there is no progress, no life.

Everyone has a unique way of finding who they are, what they stand for, and healing their mind and their bodies. For me, working with horses has been my bridge to reclaiming who I am as a woman. A disabled woman. One who still has flaws and is very much a work in progress. But one who is proud of what she has endured and survived, her stubbornness, and unwillingness to give up.

Somehow, through working with horses, I found more of myself than I ever could have expected. Have I completely healed? Not even close. I am having to undo two decades of disability trauma. Then I have to deal with generational trauma, and that makes trying to heal from that like trying to undo the world's largest knot.

However, I have arrived at a place where everything I do now is because I want to do it for myself. Not to prove to anyone that I am worthy of a seat at the table called mainstream society. Not to prove that I am more than just a disabled chick in a chair. But to prove to myself that I am very much alive. To prove to myself that disability or not, I will do what I want to do, even if that means having to go about things differently.

Life is short, too short to stay trapped in my mind forever. I realised life without a plan is more exciting than life with a plan. Freedom is having the balls to throw caution to the wind and do the damn thing anyway.

And to think all it took was three horses and a willingness to just let go.

CHAPTER 17

FAITH, FREEDOM, AND OTHER F WORDS

Disability life isn't for the meek. You are constantly challenged, so you have to learn to problem-solve quickly while still living your life, despite the hurdles thrown your way.

One of the questions I would get asked a lot, especially in my teen years as I started talking more about living with a disability, was, "How do you manage to go through all of that with a smile on your face?"

Now, some people may take offence to that question. However, I like to think of it as a major compliment.

Despite everything that life has thrown my way, and will undoubtedly continue to do so, I have been working on developing a more optimistic mindset. And there are a few elements combined that have enabled me to truly live a life that I love, despite the challenging moments. I call them "Faith, Freedom, and other F-words."

As I keep on reiterating, everyone is different. Especially when it comes to the tools they have at their disposal to get through tough times.

So, like an episode of *Sesame Street*, I feel it necessary to defuse the tension by saying that this chapter is 'brought to you by the letter F'. No, I am not only talking about the F-bomb, even though I am a pro at using that word. The tools at my disposal to get me through the difficult times are more than just dropping the F-bomb like a champion.

I am talking about Faith, Freedom, Fear, Frustration, Failure, Forgiveness, and Fulfilment. All these lovely F words combined make for a rather interesting and, not to mention, memorable life.

If there is one thing you may have realised from reading this little memoir so far, it is the fact that I am not one to sugarcoat things. I was thrown into a life resembling one hell of a boxing match, and it is only fair to be brutally honest about it.

Having said that though, life isn't all crap moments; rather, it is a tapestry of highs and lows woven together by the calm moments, resulting in an incredible artwork. To weave that tapestry, though, you need to be prepared to begin. And to begin looking at life through a different lens, especially when life decides to throw fucking curveballs at you, you must have a level of faith.

Now, because I am in a giving mood, I will spare you again from, yet, another ramble of mine. A ramble more around the concept of religion as a source of Faith. I recognise everyone comes from all unique walks of life, all with their own opinions and viewpoints on religion. I believe that it is up to people to decide what kind of religion they follow (if religion aligns with their beliefs in the first place).

I don't want to get into a debate about religion, and I also have no interest in jamming it down your throat. But I do want to be clear about my level of faith, as it serves an essential purpose for this chapter.

My parents aren't churchgoers, even though Dad went to Sunday school and summer school when he was growing up. My brother and I got baptised in the Anglican Church, but we have always been free to make our own minds up regarding religion. I studied religion at school like many others, and when I reached high school, I went to a Lutheran private school where we would attend 'chapel' services twice a week and have around two lessons a week of Christian Studies.

It's not a surprise that I had a rather complicated relationship with God growing up. For many years, I blamed him for my disability, for giving me something that would kill me, for making me endure so much at such a young age because of my disability. I didn't really want to have a relationship with Him. But at the same time, I didn't want to cut ties, as just the thought of doing so made me feel even more lost.

There were times in my life when I did end up doing a version of a prayer when I felt desperate. I remember in Year 7, I would hug the teddy bear I was given from my grandfather's collection when he passed away, before going to bed on a school night, and would either thank my grandfather, and perhaps, God for a good day, and ask if I could please have another good day the following day. Or I would thank them for an alright day, but could I have an even better day tomorrow? I would repeat that process when making my bed the next morning and ask for a good day. That was my routine for an entire twelve months. I guess that was really the first time I reached out for help from a higher power.

When I started at high school, it was around the same time that I felt incredibly lonely despite having family surrounding me. I felt mentally tired and lost. I remember that we watched *Les Misérables* in Christian Studies early in Year 9; there was a line about how, when you are desperate enough, you can surrender and call on Him, and He will listen. One night, I was crying myself to sleep, struggling with my body and many mental demons, when I decided to simply say, "I am yours, save me." I repeated it until sleep washed over me. That day changed everything for me.

I started to realise there had to be a reason why I was made the way I was. My faith was the only thing that made sense to me about why I was going through everything I had and would go through in my life.

As I grew older and experienced more trauma and anxious times, I kept reassuring myself that there had to be a reason. And of course, there were times when I did realise, 'Ah, so I had to go through that in order to handle this now.'

During the COVID times, when I had been at my lowest for years, I started quoting Jeremiah 29:11 (New International Version) to myself, "For I know the plans I have for you." Simply reciting that filled me with comfort.

It began to give me the ability to let go and believe that even if things are tough, there is a reason; I just have to be willing to hold on to find that reason.

That isn't to say that I am anxiety-free or not a control freak. Quite the opposite! I still struggle massively with my anxiety and the mental gremlins that I have yet to evict from my mind. Additionally, I still struggle with trusting everyone around me, including God Himself.

However, having faith that things will work out and that there is someone watching over me, including my grandfather and both my great-grandmothers, fills me with enough courage to keep moving forward.

With that anxiety still comes fear. I am fearful of the future at times, and not knowing what my disability will throw at me next makes me uneasy. However, despite the fear, there is a level of subtle comfort in knowing that, regardless, I am not alone and will not be alone, both in a physical sense and a spiritual one. This level of faith has kept me sane most of my adult life and has brought me back from the edge on multiple occasions, especially during 2020.

If there is anything obvious in this book, I hope it is that I don't mince my words. I am not ashamed to say that living with a disability is hard and often an uphill battle that offers only slight moments of reprieve when either the symptoms have stabilised or just during a good movie night. But how does one find freedom amid the chaos, the doctor appointments, and the uncertainty? I had to redefine what freedom meant.

For years, I would watch my family go about life with a level of ease that I craved. There was no strain on their faces when living life, no hesitation in climbing stairs, even two at a time. My mum walked into a restaurant in heels with the grace of a queen. My brother decided to drive two hours away to go fishing just because he could. My dad flew across the country for work without worrying about how to use the bathroom or how to get on the plane and stand up after three or so hours of sitting.

I would watch strangers run to catch a train, speed walking, so they wouldn't be late for work because they had gone to a coffee shop first. They danced together, whether at a club or while performing a mesmerising waltz at a wedding, without their knees giving way or being dragged across the floor too harshly, nearly causing them to fall.

I was a bystander, watching my family and complete strangers live a life in a body that didn't betray them. To me, growing up, that was the epitome of freedom.

I was born with a body that I had to fight every step of the way, literally. I couldn't just get in the car and go for a drive because I wanted to. I couldn't get to my grandparents' kitchen upstairs to say hi to everyone during family dinners, or to help with the dishes. I felt like my legs were going to crumple in on themselves while wearing a 2-centimetre heel, and attempting to dance with a partner was too risky.

My disability wasn't going to go away, and even if, for a fleeting moment, it seemed to get better, I knew it would only get worse as the years went on.

I had a choice: I could either sit at home and continue feeling trapped, ultimately letting my body win, or I could flip the script and find a way to manage my disability, reclaiming some control to live a version of life I would be proud of.

Suddenly, I started to envision what I wanted freedom in my world to look like. Instead of viewing people or utensils as obstacles and feeling 'dependent' upon them, which I believed took away my independence, I began to see them as the very things that granted me freedom.

My entire life, my mum has been my primary caregiver; we never wanted or needed any outside help. We had an agreement that if either one of us felt it was time to find someone else to assist me, then that would be the time. However, she always thought she could help take me to appointments, shopping, equine-assisted therapy, and handle all the manual tasks at home.

It was strange; having her as my caregiver didn't feel any different from growing up. I didn't feel any less dependent because she was my mum. I always viewed outside help as an obstacle, something that would mean I was dependent on others and unable to do things on my own. However, a few months ago, both my mum and I independently mentioned in the same conversation that life had changed.

She was busy with work and the family business, and I was starting to branch out and find opportunities that she simply couldn't take me to or help with. So we agreed that finding someone external was necessary for both of us—not a full-time person to assist me with everything, but someone to take me to appointments, equine therapy, and grocery shopping because, let me tell you, trying to grocery shop with a mobility scooter is one of the most difficult and frustrating experiences I have ever faced due to accessibility.

Anyway, moving on from that rant, I never truly realised how liberating having outside help can be. It has provided me with the freedom to go wherever I want, without worrying about asking, "Are you free? Can we go here today?" like a child asking her parents. I am almost 26 years old and have barely been apart from my family, but having someone external to help means I can be more independent *from* my family, which is healthy for all of us.

I realised very quickly that the help from others and my scooter are what truly give me my freedom. When I decided to have a staycation in town for the first time, the only things that made it possible for me to stay in an apartment for four days completely by myself were, in fact, my parents and my scooter.

My parents came and lifted the microwave for me so I could reach it, stacked the chairs outside to make them higher so I could sit outside if I wanted, ensured all bottles of water were open, and let's not forget the alcohol. Then they took the spare key, said see you in a few days, and left. Because of their help, I experienced what it was truly like to live on my own, even if just for a moment.

My scooter also became my ultimate freedom at that moment. If it weren't for my scooter, I would have been stuck in the apartment, unable to go anywhere. Thanks to my scooter becoming my legs, I could drive down to the shops a few minutes away, go see a movie if I wanted, or treat myself to some sushi for lunch before driving back to my apartment in the afternoon to enjoy a drink and some cheeses.

My scooter helps me travel along the esplanade on the beach, allowing me to take in the sights and sounds without worrying about falling over or how tired my legs are. It enables me to move alongside horses without concern about navigating uneven terrain or being knocked over by the gentlest nudge.

For years, I viewed my wheelchair, my scooter, and the help from others as things that kept me from being independent. However, they were the very things that granted me my freedom. I only had to be willing to reinvent what freedom meant to me. And that comes with perspective.

Perhaps one of the best gifts that comes with living with a progressive disability is being able to see life from an entirely new perspective.

I found out that my condition would kill me relatively early in life. Initially, that news terrified me, as it would anyone who receives news that their life may be cut short before they truly begin to live.

But even though it sent me spiralling for a moment or two, I started to cherish the quieter moments in life: the sunset drives in my scooter along the esplanade, listening to the waves crash on the shoreline with the seagulls happily chirping away. The cool nights sitting around the fire pit in the backyard with my family, having a few drinks and singing along to music, or simply sitting in silence with the crackle of the fire providing the soundtrack as I stared up at the Southern Cross twinkling in the sky. Even the cold mornings on horseback riding through paddocks, listening to the even breathing of my horse as its hooves crunch the frost-bitten grass below, the cold air pinching my face.

These moments, moments that most people would simply rush past, are the roses in the thorn bush that make life truly special.

There is something almost indescribable that happens to your soul when you allow yourself to savour every slow moment. It's as though your heart slows, and your senses become heightened. Time slows down, and your brain goes quiet. I don't think about what tomorrow may hold, or what yesterday told me. I am simply just being, living, breathing.

However, that level of freedom is only one part of the equation. There are, of course, the other F words to consider to truly create a unique definition of freedom.

One that doesn't need an introduction is Fear.

Our bodies, or rather our brains, are built to try to protect ourselves, with a built-in reactor. These are the Flight, Fight, Freeze, or Fawn responses. Hey, what do you know? Another bunch of F words! These F words describe how we respond to threats and fear.

For most of my life, I was a flight person. I would run, or waddle, at the first sign of something wrong, or try to avoid that potential by controlling the heck out of a situation, with most situations being completely imaginary as my mind tried to devise ways to avoid or deal with potential threats. The thought of dying, getting weaker, suffocating, or becoming completely dependent on others made me freeze. The fear was almost as crippling as my disability.

For years, I let fear control me. I was terrified to take risks, to say "yes" to opportunities, and to go after what I really wanted to do. As a result, I gave up acting, left riding horses by the wayside for years, and truly became a difficult person to live with.

The fear that I held onto for so long revolved around becoming weaker, my lung function decreasing further, and death itself, leaving my family behind. I let that fear turn into anger because I didn't know how else to deal with it, especially at a young age.

I felt as though there was really no point in doing things that brought me joy, or in trying to continue to push myself and my body to live a life that I desperately wanted. I simply gave up on life; I became miserable. Yet when I was around others, I put on a happy face, laughed, and joked around. I accepted the compliments and cheers of those around me: "You are doing so well!" or "You are such an inspiration", even though, in my head, I thought they had no clue, and that I was definitely no inspiration.

As I grew older, what perhaps started to make me turn the page was hearing more about what my grandfather had to endure, especially after returning home from the war. It's safe to say I always looked up to and admired him, but my admiration reached a whole new level when I began to understand his PTSD. He never spoke to me about it as a kid, but I would hear stories from family about his triggers and how they impacted him.

It made me realise that despite how crippling PTSD can be, he refused to let it stop him from carrying on with life, working on his hobby farm, and trying to enjoy the life that so many of those he fought with didn't have the opportunity to live. His resilience and perseverance to carry on, even when things got tough throughout his cancer battle, persisted until the end of his life. Whether or not he was scared of dying, I don't know, but if he was, he certainly didn't show it to us; he was adamant that he was not going anywhere until he said so.

If my grandmother was scared of having to live without him, she never let it keep her down. She has been able to push through despite it. She has gone on to have many incredible adventures while travelling the world, meeting remarkable people, and now, enjoying working in the garden and walking along the beach.

Both of these incredible people found the key: life goes on, whether you like it or not. The days keep coming, regardless of how scared, sad, or anxious you are. We are only on this Earth for a finite amount of time, so one needs to learn how to get on with life and push through the fear, because life doesn't wait for anyone.

Once I had this bolt of knowledge, I realised that I didn't want to sit around waiting for the Grim Reaper to come knocking on my door. The late and legendary Patrick Swayze said in one of his final interviews, "You can either get busy living, or you can get busy dying."

For me, that is so completely true. I can either sit and let fear of the future, the unknown, or what my disability will do to me rob me of any sort of amazing life, or I can get busy trying everything: exploring new places, meeting new people, riding horses, enjoying coffee dates with my mum, having dinners with my family, and singing along to *Sweet Caroline* with my brother at the footy.

In short, I can either get busy dying or get busy living. And I know for a fact that I still have a lot of life in me. Even though there are days when I am fearful and the fear and anxiety can overwhelm me, I will still work on acknowledging these feelings, allowing myself to feel everything I need to. Then, I brush myself off and get back to work.

When it is my time, I want to leave looking back on my life with such fondness, happiness, and gratitude for all the things I have experienced and accomplished, with no regrets, knowing I did everything I wanted; despite the fear, I did it anyway.

There is one topic that I don't think has been touched on much throughout this book: the power of forgiveness. I'm not only referring to forgiveness toward others, but also to forgiveness toward yourself.

People say forgiveness will set you free, but I struggled to truly believe that for most of my life until I heard the story of twins experimented on in Auschwitz during World War II. What happened to the late Eva Kor, her twin and thousands of other twins was absolutely horrendous, disgusting, and cruel. Fortunately, both Eva and her twin sister were liberated. Just barely. But not without lifelong health issues and mental trauma. For years, she was angry at the Germans and any remaining SS personnel, and to be honest, she had every right to be.

One day, someone reached out to her about a family member who had been involved in the experiments on twins during that time. He had heard that she was still alive and wanted not only to meet her but also to apologise to her. She outright refused and didn't want anything to do with him or to hear anything he had to say.

However, she realised that her anger and bitterness were what kept her from moving forward with ease. So, she finally agreed to meet with him.

He cried in front of her and took her hands as he apologised profusely for what had happened and for his involvement during the war and in the camps. He explained why he did what he did, how they were all brainwashed, and acknowledged that he should have known better but, for whatever reason, went along with it.

She simply looked at him and said, "I forgive you."

These were words she thought she would never say to the people who had murdered her sister and millions more. She said the minute those words escaped from her mouth, she immediately felt lighter. She explained that she didn't forgive him because he apologised; she forgave him for her own sake. She realised she couldn't go on living with hatred, anger, and a level of despair that only a few know too well. Forgiving him enabled her to move forward in her life and no longer feel as though she was carrying the weight of the world on her shoulders.

For me and my life, her story struck a chord. I, too, held so much anger, resentment, bitterness, and perhaps, hatred towards many: my parents, able-bodied people, God, and myself.

I was angry and resentful that my parents brought me into this world and ultimately made me this way. I was angry at God for dealing me these cards to face throughout my life. I held so much resentment towards able-bodied people for not appreciating their bodies, how easily they navigated through society, and how they continued to create a world where it felt like disabled people like me didn't belong. Ultimately, I harboured bitterness and anger towards myself—how I looked, how I walked, how much I couldn't do, and the abilities I would continue to lose because my body was hell-bent on taking it all away from me.

I carried all of this anger and negative emotion for so long. Listening to the voices of the disabled community, who were just as angry at everything and everyone, only fuelled my fire. Much like fear, my anger made me lash out at those around me and withdraw further into myself, sinking deeper into the rage.

It wasn't until I reached a level of hopelessness tied to that terrifying time in 2020 that I stopped and reevaluated. I had hit my version of rock bottom; I was tired of being angry.

I began to reach out to God again in my own way, desperate to feel calm, and I started watching sermons from a pastor on YouTube. One early morning, as I sat in the dark of my room with my notebook, my laptop being the only source of light, the pastor preached about forgiveness and the power of letting go. The sermon itself made it feel like the knot in my stomach started to dissolve, and I began slowly reflecting on my life.

After much more soul-searching in the following months, I realised that the true obstacle holding me back was my inability to forgive, as well as my habit of holding my parents, God, others, and myself to standards that didn't need to be upheld.

My parents did nothing wrong; yes, they brought me into this world, but it was merely a fluke that I ended up with muscular dystrophy. I forgave them in my mind and released them from the prison in my head labelled 'your fault.'

I forgave God when I realised that He has reasons for everything, and His plan for my life included experiences that would shape me into the person He ultimately needs me to be.

I forgave everyone else without disabilities, recognising that it wasn't their fault they were born with strong legs and bodies not burdened with additional challenges; they weren't responsible for making me who I am.

Ultimately, I forgave myself because it wasn't my fault either. I forgave myself for seeking someone to blame for the painful experiences of surgeries, for not living what was deemed a normal life. I forgave myself for not pursuing the things I desperately wanted to do, either because I lacked confidence or because my body simply wouldn't allow it. I forgave myself for the moments when I couldn't see things through, experiences I considered failures. I didn't fail; I tried, and that was more success than actually completing something in a traditionally recognised way.

There is a level of freedom that comes with forgiveness, and this power should never be overlooked. Being able to forgive everyone I had blamed for making me the way I was enabled me to start living again. I realised that life unfolds as it sometimes does, and there is no one to blame; things simply happen, and that is okay. What you do with the life you are given makes all the difference, and no amount of playing the blame game will lead you where you want to go.

It must be said, however, that life, regardless of disability, can be excruciatingly hard. No one has an 'easy' life. If there is one thing that can unite us all together under one common bond, it is the fact that everyone's life is hard. However, how you view their hardships in life, as well as taking stock of the slower, calmer, and more joyful moments, is what makes life a wonderful mystery.

Personally, I can honestly say, with all the sass and gusto, that I truly love my life. I like to say it is how a diamond is made. The rough, heartbreaking, and faith-questioning moments put me under immense pressure. However, that pressure never intended to break me; instead, it began to shape and mold me, turning those hardships into the very backbone that keeps me upright. Literally. The joyful moments and calmer moments are the polish that wipes away the sharp edges and allows the diamond to cast rainbows.

Too cheesy? Okay, I will lower the cheese factor just a fraction.

What I am trying to say is that by reinventing the wheel of what freedom means to me, rediscovering my F words, throwing a handful of F-bombs for good measure, and leaning into what faith looks like, I have been able to live a life for which I am beyond grateful. That doesn't mean it is easy, and I will always be the first to put up my hand and admit that sometimes life is shit.

But without all that, I wouldn't have really been able to value life for what it is. I wouldn't have had the opportunities that presented themselves to me, the ability to walk a red carpet (did I forget to mention that? Oops!), and the opportunity to meet some incredible people. I have a close-knit family and a tribe that is as quirky as they are feisty, and they are fiercely protective of one another. I would not have been able to receive all of these incredible lessons and blessings if I had legs that could climb stairs two at a time.

The ability to carve out a life that I genuinely love involves a lot of voluntary discomfort: going to the gym, going to venues that require me to navigate steps, and speaking up when I notice mistreatment.

But it also involves curiosity and the self-belief that I am worthy of exploring all that life has to offer, personally and professionally.

Regardless of how many tears I have cried, the pain I have endured, it is all completely worth it, and I honestly wouldn't trade what I have learnt for a second.

However, if someone were to tell me that a cure would be available tomorrow, and ask if I would take it? Well, I will let you answer that one.

SECTION 5
Lessons and Legacy

Be bold, be strong, be selfless, be courageous. Every single human on the face of the planet is unique in their own way. We were not born to be the same. We were born to contribute and leave our mark on the world.
—Rhiannon Anderson.

CHAPTER 18

FOR THE CAREGIVERS: THE ONES WHO HOLD US

They say it takes a village, and when it comes to disabled life, that couldn't be more accurate. Most people on the outside looking in only see the surface. If it's a physical disability, they may see missing limbs, a wheelchair, a breathing tube, a cane, or a guide dog. In my case, they see the waddle-walk, the scooter, and the bent arms. They see bodies that look 'different' from their own.

What they don't see is the intricate choreography that takes place behind the scenes. The extra hands that help us dress, feed us, the patience that gets us out the door, and the strength that it takes to help us live like anyone else.

They are more than our caregivers. Often, they are our families: mothers, fathers, brothers, sisters, aunts, uncles, grandparents. They are also our chosen families, friends, godparents, and friends of friends. We can't possibly forget the people who come into our lives when they receive the cry for more help: the nurses, support workers, and allied health practitioners.

Behind every disabled person is a team. A group of people who are selfless and put others before their own needs, dreams, and aspirations. They do so without complaint, and with a resilience and strength that are often either overlooked or not seen at all.

As a disabled person, it's safe to say there are many of us who hear from strangers and those in our lives all the time that we are 'inspirational'. They are in awe of how much we go through and keep pushing forward.

However, the same is often not said to those who enable us to live our lives with as much dignity as everyone on the planet has the right to feel. Their struggles often go unnoticed, as they are often not recognised for being human and having their own worries, fears, concerns, and lives.

So, it's about time that some light is shed on those who are our backbone.

If you can take even a portion out of this book as a caregiver, let it be this: you are also valued, seen, important, and loved. Please know that you, too, are allowed to admit that life at times is difficult. There is no shame in admitting that.

You perhaps have one of the hardest jobs in the world. You not only have to be present mentally, emotionally, and physically for those of us who rely on you, day in and day out, but you also hold space for your own fears, struggles, and worries.

Trying to juggle it all seems impossible; we don't know how you do it. But you do it so gracefully and with a tenacity that nothing seems to compare with.

For the parents, guardians, and chosen family who have signed up to help us live our lives, I want you to know that we are so incredibly grateful for all of you. You may be tired and don't always feel seen. I know that sometimes there are days when you wonder if what you are doing is enough. But please, I want you to know that it is enough. You are our lifeline, and you matter more than you could possibly know.

It only feels fair that I try to impart some advice from the other side of the coin. Please, look after yourself. You don't have to feel guilty or ashamed for admitting when it's too hard, and you need to step out for a minute. They often say that caring for someone you know is harder than caring for a stranger. It is okay for it to become too much at times, and you feel like you need some space. We understand that more than you know.

There will be days when we, as disabled people, will kick, scream, cry, and, yes, lash out at you. Please know it's not you that we are angry with. How could we ever be angry at people who are in our corner? We are often angry, scared, or frustrated at ourselves and our situations, and that is often taken out on you. I think it is safe to say I can apologise on behalf of the millions who receive care in their lives.

Equally, know that it is okay to admit that things are not fair, not right, or too hard. Throughout this entire book, I have spoken about the importance of living in your truth and not diminishing those thoughts and feelings to favour the positive ones. The same goes for you, too.

It is also fair to grieve the life you wished you had. For things to be different. For your family member not to be disabled. There is a grief process that comes with this journey.

Allow yourself to feel it.

We feel it, too.

There is nothing positive that comes from storing all those emotions, regardless of whether you are just starting out on this journey or have been on the road with us for a while. Those emotions will never entirely go away. Bottling them up will only do you so good for so long. Find a way to allow it to move through you. Scream, go on a journey, cry in the shower, go for a run, heck, even sign up for an Ironman competition. Find your own way to deal with those emotions. But for everyone's sake, do it healthily.

Because in all honesty, we couldn't do life without you.

Getting out of bed, starting each day, and creating our life's masterpiece, we owe so much of that to you. To the fact that you never walked away when things got hard. You kept showing up for us.

Everything we achieve is made possible because of your sacrifice. Your love. Your selfless dedication.

And while words will never feel like enough, I will say it anyway.

Thank you.

Of course, this chapter wouldn't be complete without sharing the voices of those who have carried me through my journey, quite literally at times. My family.

I wanted to give them a voice, as they know the fears, thoughts, and experiences of what it is like to be a caregiver for an entire lifetime. So, I asked my family if they would be willing to share a glimpse into the world of caregiving, as they are the ones who know it best.

I sat down with them and spoke about what they wish they knew, what life is like for them, and the lessons they'd pass on.

What follows is a blend of their words, in the hope that it will shed some light on disabled life from the perspective of those who know this life just as intimately as I do.

For my dad, he couldn't help but feel immense guilt. As a father, you want to be able to keep your kids safe. When they are hurting, so are you.

When I was first diagnosed, instead of spending sleepless nights researching, given mum had that covered, dad's head instead swum with other, more self-defeating thoughts: "Did I do something wrong? Was it my fault? Will she live a full life?"

For years, my dad carried the weight of believing that somehow my disability was his fault. Even though all the genetic testing came back, and it was determined that it was a completely random event, and neither mum nor dad had anything faulty that could have caused my disability. He had no one he could blame.

Naturally, as mum became my full-time caregiver, Dad showed up for me in his own quiet, unwavering way.

He was the one who helped me roller skate at the local skate rink, tying up my shoelaces when my mum wasn't there.

Later, growing up, there was a time when I was struggling emotionally, and Dad knocked on my door one late summer afternoon and said, "Let's go for a drive."

We went to Maccas and grabbed a frozen Coke and large chips each. For the next hour and a half, as the sun was setting, we drove around the outskirts of Toowoomba, drinking our drinks and nibbling on our food with Dad's rather interesting taste in music blaring through the speakers.

We sang. We laughed. We marveled at all the new houses being built. And soon enough, I started to feel happier. Lighter. Loved.

When I started to ride horses, he was the one who would take me to the paddock. In the early days, he would help me onto the saddle and then walk beside the horse with a steady hand, always ready to catch me if I fell. As my confidence grew, he traded his spot beside the reins for a place on the fence, with his phone in hand, snapping photos like any proud dad would.

He cares for me in a completely different way from my mum. He provides the muscle when needed. Getting into a high car, climbing stairs at the footy, and, as I said before, sitting in saddles.

Each time I ask for help, he is always there. Even when I don't ask, he somehow knows exactly what I need before I have the chance to struggle.

Over time, Dad has made peace with the guilt and grief that consumed him all those years ago. He came to understand what so many parents of kids with disabilities need to know: Being born with a disability doesn't mean you failed. It doesn't mean you did something wrong. Sometimes it's just how life happens. And no amount of self-blame or self-hatred will change that.

The most important thing is always showing up. And that is precisely what he has always done.

 For my brother, it is pretty simple.

Having a disabled sister has always been his norm. He is the younger sibling, so the minute he was old enough to comprehend what was going on, he viewed it as how our life was. Doctor's appointments? Standard. Specialists and tests? Just part of our family routine. He genuinely thought that everyone did that.

Because he didn't know any different, he never treated me any differently. We would wrestle, play the Wii, and have swimming races or handstand challenges in the swimming pool.

To him, I have always just been his older sister.

Despite this refreshing outlook, he is also incredibly protective and always on guard for any mishaps. There was an occasion when I fell between my bed frame and my bookcase while getting changed. I became trapped with my entire body weight on my toes. The pain was excruciating, and I screamed out for help.

Mum and Dad weren't home, and it was just fortunate my brother had just taken off his headphones and heard me scream. I was seconds away from twisting my knee to try and escape, risking a torn ACL, when I heard him yell, "I am coming!"

Where I was trapped made it close to impossible for him to grab me, and when he did, he had to fall back on my bed with me so he didn't drop me. After making sure I hadn't broken my ankle or any toes and my knee still had an intact ACL, he helped me pull up my pants and left me to gather my thoughts.

Honestly, I think I was more traumatised than he was. But I am still prepared to pay for his therapy.

He has never viewed life as a ticking time bomb like I do. He has never stopped to ponder what life would be like without me. When I asked him if he had ever thought about those things before writing this chapter, he looked at me and said, "No. I will worry about that when I get there. Why would I think about that when you are still here, and at the moment things are fine?"

My brother is incredibly present, and nothing much fazes him. As a result, he has never pitied me or made me feel as though he is scared.

Because he's not.

That lack of fear or unease is what has helped me immensely on my journey.

So, his piece of advice for siblings is as straightforward as he is:

"Don't treat them any differently because they aren't. And don't worry about the what-ifs because they haven't happened yet, and there is no point wasting energy on that. Just get on with life."

Truer words have never been spoken in my opinion.

Last but not least is my mum. She has been my primary caregiver for twenty-six years, and knows this world inside and out; the fears, the realisations, the worries. But she also knows how to adapt when things become difficult, without losing her sense of humour along the way. So, I thought it would be best to start with her first.

This is from my mum, to you.

"If someone told me I could travel back in time and decide between having this journey, or not having kids at all, I wouldn't have to think twice. I would take this journey in a heartbeat.

That's not to say that the journey is easy. It's the opposite. Having to watch your child struggle has been the hardest part about this entire journey.

What helped me in the beginning was that, because she was my first child, it automatically became my normal. There was no adjusting to a 'new normal'. For my husband and I, we knew no different. Rhi's younger brother was born just before she turned three. There was really nothing to compare her mobility to.

Having said that, just because it has been our normal, the balloon had to burst eventually. The moment that I realised just how 'different' our life was going to be was when we were at a playgroup.

All the other mums had gone inside to make tea and coffee, and I would think, 'Well, I'm going outside to be with my daughter because she needs my help.' There was a big sandpit she couldn't climb in and out of by herself, so I had to be there and help her. I sat and watched as she played with the other kids, laughing and having a great time. She was completely oblivious to what her body wouldn't allow her to do.

But I saw it. I saw what the other kids could do, and what she could not. It was overwhelming, not to mention confronting. I couldn't get out of that place fast enough.

When we arrived home, I found somewhere to be alone and bawled my eyes out. I wasn't crying for myself, but I was crying for my daughter. I knew that even though she was oblivious to the fact that her body would always fail her, there would come a time when it would become very obvious to her. What added to the pain was that I couldn't protect her. And as a parent, you would do anything to protect your child from whatever was hurting them. In this situation, I was powerless, and I couldn't do anything about it.

That was the moment the penny dropped. From this moment on, life was going to look very different.

Eventually, I realised something more important. This journey wasn't about me. It wasn't going to be about what I was and wasn't ready for. Nor was it about what I was grieving. I had to put my feelings aside to make sure she would have the best life possible.

Like any other new adventure, I had a lot to learn. The first lesson was to stop relying on Dr. Google. In the early days, I spent more nights than I could count on Dr. Google. I would spend hours researching what muscular dystrophy was, and how it could be cured. Desperately searching for clinical trials, drugs, diets, stretches, and operations. Anything that could give my family just a glimmer of hope that things would be okay.

At the time, I felt like I was doing everything I could to help my child. Instead, it did the opposite. I found that everything I googled made me feel hopeless. In the early 2000s, not much was known about muscular dystrophy, and anything that could be read about it wasn't that positive.

If I could go back in time, I would tell myself to get off the screen. The time I spent researching and googling could have been spent being present with my family.

The bubble had yet to burst for Rhi. What gave me real hope was watching her live. Unaware of her limitations, but still having fun and being a kid. Watching her laugh. Watching her thrive. Those precious moments are everything, especially when you have a lifetime of unknowns ahead of you.

One of the best pieces of advice that I have ever been given is this: "You have to let go of the life you imagined so you can appreciate the life you have been given."

It is okay to grieve the life you thought you would have. However, it is equally important to keep those moments of grief and anger short. If you dwell on the pain and the anger, it takes away from the life you could be living.

I found joy in the small moments. When Rhi and her brother were little, every night before bed, we would read a story. Usually, I would try to read *The Magic Far Away Tree* because I loved that story growing up. But I think in my excitement, I tried to read it to them when they were too young. After reading, I had a ritual where I would 'wipe' away the bad dreams before they would drift off to sleep.

Each little moment since then: a walk along the beach on family holidays, watching the AFL together in a sold-out stadium, nights around the fire pit having a quiet drink on a Saturday night as a family—these moments filled our lives, and we cherished them all together. We have learned over the years to never take a moment for granted and enjoy all the little things life has to offer.

This entire journey that I have been on for the past twenty-six years has made me appreciate being a mum more than I thought was possible. It has also made me appreciate our time as a family more.

Watching Rhi face her battles has also shifted my mindset on how I view my own. If she can keep showing up when things become more challenging for her, then so can I. It gives me the courage to continue to face the battles I have to face or that we must face together. Her strength is what gives me strength. It's not about comparison or invalidating my own struggles. She doesn't have a choice in whether she shows up for her battles, and that is what gives me the bravery and courage within myself to not run away from my own.

Life as a caregiver has also taught me the importance of balance. I have more than one child. Even though Rhi's needs have been more complex than my son's, who doesn't have a disability, my love and attention also needs to be felt by my son. Perhaps that is what being a mum is about when you have more than one child. Regardless of whether a disability is in the picture, every child deserves attention and love equally.

Caregiving isn't just about manual handling, brushing hair, tying shoelaces, or putting together a mobility scooter. It's all about how you do those tasks. It's about being compassionate, not just empathetic. It's important to give the person autonomy and allow them to express what they want and how they want it done. Even if you feel like it should be done differently, it's not up to you to question it.

It's equally important to never take away their sense of ownership over their life. You, as a caregiver, are their arms and legs. You are their strength. You become an extension of their body. So, make sure that they feel like your limbs are theirs. They shouldn't have to feel worried about asking for help. Rather, they should feel empowered to ask for help and express if they would prefer something done a different way.

Asking myself, "How can I make sure this person still feels in control and respected?" changed everything for me as a caregiver.

Of course, it has never been easy, and I don't think for a second it will get easier. Caregiving for someone, especially your own child, can feel like a lonely journey. Not everyone in your life will understand what you are going through. That's why your support network is everything, and sometimes, it isn't who you expect.

Your network may not be family. It may not be other parents on the same journey as you, either. Sometimes it's the people you don't expect. However, finding the people to surround yourself with who provide something different is incredibly important. There are days when you need emotional support, so you will turn to those who you know can give you that kind of support. Just like there are other days when you need physical support, and there are people in your life who can provide that.

Remember, there is no shame in needing different kinds of people at different points as you go along this journey. Give yourself the permission to grow and evolve as it unfolds.

Above all else, be kind to yourself. From the moment you wake up to the moment your head hits the pillow in the evening, the thoughts will dance in your head: *Did I do enough? Could I have done more?* Self-compassion is just as important in those moments. It's taken me over twenty years to learn that I deserve care, too, and that it isn't selfish to rest. To go out for that cup of coffee. Or to go to work without the guilt eating me alive. Because I know I can't pour from an empty cup, and if I can't look after myself, I can't show up in the way I need to for my kids.

Motherhood has not been the journey that I imagined twenty-six years ago, but it is the one that has inevitably turned me into the person I am today. In many ways, it has evolved me into a better mum. Someone strong, protective, and, above all else, grateful.

This journey has shown me that although life has carved out a different path for me and my family, different can still be fulfilling and memorable.

—Tamera.

CHAPTER 19

FOR THE DIAGNOSED: THE ONES WHO KNOW

Before we wrap up this little journey, I want to leave you with a little message from my little corner of the world to you.

I know I haven't shied away from the darker moments of disability life. That was done on purpose. Why? Because it's the reality; it's hard, gruelling, unrelenting, painful, and at times isolating. So many people say that we should always try to be positive and not dwell too much on the difficult moments, but I believe that is no longer helpful for many reasons. That kind of toxic positivity mindset often keeps others comfortable, but not you. By trying to keep everyone else happy, you end up denying yourself the right to be real about your life.

However, what is important to remember is that despite everything, you are not alone in your journey.

Let my story be a playbook of hope. Let it be proof that no matter what you go through, you will make it through the other side. There may be times when you arrive a little scared and bruised, mentally and, yes, sometimes physically. But the thing about those bruises? They become your building blocks. They shape you into the person you are becoming. Someone strong, resilient, and stubborn. Someone who is bulletproof. Metaphorically, of course.

Everyone on the face of the planet has to go up shit creek without a paddle. Our creek may look different, feel heavier, and seem unrelenting, but it is in our refusal to give up and be washed away that makes the disability community one of the strongest and most inspiring groups. And don't get me wrong here, when I mean inspirational, it isn't because you brushed your teeth or had breakfast. It is because you refuse to allow your life to be dictated by what you can't do.

Being disabled doesn't come with a set of rules all neatly bound together with a cover. Believe it or not, that can be a beautiful thing. There is no such thing as doing disabled life 'wrong'. Much like everyone else, your life is yours to live how you want. Yes, you will have the extra added elements of doctor's visits, tests, surgeries, difficult conversations, and, yes, even sometimes having to confront the concept of mortality sooner than most. But oddly enough, these elements add to the spice of life. They allow you, if you choose, to have a completely unique and powerful view on life.

The way we see life, through the lens of our experiences, might be one of the greatest blessings we, as disabled people, can receive.

Our perspective on life is, perhaps, one of our greatest gifts. We appreciate life, maybe slightly more than others, and we take stock of the smaller moments that are often brushed over by others.

This unique outlook on life, and the ability to truly understand the gift of life, in all its facets, means we often go searching for life's deeper meaning. Why are we here? Why are we born like this? Sometimes, there is simply no logical answer for why we are born disabled.

Life is only given to you once and only once. What you do with that life is completely up to you. We embrace life on a deeper level because we understand how truly fragile it is. We realise just how precious life actually is. We take immense joy in what we can do, and in simply waking up in the morning to be granted another day.

That mindset is what ultimately drives us forward in our lives. It's the fire behind our resilience—the ability to find meaning in the dark times, the joy in the smaller moments, and the immense value of each new day.

There are certainly a lot of things about this life that you didn't sign up for. The conversations with people, constantly explaining why you are unique, the arguments with those closest to you being too protective, and the endless tears, asking why this is all happening to you. Let's not even go into detail about you trying to explain the importance of health to others.

But with all the uncertainty around being disabled and what the future holds, there is also a lot of good that comes with it.

A whole new community opens up to you. Sure, it may not be the community you wanted to be in. Joining comes with terms and conditions that demand you to dig deep within yourself. It calls for a level of grit and determination that others will never have to endure.

But in my opinion, the disability community is perhaps one of the most welcoming you will find.

Those of us already within the community don't care if you were born with a disability or had an accident. We don't care if it is permanent or temporary, physical or psychiatric, if you have all limbs or some, if you use wheels or feet, if you have eyes or not, hearing or not, find tactiles painful or not.

We all see each other, and while yes, at times, we can be like a bickering family with differing opinions, we all see each other as humans.

To this day, each time I see someone from our community, we both smile and acknowledge each other with a gentle nod or compare battle stories. Why? Because we get each other, even though we may have arrived in this community in different ways, we share the same thoughts, struggles, fears, grief, and blessings.

Given the fact that our community is small and resembles a tiny fish in a big ocean, we may not come across each other for a while. But when we do, there is an immediate attachment, connection, and bond; an unconditional acceptance.

For a lot of us, we go on to do extraordinary things that we may never have even imagined.

Advocate for change and equality. Represent our country. Speak on the world stage. Share our story. Teach, parent, lead, and, perhaps, most importantly, love and receive love.

There are many of us who do incredible things, and it's not in spite of our disabilities, but more so because of the strength we have found from living alongside them.

Perhaps, most of all, we have something no one else does. Perspective. We find the joys in the things we can do. We view compromise or help not as a failure, but as a way in which we can go on living our lives. We savour and cherish each day because we get to fight, and, most importantly, live out another day that, perhaps, many told us wasn't possible.

We realise just how much of a gift life truly is and all that comes with it.

Will our surroundings and society make our journey perhaps harder than it has to be? Absolutely. But is the journey impossible because of it? Most certainly not.

The biggest piece of advice I can give you: Work on loving who stares back at you in the mirror.

Disability life is full of things to worry about. But the one thing it shouldn't control is the love you have for yourself.

Yes, I know you are probably cringing, and saying this sounds like 'fru fru'. But I say this as someone who has spent most of her adult life fighting to love what she sees in the mirror.

For years, I despised using the word 'disabled', much less being associated with the term. I went as far as to avoid people who even remotely looked disabled. I was desperate to be society's definition of 'normal', to blend in. I prayed every night for years to make it go away, to wake up with average-length arms, for my heels to touch the ground, to be able to go to the bathroom without taking fifteen minutes to pull up my pants afterward.

 But each morning I woke up and took my first step, I was still the same person. I had to do the work to truly accept and love who I saw in that mirror, disability and all.

And believe it or not, I eventually found that love and acceptance.

When you can truly love yourself, and all the bumps that come with what makes you, *you*, something shifts. You discover peace. You also realise that your self-worth was never a question; you are worthy. It was simply buried under society's noise. You will find total peace in the cards you have been dealt, and you will start to come out the other side of your acceptance journey.

For most of us, the cards we have been given in life are here to stay. How do we arrive at acceptance? Now, that is the true golden ticket.

There is so much that is fighting against you in the world, trying to bring you down. You don't need your own voice added to the war.

Letting go of control and the idea of what thought you would have, or experience, in life hurts. It's like someone took a blunt axe to your heart. However, there is freedom in letting go, in surrender. Once you surrender, doors begin to open, and your life truly begins, full of adventure and possibilities.

Now, don't get me wrong, it is okay to grieve! It's okay to grieve for the life imagined. Grieve never explored adventures, realised plans, or even the word 'disabled'. Cry. Scream. Yell. Be shit-scared.

Take your time to work through it. Don't let anyone tell you to move on and accept it when you aren't ready. It's your timeline, not theirs.

It may take you a few weeks, months, or, even like me, years, but you will eventually arrive at a place where saying, "I am Disabled" won't be a punch to the stomach. Instead, you will recognise that it is a part of who you are, not *all that you are*.

And when you arrive at that place, own it.

Live loudly. Live proudly. Live unapologetically. It is your life, and yours alone.

At times, you will need to stand up for yourself, regardless of who that is, including the people with fancy white coats and the stethoscopes around their necks. And that is your right. It's your life, your body, your voice. You deserve to be heard. Everything you think and feel is valid.

The bullies will come whether it is at school, at work, out shopping, or online—even your own circle. But remember, as the line in *Cool Runnings* says, "People are always afraid of what's different."

It says more about them than you. Their fear is not your burden to bear. It is theirs. They just haven't figured out they are different, too.

Remember, being different is nothing to hide or be ashamed of. Our differences are something to celebrate.

So, let me leave you with this:

Be bold. Be strong. Be selfless. Be courageous.

We weren't born to be the same. We were born to stand out. We were born to leave our mark on the world.

For us in the disabled community, our mark can and will be louder than anyone else's. It's unfinished history.

Don't ever be ashamed of your disability and all that comes with it. Embrace it. Use it as the match that lights the fire to living your life. A life that is on your terms.

Whatever you choose to do, do it because you love it.

Surround yourself with those who lift you up, figuratively and literally. Find the moments that make you laugh so hard that tears stream down your face. Find the quiet moments in between the doctor's appointments.

Carve out your journey one moment at a time.

You aren't alone, you will never be alone.

Disability life isn't all sunshine and rainbows, but it isn't all thunderstorms either.

You are seen. Heard. Worthy. Enough.

You are perfectly you.

Celebrate your journey. Be proud of your story. The summits you have climbed. The silent battles you have won.

Write down your victories. Not just the trophies, the titles, the engraved plaques—but the small moments. The quiet wins. The victories that no one sees, the ones that you fight within your own head, the ones you fight at home when no one is watching. The things you thought you couldn't do but did anyway, on your own terms, and in your own way.

If you are breathing, no matter how, you are worthy of all the love, positivity, and opportunities the world has to offer.

We see you.

We feel you.

We celebrate you.

We love you.

We honour you.

Welcome to the family.

CHAPTER 20

THE LEGACY OF LIVING ABLED: A LIFE WELL-PLAYED

When people think of legacy, they more than likely think about the movers and shakers of the world; the celebrities, scientists with their names immortalised on the front of buildings, the sports stars with their statues at the front of stadiums.

A while ago, I was in the car with my mum on our way to pick up some new riding sunglasses, as the ones I was using were giving me headaches. As we stopped at a red light, a funeral procession passed us; first, the hearse, followed by a steady stream of cars with their lights on.

As I watched the procession pass us, the light turned green, and we carried on our way. I struggled to comprehend how everyone seemingly continued on with their day, heading to work, heading home, running errands, or going on a holiday. Time kept moving forward. Someone had died, and their family was facing the worst day of their lives, but the rest of us carried on.

It was a strange concept to me that, despite death, life moves on, and so do we.

I didn't know who was in the casket, but during the rest of the trip, I couldn't help but ask myself, "What was their life like?", "Were they married?", "Did they raise a family?", "What did they enjoy doing the most?", "Did they live a full and happy life?"

So many questions flooded my head, wondering about the life of the person in the back of the hearse.

That's when it hit me: a legacy isn't about how many buildings are dedicated to you, how many statues are made apparently in your likeness, how many movies you starred in, or your investment portfolio.

Legacy doesn't have to be defined by the moments that make headlines. It's often found in the quiet—the values passed down from generation to generation that quietly shape how we live and who we become.

The people who have walked alongside me, and the principles they've instilled in me, are their never-ending legacy.

It's the way my grandfather stood his ground when the odds were stacked against him—and the way I now do, too. It's the soft light of golden hour casting its glow on the paddocks, the cows calling in the distance—echoes of the past carried within me.

It's my grandmother, teaching me that even in the hardest moments, life still holds more to live for. It's my parents, showing me what unconditional love really looks like, and how to show up for people when it matters most. It's my great-great-grandfather's love of horses as a drover, somehow carried through the bloodline. It's the grit, the quiet determination, and the instinct to 'saddle up' when life throws a curveball—because the ride is still worth taking.

Legacy isn't always loud. It's often built in the mundane, the unseen. Passed down not in statues or plaques, but in the way we live, love, and keep going.

Your legacy is the thing that people talk about at family dinners when you are no longer at the table. However, legacy isn't only what you end up leaving behind; it is what you build while you are still here. Its foundations are built in the present moment, how you show up, the courage you wear like armour, and the lives you touch without you even realising. It is the ripple effect of what it means to live.

Someone asked me a while ago what *Living Abled* meant. What it stood for. It took me a while to formulate a response that accurately summed up everything that *Living Abled* was at its core.

When I first came up with the name five years ago, it was purely the name of my blog. It gave me the place to write, process, and share a glimpse into my life; how I viewed my diagnosis, offering advice to those newly diagnosed, and a place to structure the multitude of thoughts in my head.

Five years ago, *Living Abled* meant that, even though I was disabled, I could live 'abled' just like everyone else.

I had yet to really peel back the layers of my own internalised ableism and deconstruct the way in which I wanted to live my life. So, I guess you could say that *Living Abled* was created on the grounds of unawareness and a lack of self-worth.

However, after plenty of reflecting, and a lot of work on cleaning out the ableist skeletons in the closet, as well as emotional baggage over twenty-five years, *Living Abled* suddenly started to take on a new form.

Living Abled, to me now, means turning the tables on what I once believed was impossible.

It's about living a life that is authentic, fun, exciting, and memorable. Despite the hardships and the challenges, it's a life full of adventure and joy.

Living Abled isn't so much about the physical ability of my own body, but rather the mental freedom of having the shackles come off and no longer looking at my disability as a curse, and something to be ashamed of.

It is the pieces to my jigsaw puzzle, and the foundation to creating a life that is never dull. It's about owning and living in my own truth, admitting when things are hard, and not feeling as though I need to hide that part of life any more. It's the freedom to live life on my terms, for me and no one else.

Living Abled has given me opportunities that I could never have imagined.

What started out as a desperate effort to survive 2020 blossomed into five years of blog posts, friendships made, and podcast interviews. Perhaps the best thing of all is the messages I receive from people all over the world saying that my posts gave them hope for their family members going through MD, or from others who say I have made them look at life in a completely different way.

One of the first messages I received, sometime after starting my blog, was from a father in India whose daughter had just been diagnosed. He messaged me saying that reading my blog has given him hope that his daughter will be okay and still lead an abundant life, and that he now knows a little more about what to expect going forward.

His message caught me off guard, but it immediately made me realise that my life and my journey had become larger than just words on a page.

People were feeling less alone. Families were finding hope.

Everything I had gone through in my life up to that point, all the surgeries, roadblocks, the continuous loss of ability, the fear, anxiety, and uncertainty, suddenly all made sense. Those moments that I thought would break me, but instead rose from, became the moments that enabled me to write a blog that gave people hope for their future, or the future of their loved ones.

Suddenly, all those moments became worth it.

That, to me, is legacy.

At the same time, I know that this is just the beginning. Legacy isn't a finish line. It's an ever-evolving, living, breathing thing.

I hope that *Living Abled* does not become limited to a place where people can go to make sense of their journeys, but that it becomes a movement where people can start to put the pieces of their own lives together. Where they decide that they are more than worthy of a masterpiece of a life.

Living Abled isn't about blending in; it is about standing in truth, admitting when things are hard, and rising against the challenges. It's about standing out from the crowd. Living a life that is built on thinking outside the box and turning the impossible into the possible.

By throwing caution to the wind and purchasing the name that day in May all those years ago, I was enabled to embark on my own journey of self-realisation, and it helped me see that being a solicitor, reading legislation 24/7, and being scrutinised through a pair of glasses is not my legacy. It's the ability to help people find a way to push beyond the trials and tribulations of life. To be true to themselves and not run from the hard moments, to allow those times to flow through them and face them, instead of pushing them to the side. To help people realise that no matter their past or diagnosis, they are worth living a life that they can truly say they love.

The concept of the inner child isn't new, but it's powerful for a multitude of reasons. For many of us, it becomes the quiet voice shaping our decisions more than we realise. Sometimes, it's the one urging us to hold back out of fear—the fear of rejection, failure, or embarrassment—fears we first learned as kids. Other times, it's that same voice bubbling with excitement, pushing us to leap with curiosity and see what might unfold.

Often, our inner child doesn't need to be silenced or "healed away". They just need to be seen. Held. Reassured. And told, *I've got this now.* To be able to breathe a sigh of relief and be shown we don't need protecting any more. We need to start living again.

The day I stood in the round yard with Larry, tears running down my face, I felt like that little girl inside me—quiet, lost, scared—was curled up in the corner, begging for someone to take over. And when Larry burst through the barriers, my inner child had built to keep us safe from the outside, I realised that it was time to step out into the light. I had to take care of us—both of us.

Some people say we need to let our inner child go, to move on from the scars of yesterday. But that never made sense to me. Everything we experience brings us to where we are now. Those moments aren't distractions from the path—they *are* the path. They are the stepping stones to our present and our legacy.

So no, I won't let her go. I'll walk forward with her. I'll take the reins, gently, intentionally, and show her that we can do this. That we are safe now. That our life can be meaningful, full of light and laughter, even when it's hard.

Everything I do now, I do for her.

Of course, as with everything in life, there are setbacks. I am not perfect, nor will I ever be perfect. There are moments when I go back to my default setting; the insecurities, anxieties, and fears come rushing back. My mind becomes loud, my heart starts racing, and I have to use all my strength to remain on my feet.

At the moment, I am starting to realise that I am not getting any younger. In four short years, I will be thirty. For someone with muscular dystrophy, that is practically middle-aged. And when my parents first received my diagnosis all those years ago, the prognosis wasn't positive. Like I said at the beginning of this book, I shouldn't be here right now.

Living with numbers in your head is like a clock ticking down. I understand the importance of how fragile and quick life is. The saying is so true: "We are here for a good time, not a long time."

Growing up, I was terrified that I would leave this world before I had a chance to live in it truly. I feared my life would have no meaning, that I wouldn't do anything that truly mattered or made a difference.

For years, I wanted to make the pain and sleepless nights my parents endured in those early days, and perhaps, still to this day, worth it. I wanted to make sure that my life wasn't wasted, not for me, but for them. I wanted to ensure that when I leave this world, they will never have a single regret. I wanted to show them that whatever I did in life was a result of their unconditional love and belief in me, and that because of them, my life meant something.

For years, I thought that 'something' had to be big. For it to matter, it had to be spectacular.

However, as life has continued, and I surpassed the expectations of the doctors, the predictions, and the science, I learnt something more powerful:

Living a full life doesn't require anything spectacular.

Life is about being present, creating the little moments, and the surprises that will be cherished. It's about being real not only for yourself but for those around you, and when things get tough, it's about choosing to rise again and again.

With each stroke of life's pen, we write our legacy. With each sunrise and sunset, our stories are shaped, not just in what we leave behind, but in how we live while we're here

And I have unknowingly been shaping my legacy for the past twenty-five years.

What do I want it to say?

Strength.

Courage.

Determination.

Fun.

Joy.

The ability to hang on when my back was against the wall, when I had no other choice but to 'saddle up'.

I want to prove that just because people say, "this is how it is", doesn't mean it has to be.

I said, "Watch me."

But perhaps more than that, I didn't just survive.

I lived. And I continue to do just that.

And that, in itself, is my legacy.

Epilogue

When I decided to write this book, I honestly thought I would just be sharing my story, which I've told many times before, whether as a speech or as a snippet in one of my blogs. However, a 1,500-word blog is just a tad different from sharing your life as a book. I didn't realise that I signed up for unearthing parts of my life that I had buried for many years.

I couldn't tell you how many times I have cried while writing these chapters. However, the tears weren't just because I was reliving the past in vivid imagery in my head as I recounted the memories. It was because I was healing the sides that my memory had long kept sealed out of self-preservation. Clearly, it doesn't matter how much work you think you put into healing past wounds; healing never ends.

I have always been one to be honest, brutally so. But I didn't expect to pour my heart out like I did during this process. I didn't have storyboards or plan this book out in detail when I started writing. I wanted the process to allow my mind to wander and let the story unfold. I didn't expect it to unlock sealed vaults.

This book has truly been a full-circle moment. I have been able to explore parts of my life that I never would have had the courage to do. In a way, it has also allowed me the opportunity to make peace with all the conflicting feelings and emotions that have been lurking in the shadows for my entire life.

In a strange way, this full-circle moment has enabled me to really make peace with all that I have been through. Even when, at times, I felt like the perfectly sewn stitches in my life began to unravel, they were simultaneously being stitched back together. Each chapter I wrote opened up another vault, and instead of trying to bury the feelings that washed over me, I put all I had learnt into practice. I allowed myself to feel everything and let it pass through me.

I never expected when writing this book that it would have such a profound impact on me. I thought I was writing for those in my life to allow them into my world more than talking ever could. I thought I was also writing this for the people who may eventually stumble across it on a bookshelf, be it online or in a cosy bookstore. I wanted to show what it means to be able to have a meaningful life, regardless of the uncertainty, fear, and loss that disabled life can bring. That life truly is a masterpiece if we take hold of the brush.

But in all honesty, I think I wrote this for the little girl who didn't have the courage to speak. And perhaps, even now, I wrote it for the woman I am now, to remind her that her voice is still important. For both versions of me, young and old, I have been blessed to live an incredible life so far, and all the hardships have been worth it.

I am fortunate enough that, through my experiences, I have been able to throw caution out the window and explore what life truly has to offer. The curiosity I had many years ago is still in full force today. I have been able to try so many different things in my life. From law school, public speaking, QAFLW Statistician, working within the legal industry, life coaching, and writing. There have been so many things I have been able to achieve and experience in my life, not only because of my disability but because I decided to throw out the rule book of what society expected from me, which, in turn, helped me discover what I wanted life to look like for me.

So, where am I now?

I will always be a work-in-progress, continually learning and unlearning, exploring, and challenging myself. But I am more at peace and proud of how far I have come, and, as a result, even more open to anything that this life has to offer me.

I am building a life that truly feels like mine, full of quiet mornings with my dog, unexpected pivots, and choosing to let go of competition or feeling as though I need to be more.

So, starting February 2026, I am returning to university to study a Master's in Business, majoring in digital marketing. I always knew I would go back to university eventually, but I honestly thought that I would be studying a Master's in Human Rights. I didn't foresee a business master's on the cards a couple of years ago, but it's a journey I cannot wait to begin.

I am in the early days of building businesses that have been born out of my desire to create and to help others. Life coaching through *Living Abled* enables me to guide and help people who feel lost and consumed by fear and uncertainty in their lives. To help those break free from the expectations around them.

Phoenix Marketing was born by sheer chance. An opportunity to help my parents in their business tickled the creative side in me, and I never expected to fall madly in love with digital marketing.

By throwing caution to the wind and allowing life to steer me in any direction, I am doing things in my life that I never thought I would do, including writing this book.

Everything I have done in life up to this point was despite muscular dystrophy.

But now, everything I will do will be alongside it.

Before I close out this story, it only feels right to offer a final word to the companion that's been with me every step of the way.

To the companion that I didn't choose, the one that shaped me, broke me, but ultimately, strengthened me. This letter is for you.

Dear Muscular Dystrophy,

Where do I even begin? It has been 24 years since you and I started life together. Every day has created incredible blessings and, at the same time, astonishing heartbreak.

In every sense of the word, we grew up together. However, that isn't to say that always being with each other 24/7 hasn't had its trying moments. Throughout my childhood, you were the thing I couldn't understand. People told me about you and your potential impact on my life, yet I still couldn't put everything together.

You were and still are the world's most complex Rubik's cube; even experts couldn't and still can't figure you out completely. There are questions upon questions, and rarely are there concrete answers; you are constantly evolving, making people wonder what kind of sub-branch you are. Ullrich's to one, Bethlem to another.

Safe to say, there is never a dull moment with you.

As much as your elusive nature surprises me, you are the thing that constantly tries to raise the stakes in a way that is like tying someone down to train tracks and asking them to move. It's simply terrifying, yet at the same time, the adrenaline and desire to beat you is intoxicating.

I often think we have a toxic relationship. You take and take while you force me to give everything 100 percent of the time, physically, emotionally, and mentally. I still don't understand why you do that, but I guess your gifts and blessings come out in other ways.

You have made me question my life too many times to count and stopped me from doing what I love most—chasing after my younger brother, dancing, running, climbing, jumping, and potentially having children one day. But the one thing you constantly try to challenge and take from me is my independence.

There are days when you make me feel weak, tired, scared, my arms getting shorter, my legs getting stiffer. Walking one kilometre feels like a marathon. But perhaps, the most significant thing I must comprehend is that you are suffocating me ever so slowly, taking away lung capacity a percentage at a time. Watching the numbers on the screen during every lung function test is like watching my future tick down one number at a time; it's simply paralysing, and yet, motivating at the same time. I have to fight you on everything. Can't you give me one thing in the physical realm, like the chance to breathe a full breath again?

It can be a cruel hand you play, taking a little something away when you feel like it. I am at your complete mercy, almost making me bow down to you, as your unrelenting motivation to try and break me never ceases.

So many questions in my head play almost like a broken record: What will my life be like with you? What will you take next? What are you truly capable of? Will you show me your hand at least once?

The truth is, I have seen what you are truly capable of. I have seen what your extended family does; I have been to funerals and watched those I care about most slowly decline as you continue to take. I have been a sounding board, an ear, and a shoulder to cry on as they worry and are uncertain about their future. I do this, all while you sit in the background, working your own Voldemort powers over me.

Not only do you have complete control over our bodies, but it's like you have control of our minds as well. Making us question our worth, value, and our place in this world; our confidence so quickly shattered by one glimpse from a stranger, making us want to hide away like a hermit, and never truly experience what life has to offer.

Did you know that I have friends who tell me they think they will never find love and happiness because of you? I have gone through my doubts because of you as well, but I simply ask that you give them at least someone who loves them unconditionally.

I have had to watch my parents come to terms with the reality you bring. Sharing many tears, fears, and multiple heartbreaking conversations that will potentially haunt me forever. Because the reality is, no parent should ever have to contemplate the thought of possibly outliving their child. And no child should ever have to discuss mortality with their parents.

Watching my brother learn about you and be my biggest cheerleader has been heartwarming, but it has also been incredibly difficult. Listening to his friends be so accepting of you and wanting to know more about you, I could tell, made him relax.

Perhaps the one thing you haven't taken away is our typical sibling bond, and for that, I thank you.

You have made me contemplate things that no young human should ever have to consider. People I once thought would be in my life forever walked away because of your never-ending quest to take from this world. How should anyone ever be forced to go through that?

However, just as much as you take, you have been perhaps the biggest blessing in my life. You have made me grow up faster than I should have. Doctors' offices as a young child, hearing difficult conversations the doctors were having with my parents, hearing my parents' concern for the quality of my life in the future.

Having to explain to every person I met who you were and what you were doing to me. Sometimes, no matter how hard I try to explain to people about you, they still don't fully understand. But at the same time, you constantly showed me just how strong we are together. Growing up faster meant I learnt how to have serious conversations earlier and find the deeper meaning of life.

We work oddly, but in a good way, together. You know how much I love a challenge, and you always amaze me with what challenges you can cook up.

To meet your challenges, you have had to make me change. You had all the power when we started learning to live with one another. But I am taking some of the power back.

Years ago, I was anxious, shy, completely introverted, unsure of myself, had body image issues, contemplated hurting myself, and had self-worth issues. I felt like I didn't deserve love and happiness. However, little did I know that I would combat all of these things simply by getting to know you more and accepting you instead of being in denial of you.

That power struggle has ultimately led to some incredible moments I will cherish forever—meeting new friends, creating a blog, finding a potential career path I love, speaking at functions and panels, and taking trips of a lifetime. Living Abled was started because of you, to help people know more about you and your muscular dystrophy family, while helping those who live alongside you find their zest for life again. There is something magical about having you in my life, and I would be lying if I said I hated you completely.

Because the truth is, I don't hate you. Shocker, I know.

I am blessed to have you in my life for all the incredible moments we create together. The good ultimately outweighs the bad. You may continue to get the upper hand, but I enjoy the challenge of taking you on.

I thank you for the memories, the adventures, the good times, as well as the bad times.

Even though I still contemplate what life would be like when there is something that could finally free me of your vice-like grip, I don't know who or what I would be without you. No one knows exactly what the future holds, even with you being by my side, I also don't know—that's why I am determined more than ever to keep Living Abled My Way with you.

I know there are more pieces to your puzzle—our puzzle—to solve. And I am ready for it. Bring it on.

With gratitude, your frenemy,

Rhi, 2023

So here's to the next chapter and whatever it may hold.

This is not the end.

It's only the beginning.

ABOUT THE AUTHOR

Rhiannon Anderson is a writer, entrepreneur, and advocate redefining what it means to live boldly with Muscular Dystrophy. A law graduate turned Blogger and Life Coach, she combines humour, resilience, and raw honesty to challenge stereotypes and inspire others to embrace life beyond the unexpected.

As the founder of Living Abled, she empowers people to recognise their unique potential despite their challenges. Through Phoenix Marketing, she helps brands find their unique voices and share their stories.

When not working, she finds joy in life surrounded by her dogs and family, spending time on the land with horses and cheering for her favourite Aussie Rules Football team. With a passion for storytelling and connection, Rhiannon encourages others to embrace resilience, challenge expectations, and live authentically.

LinkedIn: https://www.linkedin.com/in/rhiannon-anderson
Facebook: https://www.facebook.com/livingabledcoaching
Instagram: https://www.instagram.com/living_abled/
Website: https://Livingabled.com.au

Loved this story?
Let's keep the conversation going.

You'll find me on socials sharing more real talk, rolling through life one F-word at a time (faith and freedom... mostly), and cheering others on as a life coach for adults who are ready to step into their truth and create a life that is meaningful and without barriers.

I'm also available for public speaking—whether you're looking for a keynote that blends heart, humour, and hard-won truth or a conversation around disability inclusion in the workplace. I speak with businesses and organisations about breaking stigma, building accessible environments, and redefining what it means to *truly* include everyone.

Follow me on social media:
Facebook: https://www.facebook.com/livingabledcoaching
Instagram: https://www.instagram.com/living_abled/
For coaching, speaking or workplace enquiries:
Email: Rhi@livingabled.com.au

www.ingramcontent.com/pod-product-compliance
Lightning Source LLC
Chambersburg PA
CBHW071705120626

46550CB00001B/107